Encountering Nationalism

21st-Century Sociology

SERIES EDITOR: Steven Seidman, State University of New York at Albany

The *21st-Century Sociology* series provides instructors and students with key texts in sociology that speak with a distinct sociological voice and offer thoughtful and original perspectives. The texts reflect current discussions in and beyond sociology, avoiding standard textbook definitions to engage students in critical thinking and new ideas. Prominent scholars in various fields of social inquiry combine theoretical perspectives with scholarly research to present accessible syntheses for students as we move into a new millennium with implications for rapid social change.

Already published:

1 CULTURAL THEORY: AN INTRODUCTION   *Philip Smith*
2 CULTURAL SOCIOLOGY IN PRACTICE   *Laura Desfor Edles*
3 CLASSICAL SOCIAL THEORY   *Kenneth H. Tucker, Jr.*
4 MULTICULTURALISM IN A GLOBAL SOCIETY   *Peter Kivisto*
5 THE WORLD OF CITIES: PLACES IN COMPARATIVE AND HISTORICAL PERSPECTIVE   *Anthony M. Orum and Xiangming Chen*
6 ENCOUNTERING NATIONALISM   *Jyoti Puri*
7 THE VIRTUAL SELF: A CONTEMPORARY SOCIOLOGY   *Ben Agger*

Forthcoming books in series:

NEW TECHNOLOGIES AND SOCIETY   *Douglas Kellner*
RACE, CLASS, AND GENDER   *Lynn Chancer and Beverly Watkins*

Encountering Nationalism

JYOTI PURI

Blackwell Publishing

350 Main Street, Malden, MA 02148-5020, USA
108 Cowley Road, Oxford OX4 1JF, UK
550 Swanston Street, Carlton, Victoria 3053, Australia

First published 2004 by Blackwell Publishing Ltd

Library of Congress Cataloging-in-Publication Data

Puri, Jyoti.
Encountering nationalism / Jyoti Puri.
    p. cm. – (21st-century sociology)
    ISBN 0-631-23105-6 (hb) – ISBN 0-631-23106-4 (pbk.)
    1. Nationalism. 2. Nationalism–Social aspects. 3. National characteristics. I. Title.
II. Series.

JC311.P87 2003
320.54–dc21

                                                                        2002156496

A catalogue record for this title is available from the British Library.

Set in 10/12.5pt Photina
by Kolam Information Services Pvt. Ltd, Pondicherry, India
Printed and bound in the United Kingdom
by T. J. International Ltd, Padstow, Cornwall

For further information on
Blackwell Publishing, visit our website:
http://www.blackwellpublishing.com

Contents

Acknowledgments

Books are rarely written without accruing debts. Steven Seidman recruited me to write this book and several people have helped me put it together. Above all, I am grateful to Hyun Sook Kim, dear friend and colleague, for her input and advice, particularly on all matters of the state. I have benefited time and again from her wise counsel. Cailin Duram, Colleen Johnston, and Denise Oberdan at Simmons College were generous with their time and effort. I solicited help from them repeatedly, especially Cailin, to "get the facts right." One cannot always count on getting thorough and supportive assessments from anonymous reviewers; fortunately, I did. I hope the two reviewers will recognize their imprint on various chapters of the book. Ken Provencher at Blackwell was consistently helpful and supportive, which made my task that much easier. Many thanks also to Mary Dortch for her skillful editorial touches to each page. How does one begin to acknowledge a debt to those who provide sustenance endlessly? My gratitude to Rohin Mhatre.

I dedicate this book to immigrant communities living in the USA who were affected by the nationalist backlash of September 11, 2001.

Parades, Flags, and National Pride

September 11, 2001 has moved from the present to history. Especially for those living in the United States and in Afghanistan, the events will surely not be easily forgotten; an untold number of people lost their lives on September 11 and in its aftermath. Where were you when the planes hit the twin towers in New York City? How did you feel when a plane destroyed part of the Pentagon in Washington DC? When did you hear about the plane that crashed outside of Pittsburgh, Pennsylvania, killing all the people on board, including the hijackers? Where were you on October 7, 2001 when the United States started its relentless bombing of Afghanistan? How many Afghan civilians lost their lives in the war? Were you too young then to remember the details? "Stunned and bewildered" was how many people in the United States reported feeling immediately after the attacks. Some fervently hoped that no Islamic group had anything to do with the attacks; others were sure that it could not be anyone else. For many, at least initially, the scale of the devastation and its unexpected force made it difficult to give in to the grief and anger that were at the edges of the shock. Grieving would mean coming to terms with the extraordinary scale and deliberate, methodically planned nature of the devastation. For other people, anger was their primary response and means of coping. If the question "Why would anyone do this to us?" marked the bewilderment, then "How dare anyone do this to us?" registered profound anger at the attacks. Two sentiments were widely expressed within hours of the attacks: a deeply felt patriotism, and demands for retribution against the outsiders who were responsible. Others among us feared the retaliation against more readily available targets within the United States: Muslims, people from the Middle East, and all those groups who could be easily mistaken for them.

There are various ways of understanding the enormity and scope of these events, but little gives us better insight into the responses and actions following September 11 than the concept of nationalism. That nationalism was the idiom through which the events were interpreted is in little doubt. Within minutes of the news breaking, the violence was seen as an "attack on America." Major television channels used variations of this phrase to headline their coverage; "Attack on America" was how CBS and NBC described their reports, while ABC used the phrase "America Attacked," and CNN called its coverage "America Under Attack." The language that we use to describe events shapes how we make sense of them while also reflecting how we interpret their meanings. Which is also to say that the events might be framed in a different way; that is, we might have interpreted them through a different lens or put a different twist on them.

Typically, most of us see our own nationalism as loyalty or love for country, i.e. patriotism, whereas nationalism elsewhere is likely to be associated with fanatical militancy. It seems easier to think of things that can be associated with nationalism – flags, wars, passports, place of birth or belonging – than it is to pin nationalism down to a definition. Like many other social concepts, such as racism or sexuality, nationalism is so deeply embedded in our lives and so self-evident that it makes any explanations seem redundant. Considered more broadly, though, nationalism refers to relatively recent beliefs and practices aimed at creating unified but unique communities within a sovereign territory. In this definition, such forms of community are thought of as nations and sovereign territory is associated with the concept of the state. (Given the interchangeable and confusing ways in which the three concepts of nationalism, nation, and state are used, the following chapter explores these concepts and their varied relations more carefully.) Sameness and difference are the foundations upon which nationalism rests: individuals in a nation are essentially similar and equal, but each nation and its people are distinct from others. Nationalism is seen to unify people and provide a sense of belonging to a community that takes precedence over all else, whether family, or ethnic or local group. It is believed that we realize our potential as individuals by virtue of belonging to this national community; in that, nationalism conjoins our individuality to the collective. Taken as a whole, the interests of the people of each community are seen as synonymous with the interests of the nation. Political maps exemplify how our notion of the world is represented through national and state boundaries. Each nation is seen as independent, with a sovereign territory that it has rights over, and the right to defend. We find nothing unusual about the fact that each person has a nationality that affects whether she or he can exist in the eyes of the state, or can work, travel, have rights, or be expected to take on some responsibilities, and so on.

Taken together, these factors made it difficult for the attacks of September 11 to be seen as anything other than an attack on the (north) American nation, its people, and its sovereign territory.[1] That the attack on the World Trade Center represented an attack against international trade and finance as much as it represented an attack against American interests seemed only secondary. This language of an attack against America, American citizens, and the American way of life set into motion a groundswell of nationalism. The power of nationalism rallied people together at a time of great uncertainty and anxiety. Even though we may turn to our families, our friends, our co-workers, and other communities that we belong to in moments of crises, coming together to share grief and mourning with a national community was, at that time, just as important. It was not uncommon for people to express privately and publicly that they had never felt more "American" in their lives than at that time; they felt connected to the national community of fellow Americans in their grief and outrage.

The Power of Nationalism and Nationalism as Power

The crisis of September 11 revealed the force of nationalism in the United States in various ways. Political leaders urged people to come together as Americans and do their part in this war against terrorism; patriotism was used to mobilize the public to give blood, donate their money, and defend the territory. At the same time, with few exceptions, national and local political leaders repeatedly invoked the language of war and militancy to console a grieving, anxious American people. The rawness of the initial shock and anger gave way to a powerful rhetoric of American fortitude and a demand for retribution. The spirit of nationalism and love of country were used to build support for military strikes initially against Osama bin Laden, the assumed initiator, Al-Qaida (the group inspired by and sheltering him), and the Taliban, and later against Saddam Hussein's regime and other militant Islamic groups believed to support anti-American insurgency.[2] Numerous national and local political leaders used words such as "evildoers" and "Muslim fundamentalists," in order to identify the enemy. It was not uncommon to hear news analysts and experts saying that enemy groups hate America for its freedoms, its way of life, its material superiority, and the rights that American women enjoy. If these attitudes helped identify the enemy and its motivations, then it also helped characterize America as a free, open, and powerful nation. Exacerbated by prominent political leaders like President Bush and Senator McCain, this nationalist rhetoric was put into practice by the military on October 7, 2001 in the war against the Taliban government in Afghanistan, a war to prevent it from providing support to terrorist organizations.

That political leaders deployed the power of nationalism to political ends is indisputable. But it was also popularly expressed. Americans of various persuasions – conservatives, liberals, African Americans, Asian Americans, Latinos, whites, Christians, Jews, Muslims, women and men – felt the tug of nationalism and, in numerous cases, responded to it. Ordinary Americans from all walks of life expressed their patriotism and their anger against the perceived enemy. Flags are a particularly handy way of showing one's love for country to fellow citizens and to the enemy at a time of war. Vast numbers of homes, gardens, and cars were decorated with the red, white, and blue colors of the (north) American flag. In some neighborhoods in the country it was harder to find homes that were not marked by the national colors. Walmart reported that it sold a staggering 88,000 flags on the day after September 11 and businesses that make flags had a hard time keeping up with the unprecedented demand. Graffiti, clothes, and clothing accessories in red, white, and blue enabled people to wear the love for their country on their sleeve, as it were. Those who had never before felt this need to express their nationalism were moved by the extent of the national tragedy and looked to the national community for comfort and unity. Indeed, those who ordinarily feel ambivalently about nationalism responded to its power and its promise despite themselves.

There is no doubting the depth of nationalism's influence. I once asked a friend, "What is most precious to you?" After due reflection, her response, which would probably be true for most of us, was, "My life." That some of us would sacrifice our lives for the nation is a sobering thought. In fact, in his influential book, *Imagined Communities: Reflections on the Origin and Spread of Nationalism* (to be discussed in greater length in Chapter One), Benedict Anderson wonders why nationalism has the ability to make people love, die, and kill for their nation.[3] The answer to this question is often more complicated; for example, in many countries it is men from the lower socioeconomic classes who are the foot soldiers who die and kill. But Anderson's point is well taken; it is a rare concept that would elicit the sacrifice of the lives of people on a wide scale. This is a sobering reminder of the men and women in the US armed forces who lost their lives while defending the nation after September 11. They were later hailed as heroes and their lives commemorated as sacrifice for the national community.

If these observations indicate "the power of nationalism," then they also compel us carefully to consider nationalism itself as a form of power. Nationalism may be awe-inspiring in its ability to connect and unify people at a time of crisis or allow political leaders to whip up public support for retaliatory action. But nationalism is an expression of power, more broadly conceived. Power is the ability to shape beliefs and practices. It is the foundation upon which human relations and social institutions are built. As a form of power, nationalism has some similarity to ethnicity, religion, sexuality, race, or the family in making us function in socially patterned and socially regulated ways. Frequently, scholars consider nationalism as power wielded by the nation's elites and therefore see nationalism as a dangerous or ideological phenomenon. For example, some see nationalism as an ideology or a kind of false consciousness that is imposed on people despite their best interests.[4] But others take the point of view that power exerts social control by both making things happen and preventing them; it is both productive and restrictive.[5] This is what makes nationalism's influence awesome: as a mechanism of social control it works by permeating our pleasures and desires, by enabling us as citizens, and by making it seem perfectly "natural" and "normal" that each person has a nationality. The passion, love, and devotion to country that is expressed by ordinary people, by writers, and by poets, are resounding reminders of how the spirit of nationalism is not simply inflicted but also desired.

The surge of nationalism in the United States after September 11 tells us much about its functioning as a form of power. Power shapes our individual selves. Not surprisingly, Americans were widely called upon to do their duty to national interests in the aftermath of September 11. In an interview on CNN, the Republican Senator from Virginia, John Warner, called upon every person to think of himself (sic) as an agent. He clarified that this did not mean spying on one's neighbor, but reporting odd behavior. Indeed, the *Christian Science Monitor* reported that 435,000 tips of "anti-American activity" were received post-September 11.[6] In one case, the FBI investigated a tiny art gallery in Houston that was opening an exhibition on US covert operations and government secrets. In another case cited in the article, a 60-year-old retired telephone worker was approached by the FBI about political views that he had aired at his gym. Consider also what happens when intelligence work on behalf of national interests is mixed with racism and xenophobia. Passengers on a commuter train in Rhode Island reported a fellow passenger to the police for "suspicious behavior." As it turned out, his turban and brown skin were what constituted his suspicious behavior in the eyes of the other passengers. If the weeks and months following September 11 give us some insight into how nationalism as a form of power can make some things happen, then they also indicate the pitfalls in the beliefs and practices that are set in motion.

Clearly, power permeates our interpersonal relations and gives us unequal access to material and nonmaterial resources. A chief characteristic of nationalism is that each nation is internally unified, but this belief is fraught with the reality of differences among citizens. When politicians speak of the American nation or the American people they can do so by sweeping important differences of class, race, ethnicity, gender, sexuality, geography, or religion between millions of people under the national rug. Furthermore, we expect that the people of a nation are equal, or ought to be equal if they are not. But this is the fundamental flaw of nationalism: although the nation may be seen as a community of equals, inequalities are rife. Not only do aspects such as race, class, gender, place of birth and belonging, sexuality, ethnicity, and religion make people different but these aspects also explain why not all citizens are treated equally. These inequalities are not simply incidental, but are a routine part of our lives; they are built into the social and legal infrastructures. All kinds of people may be (north) American citizens, but racism and xenophobia filter who truly belongs and who is denied full rights of inclusion into the national community.

Creating internal frontiers: racism and xenophobia in nationalism

The point that I am leading up to is the anti-Muslim violence that came within minutes of the tragedies. Racial verbal and physical assaults occurred immediately. These assaults were against Muslims of diverse origins, people of Arab origin, Sikhs, Hindus, Iranians, and Christians who were visibly different. A Pakistani family's house was burned down in Sacramento; the Islamic Institute of New York received phone calls threatening that the streets would be painted in the blood of its school's students; in Gary, Indiana, a man fired more than 21 shots from an assault rifle at an American of Yemeni origin; an elderly Sikh man was beaten with a baseball bat; and another Sikh man was shot dead at his gas station in Mesa, Arizona. The list is too long to complete, and it appears that many of the physical and verbal assaults were never reported for fear of further retaliation. Sikh men wearing turbans were especially targeted because they looked like Osama bin Laden in the eyes of their assailants; this, despite the fact that Sikhism is a different religion from his. While

some lamented the fact that assailants could not tell the difference between a Sikh and a Muslim, between an Arab and a South Asian, the
scope of the violence forced otherwise distinct groups to identify with the
widespread victimization. At the very least, the confusions between
the enemy and immigrants protected any group from being singled out.
Attacks against Jewish Americans were also reported later.

Why were racism and xenophobia so swiftly expressed? Lessons learned
after the bombing of a federal building in Oklahoma City in 1995 did
temper public reaction momentarily. At that time, immediate speculations
that it had to be the work of Islamic terrorist groups were proven wrong;
terrorism turned out to be of a white, Christian variety. But on September
11, 2001 any restraint quickly disappeared upon reports of Middle-
Eastern sounding hijackers. Racism and the xenophobia against people
perceived to be Muslims, foreigners, and others were swiftly expressed
because these sentiments already existed. There is a deeprooted history
of anti-Islamic sentiments in the United States that can be traced back to
black nationalism and its links to Islam. The violence of September 11
catalyzed rather than caused the racism. Furthermore, the racism and
xenophobia were not merely expressed against brown- or olive-skinned
women and men; this time, they were charged by the vigor of nationalism.
Anecdotal reports suggest that in some cases perpetrators of racism saw
their crimes as acts of patriotism. A 75-year-old man in Huntington, NY,
tried to run over a Pakistani woman in the parking lot of a shopping mall.
The man reportedly screamed that he was "doing this for my country." He
then followed the women into a store and reportedly threatened to kill her
for "destroying my country." The racism and xenophobia in the aftermath
of September 11 was the other side of nationalism and patriotism.

But the line between "us" and "them" that seems to be characteristic of
nationalism is rarely sharp, and more often than not is unstable. Even
though nationalism, racism, and xenophobia can draw lines between
insiders and outsiders, between foes and friends, between the American
people and the Taliban/Afghans, the divisions are far more ambiguous
and complicated. Initially, most political leaders' references to the moral
attitudes and ties that make people Americans made little allowance for
some Americans being Muslim. But a few days later they started to
caution people against persecuting Muslims and brown-skinned, foreign-
looking people. Attempts were made in political speeches to remind audiences that America included all manner of people – even Muslims and
Arab Americans.

Recognizing that the racist and xenophobic attacks after September 11
were about the internal frontiers of nationalism, President Bush and

others attempted to revise these boundaries.[7] He and other leaders spoke out against the racism and xenophobia that was fairly widespread across the nation. The President, for example, visited a mosque in Washington DC to make the point that retribution was being sought not from Muslims in general but from groups of Muslim terrorists. Nonetheless, rather than diminishing the interior boundaries between "real" Americans and brown-skinned immigrants, these political leaders differentiated between "good" immigrants and "bad" immigrants. Even though "good" immigrants were partially incorporated into the national community, the distinctions between "real" Americans and "good" immigrants remained intact. In one of his many speeches delivered to Congress after September 11, President Bush reminded his fellow Americans not to pick on those who look different from them. At first glance, this was an important statement coming from the President, but the limits of liberal attempts to *include* people in the national community were equally vivid. References to his fellow Americans and those different from them once again distinguished between Americans who represent the norm and those who do not because they seem different. Simply trying to include different people into the national community without redefining the national community as inherently diverse ended up re-emphasizing the distinctions between "regular" Americans and those who, regardless of their birthplace, will always remain outsiders in many respects because of their race and religion.

Another important reason to complicate the distinctions between "us" and "them" that seem so central to nationalism has to do with the impact of nationalism on American Muslims, and Arab-American immigrant groups, and others who were targeted in the aftermath of September 11. What complicated the positions of these groups is that anything less than unequivocal support for American nationalism and American foreign policy was considered akin to sedition and, moreover, support for the terrorists. Particularly for relatively recent immigrants this was not easy to negotiate. Most immigrants are tied to American soil because of a variety of factors: livelihood, property, lack of alternatives, desire to raise their children in America, desire to belong to the American national community, among others. Not surprisingly, many such groups condemned the violence of September 11 in no uncertain terms and rallied behind (north) American nationalism. I received a number of personal emails from South Asian friends and family members urging each other to stand up and be counted. A coalition of Muslim advocacy groups urged Muslim doctors to help in efforts at the World Trade Center site and encouraged Muslim Americans to donate blood. Arab and Sikh taxi drivers in New York City offered free rides to people who were attempting to track down loved ones feared lost in the attacks. Reportedly, these taxi drivers also clearly displayed the American flag and carried messages such as "God bless America" to show their patriotism and also to avoid harassment and assault.[8] That such groups would identify with the American national community is not unusual. What is noteworthy, however, is that these groups were unable freely to express any reservations about the war against Afghanistan for fear of retribution. The ongoing threat of physical and verbal violence against Muslim Americans, Arab Americans, and South Asians narrowed the possible responses from immigrants and citizens of color. Paradoxically, these groups became both collaborators in the surging nationalism, patriotism, and jingoism and the targets of the underside of nationalism, in the form of racism and xenophobia.

Institutional power of nationalism: quelling dissent

By now, it is surely clear that power is hardly limited to relations between individuals but also is institutionally exercised. That nationalism can move people to act in certain ways, give pleasure, fuel retribution against others, create and enforce social laws, govern who has the right to enter and exit national boundaries and who is entitled to the benefits of citizenship, gives us some measure of the expansive scope of nationalism spanning interpersonal and institutional realms. Its institutional forms lend force to the inequalities between individual people. We may downplay the racist, homophobic, or sexist behaviors of individuals by saying that they spring from ignorance or misplaced anger. But when representatives of the law or the Church or immigration laws enforce these viewpoints, racism, homophobia, or sexism become far more powerful. If the positions of leaders like President Bush and Senator John Warner give us some indication of the role of the legislative arm of the state in supporting expressions of nationalism, then the passing of the Patriot Act in the aftermath of September 11 is a sobering example of the power of institutions to enforce nationalist beliefs. Writing about the act, Patricia J. Williams questions the unprecedented merger between intelligence agencies and law enforcement sanctioned by this act.[9] She worries that the expanded power granted to law enforcement agencies, coupled with lowered standards of accountability, could seriously compromise civil liberties and promote paranoia.

Institutional attempts at quelling dissent were another aspect of the power of nationalism after September 11. In the wake of the discussion on the appropriate retaliation against terrorist groups and the Taliban, then accused of sheltering Osama bin Laden, critical or alternative positions were dismissed as anti-American. What I suggested before about minority groups' inability to freely express sentiments contrary to majority public opinion was more widely true for groups that questioned US foreign policy or advised against the bombing of Afghanistan. From conservatives to liberals, from Democrats to Republicans, the scope of acceptable positions became narrower in the first few months after September 11. In the mandate given by the Congress to the President to declare a war in response to the violence, there was only one representative, Congress-woman Barbara Lee, who declined. Reportedly, she was subjected to death threats as a result of her position. Again, what is unusual about this is that political dissent was quelled by charges of anti-Americanness; it would have been seen equivalent to inciting anti-American hatred. At its extreme, political dissent from US foreign policy or the popular public response was assumed to indicate sympathy with the terrorist groups. Rather than provoking healthy discussion and difference of opinion on a matter of crucial importance, nationalism prevented such differences.

Nothing better illustrates how the spirit of nationalism can be used to silence political differences than the task of the American Council of Trustees and Alumni (ACTA), which was founded in 1995. As its mission statement lays down, this organization is dedicated to academic freedom, quality, and accountability.[10] But Lynne V. Cheney, wife of Vice-President Dick Cheney, Senator Joe Leiberman, and other members of government joined together in targeting the academy for failing to participate in American patriotism and, worse, for inciting anti-American sentiment in students. A report on ACTA, published in November 2001, accused universities of "failing America" by refusing to take unequivocally patri-otic stances. President Bush's comments that there is no neutral ground, that governments and people either concur with or are against the United States, provided the political outline for the report. Citing selected com-ments from professors and deans at various universities in the nation, the report summarized its concerns in these words:

> Rarely did professors publicly mention heroism, rarely did they discuss the difference between good and evil, the nature of Western political order or the virtue of a free society. Indeed, the message of much of the academe was clear: BLAME AMERICA FIRST.[11]

There is much that can be said about the ACTA report. Never mind the glossing over of the differences among the positions taken in the academy.

Never mind, also, the fact that the academy is supposed to foster critical thinking and not easily capitulate to public opinion or state policy. Instead, I would like to draw attention to three points. First, giving the events and aftermath of September 11 due consideration by looking at history, contemporary politics, or America's role in the Cold War is not akin to blaming America. Second, there may not be neutral ground in this conflict, but serious and broader understandings of these events complicate simple distinctions between "good" and "evil." The moral equivocation among some academics might have occurred because they see victims on both sides of the conflict. Third, since when did expressing political difference come to signify sedition? Some would argue that disagreeing with state policy and popular public sentiment is a deeply American tradition that can be traced back to the revolutionary war against British colonialism.[12] Yet the report on ACTA simplifies a complex situation, and its identification and criticism of individual professors, deans, and groups in the academy in the name of patriotism threatens and silences different perspectives.

Cornerstones and Contradictions of Nationalism

One question that I often pose to students when we discuss nationalism in the classroom is "How do you identify nationalism?" Invariably, much of the discussion pivots around flags, maps, language, and intangible but influential ties between members of a national community. Isn't it strange, then, that despite the tremendous force of nationalism, it seems both very specific and very abstract? As noted earlier, it's not just that most of us have an easier time coming up with examples of nationalism than its meaning; rather, the symbols and rituals of nationalism are what give it shape in day-to-day life. Clearly, at moments of crisis, symbols such as flags at half-mast or the memorable photograph of the crew at the site of the World Trade Center hoisting a tattered flag as an act of defiance and fortitude, are the specific instances that gives shape to the nationalist spirit. In general, however, symbols such as flags, and repetitions throughout the media of national community and national interests, and the national map displayed on television weather reports, are a few of the ways in which we are constantly reminded of the American nation. Notwithstanding state institutions that enforce law, defend territories, and collect taxes, the intangible spirit of nationalism relies on its constant reiteration. Symbols such as the flag, together with a national language and depictions of the national character not only buttress the power of nationalism, but also are the very expressions of nationalism as a form of power.

Perhaps the most curious aspect of American nationalism post-September 11 was a disavowal of its nationalism. However paradoxical this may sound, the widespread opinion was that what was being witnessed in response to September 11 was patriotism, not nationalism. In a radio conversation regarding the recent rise of nationalism in the United States, a news commentator corrected me, saying that patriotism (good nationalism) rather than nationalism (the retrogressive variety) is what is true of American society. By implication, nationalism, in all of its dark and negative connotations, exists elsewhere. Somehow, nationalism has come to be associated with an unpredictable force more closely associated with the Third World and thus to be condemned. These differences between the First and the Third World, between "good" and "bad" nationalisms, and about nationalism as a progressive versus a retrograde force, plague discussions of nationalism. Taking issue with such divisions, an important commentator on the commonplace nature of nationalism, Michael Billig, says that this approach ignores the proliferation of nationalism in the West, seeing it as a property of extremists, guerrilla groups, and propagandizing states.[13] He writes,

> "Our" nationalism is not presented as nationalism, which is dangerously irrational, surplus, and alien. A new identity, a different label, is found for it. "Our" nationalism appears as "patriotism" – a beneficial, necessary and, often, American force."[14]

Building upon this theme, the position I take is that nationalism is both "here" and "there," it is both progressive and retrogressive, and it carries both possibilities and dangers.

Another paradoxical cornerstone of nationalism is that each nation is thought to be fundamentally unique. It is held that all nations are constructed on the basis of a single model but each nation is somehow unique. Culture, language, history, tradition, race or notions of racial stock, religion, sexuality, and attitude to women are among the chief ways in which nations are distinguished from one another. But since these differences between nations are established in relation to one another, like any other national identity, American national identity is given shape against what it is not; after September 11, Afghanistan provided the mirror image – the opposite – of American national identity. From the American perspective, if the differences between the two nations were differences between good and evil, between morality and malevolence, then religion, race, and, most of all, women crystallized their unique and opposed national identities.

Women as markers of national identity

The war against Afghanistan and the ruling Taliban was partly justified by the American national state as a war against a reprehensible regime, as measured by its support to terrorists and its oppressive treatment of women. If the men were characterized as evil, warmongering, fundamentalists, repressive, and irrational, then Afghan women were characterized as oppressed, passive, and abject victims. These characterizations did not take into account the history and origin of the Taliban and their repressive measures, or the ways in which Afghan women both colluded with and resisted the Taliban. Despite the fact that the Taliban seized control over most of the country in 1996 and a wide range of international feminist and human rights groups had expressed significant concern about the increasingly harsh control of women, there was little attempt by the United States to hold the Taliban accountable; on the contrary, state officials were reportedly attempting to strike deals for an oil pipeline with the Taliban. Soon after the start of the US military's bombing of Afghanistan, though, Afghan women's status was in the limelight. The discarding of the veil by some Afghan women after the surrender of the Taliban in key areas was mistakenly seen as a sign of their liberation and an endorsement of US intervention in Afghanistan. As the interim government was established, depictions of Afghan men as brave, proud, and resilient, and Afghanistan as a nation under siege started to emerge. What is striking is how characterizations of Afghanistan seem tied to US foreign policy.

Yet again, these characterizations of Aghanistan in the United States tell us more about American nationalism and national identity. Parallel to the more abject images of Afghan women and men were more potent images of American women and men. In response to the common question "Why do they hate us?," the freedom of American women was repeatedly cited. Political leaders and news commentators and analysts who took this point of view suggested that the freedoms that American women have access to are objectionable to fundamentalist and terrorist groups. Never mind the similarities between the lives of elite women in Afghanistan and in the United States; there is no denying the differences in the lives of most women in Afghanistan and those in the United States. Yet freedom and repression are relative terms that do not acknowledge that women's fundamental rights to freedom from poverty, freedom to make reproductive choices, the right to earn wages comparable to men, the right to basic health care are embattled in both countries. The parallel representations of the heroes in the aftermath of September 11 have almost exclusively been men in their roles as firefighters, as policemen, as soldiers, and as political leaders. As one insightful interviewer of the men and women working at the World Trade Center crash site noted, the attacks of September 11 were seen as attacks against American masculinity; not surprisingly then the scores of women who actively supported the work at the site were ignored in favor of the icons of American masculinity.

Approaching Nationalism

Reflecting back on the events of September 11, 2001 and its aftermath helps realize that the power and pitfalls of nationalism are not just limited to (north) America. Lest the discussion on September 11 and American nationalism give the misleading impression that nationalism is a factor of crisis and unusual events, I want to note that these moments of crisis merely make nationalism more visible and present in our consciousness. Developing this approach, Billig compellingly turns our attention to the everyday, ever-present but less visible forms of nationalism that are deeply ingrained in our consciousness.[15] In the United States, countless numbers of flags usually hang unnoticed and anthems are routinely sung at sports events. The President of the country typically ends speeches with "God Bless America," thereby calling on God to serve the national order.[16] Billig uses the term "banal nationalism" to make the point that nationalism is neither unusual nor uncommon but a humdrum part of our daily lives.[17] Indeed, he puts his finger on a central characteristic of nationalism: its ordinariness, which attests to its power to make itself seem part of the "natural" environment of societies. Therefore, the intangible, elusive nature of nationalism might be an indication not of its insignificance but of its extensive reach.

The look back at the aftermath of September 11, 2001 surely also clarifies that nationalism is neither inherently good nor inherently bad. As a belief system that has considerable consequences in our lives, nationalism is not innately a positive force nor is it innately a problem. On the contrary, nationalism emerges as a complex set of beliefs and practices that defy facile moral characterizations. Nothing less than a nuanced and even-handed approach is called for under these circumstances.

There is good reason to be critical of nationalism as a coherent, stable belief system. If, indeed, nationalism is based on networks of power that produce the illusion and reality of unity despite the differences between people, then looking for the contradictions gives insight into the workings and mis-steps of institutional forms of power. Examining the contradictions of nationalism following September 11, its promise of patriotism as well as its positioning of minority and immigrant communities allows us to challenge its influence. Rather than capitulate to its seduction, we are better able to see both how it can play a powerful role by uniting vast numbers of grief-stricken Americans while simultaneously making other groups vulnerable. The study of nationalism, then, has to be done thoughtfully. It is not to say that we cannot entertain the question that nationalism is genuinely shared by a group of people or questions of national history and culture, but all these need to be explored through a critical lens.

The classifications of nationalism are no less questionable. By that, I refer to national identities, differences between nationalism and patriotism, differences between insiders and outsiders, and distinctions between citizens and non-citizens. We need to take a skeptical approach to these categories for three reasons. First, national identities do not have any inherent essence, but are defined in relation to each other. In some ways, national identity is defined in opposition to another; as mentioned, before the fall of the Taliban American nationalism was characterized in diametrical opposition to that of Afghanistan. That these definitions of themselves rather than any innate or fixed notion of American identity tells us the importance of taking a thoughtful approach to the classifications of nationalism. Second, as we explored above, differences between national identities or between insiders and outsiders are hardly fixed. The interim, United States-backed government in Afghanistan and the presence of "good" immigrants in the United States indicate that classifications of nationalism are unstable and not simply twofold. In subsequent chapters, as we consider nationalism's links to colonialism, gender, sexuality, or ethnicity, I will suggest going beyond the superficial differences between the colonizers and the colonized, women and men, or hetero- and homosexuality. Third, a skeptical approach to classifications related to key concepts explored in the following chapters should also help us remain critical of the inequalities that frequently exist between categories. National identities, women and men, the colonizers and the colonized, do not simply acquire meaning in relation to one another; they are also unequal classifications.

Currently, the central challenge facing nationalism is the rise of ethnic political movements that struggle for greater autonomy within the confines of an existing state or seek to forge an independent state. Sometimes violent and bloody, these movements threaten to destabilize existing national states and an international order, or splinter these states into myriad unviable nation states. Yet the implications of these trends are less than clear. To what extent do these movements signal a tension between the model of nation state – one people, one territory – and the reality of most national states: many competing and unequal peoples living within a unified political territory? Did the wave of newly independent states at the end of formal colonialism mark the end of the revolutionary potential of nationalism? And, therefore, do these contemporary ethnic political movements point to the more repressive and regressive aspects of nationalisms? What do these movements portend for the future of nations and their states? Also, to what extent are these political and separatist movements exacerbated by the changing role of the national state amidst cross-border flows of people, finance, trade, and information? Alternatively, the question is whether these movements appear to be more violent and intransigent as a result of our analytical tools. In effect, what may have changed is our perspective on nationalism; in other words, we are now more likely to discern the violent, exclusionary nature of nationalism.

Locating this Book

This book is primarily directed at readers curious about the meaning of, and matters related to, nationalism. I do not assume ready familiarity on the part of readers with the concepts of nationalism, nation, or state. My intention here is to render the meaning and importance of these concepts intelligible through clear prose and useful examples. By bringing together these varied and sometimes competing insights across a range of disciplines my purpose is to inform rather than to persuade. Yet no doubt my "take" on nationalism will filter through the pages of this book and readers will consider whether they disagree or agree. Since this book will be more widely distributed in the United States and Western Europe, I have concentrated on examples that more easily resonate with a range of readers in these settings. At the same time, examples and discussions relate to contexts outside the Euro-American context and I hope that, where possible, this book will be of interest to readers elsewhere. For this reason, I have tried to mix internationally publicized matters of nationalism with examples that are less widely known.

In a nutshell, this book is an account of nationalism and its central aspects. The quick version is that even though there is considerable debate about the lasting power of nationalisms and nations, they continue to have great impact in our lives. To do better justice to the beliefs and practices of nationalism, this book-length account is devoted to examining its important facets. Yet neither this book nor any other can provide a complete overarching understanding of nationalism; in the most optimistic case, we aim to do our best. Nationalism is too broad and wide-ranging a concept to allow any author to capture neatly its complexities, contradictions, and diverse trajectories. But this is true of a wider field as well: knowledge is by its nature incomplete and ongoing.

Knowledge is biased as well as partial. The overview of the various theoretical perspectives in Chapter One helps make the point that theoretical approaches are less objective statements of fact than they are disciplinary and personal ways of understanding and analyzing a concept as complicated as nationalism. If there is one thing that these approaches illustrate, it is the point that there is no single account of nationalism or no single way to tell its story. On the contrary, the disciplinary perspectives and the way scholars conceptualize power with respect to nationalism produce multiple, competing accounts of nationalism. Indeed, the variety of lenses produces a range of insights and incongruences. As the discussion in Chapter One will indicate, sometimes it is not clear that investigators are looking at the same concept. If there are those who laboriously work on nationalism in order to find a comprehensive, useful theory of it, there are others who argue that no single theory of nationalism could be useful, because just as there are many nationalisms there are numerous explanations.

Perhaps the breadth and the complexities of nationalism explain the substantial body of literature that has emerged since the early 1970s attempting to answer questions about the definition and meaning of nationalism, its origins, its crucial aspects, and its links to broader social processes such as capitalism, colonialism, as well as their cultural and political consequences. Not surprisingly, as a topic of inquiry it cuts across several disciplines. The origins and history of nations around the world, the area of international relations, cultural and political forms of nationalism, links to the state, racism, fascism, ethnic conflict, gender, sexuality, genocide, immigration, diaspora, are only some of the aspects that are considered by various disciplines. Political science, sociology, international relations, history, women's studies, literature, and anthropology are the disciplines that typically engage with questions of nationalism. Analyzing the concept of nationalism from any single disciplinary perspective is no easy task either, nor is it always useful. Where the boundaries between these disciplines are very strictly observed, the study of nationalism seems analogous to the blind men of fable who tried to describe an elephant through its individual parts. This also explains why the bulk of the literature on nationalism based in political science, international relations, and, to some extent, sociology continues to ignore the links between nationalism and gender. In political science and international relations, along with the omissions there are also insights about the role of the state and the institutions that enforce nationalisms.

Given the sheer breadth and depth of aspects of nationalism and the fact that issues cannot be neatly divided as a political science or a sociological matter, the trend in the study of nationalism is toward interdisciplinarity. Interdisciplinary studies on nationalism are important for another more compelling reason: some of the most groundbreaking and fruitful insights on nationalism come from work that cuts across disciplinary perspectives. In this book I borrow from numerous areas of study in order to make sense of nationalism. Nonetheless, my background is in sociology and women's studies, and that will shape my approach and argument here. Sociological insights about the links between personal and collective matters, about the importance of understanding group practices and patterns, about paying attention to the influence of social institutions are no doubt useful to any study of nationalism. Feminist insights further enrich the contributions of political science, international relations, anthropology, colonial studies and history toward a critical understanding of nationalism. Our societies remain at odds owing to inequalities of class, gender, race, sexuality, and ethnicity, among other factors. Perhaps no group has more effectively contributed to the nuances of nationalism's flawed promise of a united community than international feminist scholars. While I draw upon the insights of modernist approaches to nationalism, my approach is strongly shaped by postcolonial and feminist criticisms of modernist theories; this will become clearer in the following chapters.

As befits a feminist sociological perspective, I should complete this introduction by locating my subjective position on nationalism. I grew up in India, which became independent from British colonialism and was partitioned from East and West Pakistan in 1947. Coming of age in the 1980s, my middle-class urban-educated cohort was shaped by the legacies of nationalism that had led to political sovereignty as well as forging of the two separate nations of India and Pakistan. We were heavily influenced by the idea that over and above our class, ethnic, regional, religious, and caste differences we were all Indian, that our individual and communal interests were synonymous with national interest, and the progress of each group was tied to national progress. To take on board this ideal was no small achievement for a densely-populated, highly stratified, linguistically, ethnically, and religiously diverse country that was forged into a nation through the encounter with colonialism. I remember well the television documentaries, advertisements, textbooks, popular films, political speeches, national rituals, and state policies on centralized administration that frequently played on these themes through the 1970s. I think we learned early to be cynical about the vested interests and greed of politicians but maintained faith in the future of the nation.

By the 1980s, however, the promise of the nation became increasingly harder to reconcile with growing communal tensions in numerous parts of the country – often due to the tensions between Hindus and Muslims but also those between upper-caste and marginalized Hindus. The secessionist movements in Punjab and Kashmir, the movements for cultural and political autonomy in the Northeast states disabused us of our liberal perspectives on national unity. State-sponsored violence to quell secession and political dissent was as troubling as the realization of what it took to "unify" peoples who did not see themselves as Indian. More immediately, I believe that the political implications of differences among my middle-class cohort, based on religion and ethnicity, were beginning to become clear as we thought ahead about higher education and job opportunities. No less troubling was the inconsistency of womanhood; even though many of us had embraced the ideology of the modern educated but culturally Indian woman, we were also faced with its limitations in our personal and public lives. It is this paradox of the promise and pitfalls of nationalism in India, which were further complicated in the United States owing to racism and xenophobia, that has left its impression on me.

To recapitulate, this book presents a partial and considered account of nationalism. I chose to focus on aspects of nationalism that are either influential and, therefore, relevant in our contemporary lives or have been neglected in the bulk of the literature on the topic. While the salience of ethnicity and religious fundamentalism seem entirely relevant in the changing face of national and international politics, issues of gender, race, and sexuality have not been given adequate attention in the dominant scholarship; they have been relegated to scholars working at the margins of academic hierarchies. As a result of the Eurocentric approach to the origins of nationalism there is far less attention paid to the links between nationalism and colonialism than one might expect. The insightful scholarship from researchers working in gender, colonial, sexuality, and literary studies have, since the 1980s, provided an important basis upon which this book can build.

Therefore, Chapter One explores theoretical perspectives on nationalism, but also carefully considers the concepts of nation and the state. In keeping with the more carefully elaborated approach to nationalism in this chapter, successive chapters trace the many strands of nationalism's links to the modern state. Chapter Two highlights the importance of colonialism and race in the meaning and proliferation of nationalisms in the nineteenth century, by way of mapping their enduring legacies. Chapter Three focuses on the links between nationalism and gender, Chapter Four on sexuality. Chapter Five looks at the role of religion and ethnicity in the contemporary resurgence of nationalism. The sixth, concluding, chapter explores the importance of understanding nationalism from a globalizing, transnational perspective.

NOTES

1 I put "north" in parentheses to make the point that there is more than one America. Even though "America" is frequently associated with "the United States," people living in Central and Latin America also think of themselves as Americans. Therefore, I will periodically put the qualifier "north" before America or use the terms "South," "Central," or "Latin America" to register the differences.

2 While this book was in production the USA invaded Iraq to oust Saddam Hussein and his regime.

3 Benedict Anderson, *Imagined Communities: Reflections on the Origin and Spread of Nationalism*, rev. edn. (London and New York: Verso, 1991), esp. p. 7.

4 Here, I especially refer to the work of Elie Kedourie, *Nationalism*, 4th, expanded, edn. (Cambridge, Mass. and Oxford: Blackwell, 1993). Kedourie's work will be more carefully taken up in Chapter One.

5 Michel Foucault is best associated with this view of power. Unlike others who take the position that power is the ability to prevent, restrain, and control, Foucault argues that power operates by specifying what is possible: power operates in a "productive" way by shaping what is normal, desirable, or pleasurable. This is also what makes power not simply an external imposition but part of our subjectivity and social relations. See *Discipline and Punish: The Birth of the Prison*, trans. Alan Sheridan, 2nd edn. (New York: Vintage Books, 1995); *The History of Sexuality*, trans. Robert Hurley, 1st American edn. (New York: Pantheon Books, 1978).

6 Kris Axtman, "Political dissent can bring federal agents to the door," *Christian Science Monitor*, January 8, 2002.

7 The concept of internal frontiers was developed by Johann Fichte. His reference to interior frontiers is particularly helpful because it reminds us that making

internal distinctions between members of the nationalism community is essential to nationalism and, at the same time, nationalism is defined by an intangible "moral attitude" and "invisible ties" that make an individual a member of a nation. See Ann Laura Stoler, "Sexual affronts and racial frontiers: European identities and the cultural politics of exclusion in colonial Southeast Asia," in Frederick Cooper and Ann Laura Stoler (eds.) *Tensions of Empire: Colonial Cultures in a Bourgeois World* (Berkeley, Los Angeles, and London: University of California Press, 1997), pp. 198–237, esp. p. 199.

8   Chastity Pratt and Melanie Lefkowitz, "Volunteers help families, hope to avoid harassment," *Newsday*, September 16, 2001.

9   Patricia J. Williams, "By any means necessary," *The Nation*, November 26, 2001.

10   *Defending Civilization: How Our Universities are Failing and What Can Be Done About It* (Washington, DC: American Council of Trustees and Alumni, November, 2001).

11   Ibid., p. 3.

12   This was the position taken by a professor at Tufts University, Medford, Mass. in an effective response to ACTA's report. See Martin J. Sherwin, "Tattletales for an open society," *The Nation*, January 21, 2002.

13   Michael Billig, *Banal Nationalism* (London, Thousand Oaks, Calif., and New Delhi: Sage Publications, 1995).

14   Ibid., p. 55.

15   Billig, *Banal Nationalism*.

16   Ibid., p. 75.

17   Ibid., p. 6.

CHAPTER ONE

Vexed Links: Perspectives on Nationalism, the State, and Modernity

[I]t is surprising to recall that not many years ago nationalism was considered one of Europe's most magnificent gifts to the world.[1]

"Nation," "nationalism," and "the state" are loosely and interchangeably used concepts in everyday parlance. The terms often seem confusing and imprecise. The premise of this chapter is that they are not interchangeable. But giving precise, unequivocal definitions of these concepts is easier promised than delivered. Depending upon their theoretical perspectives, influential scholars of nationalism, nation, and the state develop somewhat different definitions and meanings for them. Therefore, in lieu of singular definitions, this chapter will explore the multiple meanings of nationalism, nation, and the state, and address their historical and varied linkages.

A second task in this chapter is to identify and analyze the foremost theoretical perspectives on these matters. Understanding the nuances of theories underlying different definitions of nationalism – their insights as well as their limitations – will be helpful in engaging with nationalism at a more profound level. Indeed, developing theories is no esoteric process; in order to make sense of the world around us, we "theorize" constantly. "Theorizing" is shorthand for how we interpret, name, and explain events, and react to them. Our concepts, such as "state," "nation," and "nationalism," are attempts to describe and interpret complex social realities even as what we perceive and make sense of as reality is filtered through our notions of these concepts. Theorizing, then, encapsulates a complex relationship between reality and the abstraction necessary to make sense of it and to find how best to align complex, unstable, and linked empirical and conceptual worlds. Theory filters what we recognize as experience and what that experience means to us; in this sense, theoretical perspectives are not unbiased, ever complete, or incapable of change. And without doubt it is possible to shift one's theoretical perspective and to look at the same concept, social phenomenon, or object with fresh eyes.

Here, I am reminded of a television show of the late 1980s and early 1990s, *In Different Worlds*, which I used to watch periodically several years ago. It was a popular show in the United States, in which the plots revolved around students attending a black university. It was only in the midst of a casual conversation with a friend that I realized that all of the student characters were black! Owing to my cultural background up to that point, which was the vantage point from which I was interpreting the show, I could enjoy it with a partial understanding. Watching it with a different understanding of the student characters gave me a different angle into the otherwise same show. Most other viewers in the United States at the time would surely have had less difficulty in placing the race of the characters on the show, but their overall perceptions and reactions would have varied in other respects. One's vantage point may shift to provide renewed or different understanding of a social occurrence, but there is no one position that provides complete or unbiased understanding.

Multiple theoretical perspectives that help us understand, explain, and respond to events do and should exist. These perspectives are mediated not only by our personal experiences, but also, as suggested in the Introduction, by our disciplinary orientations, political events, the cultural context, and the broader historical moment. Since no single perspective can provide us with a complete understanding of these events, alternative perspectives not only yield different insights but also give us indications of what is at stake beneath the differences. Why, for example, does nationalism seem to be dangerous when considered from one perspective and a kind of daily plebiscite from another vantage point? This chapter will also address the problems that arise when theories are generalized beyond the specific cultural, historical setting from which they were initially drawn. Why do the bulk of the theories of state, nation, and nationalism remain rooted in western contexts or, worse, get exported as universal measures to the Third World? This is the concern underlying the opening quotation from Partha Chatterjee: prevalent Eurocentrism in dominant theories encourages the view that nationalism is a western invention that was corrupted in its export to other sites.

In order to sidestep the limitations of some of the theoretical perspectives explored in this chapter, I will argue in favor of taking a "culturalist" approach to nationalism. In keeping with the position outlined above, I do not assert that this culturalist approach is either complete or unbiased, rather, that it is more useful. It allows us to consider the multiple origins of nationalism, and that there may be more than one variety or model of nationalism. It allows for the importance of understanding the interplay of nationalisms and modern states without reducing them to one another, for acknowledging nationalisms as contested forms of power, and for locating the politics of nationalism at the institutional but also the more mundane, unremarkable level. While I will elaborate on this culturalist approach to nationalism, it is necessary to clarify what I mean by the underlying notion of culture. I understand culture as not just a way of life, including traditions, food, religion, language, but more broadly as the framework through which we make meaning: of ourselves, our environment, and our social relations. Like meaning, cultures are plural, unequal, fraught with power and contestation, variable with place and time, and dynamic. Not just something we do at the end of the work day, culture is also the realm through which we make sense of fundamental aspects of ourselves, including gender, race, sexuality, nationality, citizenship, personhood, and other subjective and objective aspects of ourselves. Culture, then, is thoroughly political and politics is thoroughly inflected by cultural meanings and differences. In sum, "culture" is shorthand for the historical, specific social context within which we live, make sense of our beliefs, practices, desires, and identities, and reproduce and challenge forms of power and social inequalities – such as those to do with race, gender, age, nationality.

This chapter starts with a discussion of the concepts of state, nation, and nationalism, and their variable linkages. The following section focuses on theories of state and nationalism seen through the lens of a culturalist approach. The focus is on the strengths and limitations of modernist perspectives as well as alternative approaches to nationalism. The chapter concludes with a brief overview of the central points.

The Concept of the State

While it is widely agreed that states, in their varying shapes and forms, have long existed over the course of human history, anthropologists and historians, in particular, underscore the concept of state formation to note that states are neither natural nor inevitable. On the contrary, states emerge in some cultures under suitable historical circumstances, and critical writers highlight the importance of cultural and historical contexts for state formation.[2] In the introduction to a useful volume on states and state formation, *State/Culture: State-formation after the Cultural Turn*, editor George Steinmetz is careful to note that "state formation" does not refer to the mythic, initial moment when the state emerges.[3] Instead, he sees state formation as the "creation of durable states and transformations of basic structural features of these states."[4] The concept of state formation sees past and contemporary states as always and continually in formation. Furthermore, there is no natural progression or developmental trajectory of state formation. Scholars of state formation note that there have been various kinds of states at different historical moments.[5] Over the last five hundred years, one can speak of absolutist states, national states, colonial states, theocratic states, postcolonial states, and postindustrial states.

What does hold more generally true across the different classifications of relatively recent states is that there is little about our lives that does not come directly or indirectly under its purview: birth, death, taxes, marriage, sexuality, health, education, property, and commerce, to name some aspects. The institution of marriage may be considered a personal matter but the United States' General Accounting Office, for example, in 1997 listed as many as 1,049 federal laws relating to the benefits, rights, and privileges contingent on marital status.[6] At the same time, individual states within the country (not to be confused with the concept of the state under discussion), have several hundred more laws about marriage, the vast majority of which do not recognize civil or marital unions between same-sex partners. Indeed, it is difficult to consider contemporary life without the presence of the state.

Perhaps therefore, we may find it difficult to identify the state, since it seems to be either too abstract or too diffuse. "The state," as such, cannot be pinpointed. Rather, we identify the political institutions, social structures, rituals, and symbols that make up the state, giving it both meaning and power. We are also likely to think of the state as a "thing"; in its noun form, we infer the state to be a fixed, permanent, singular entity. But the state is neither continuous nor unchanging. We may personify states as autocratic, liberal, weak, or failed, but these characterizations have been rightly challenged because they are underpinned by perceptions of fundamental differences between western and Third World states.[7] Furthermore, we have a tendency to speak of the state as a coherent unit. In their introduction to a helpful collection on postcolonial states, *States of Imagination: Ethnographic Explorations of the Postcolonial State*, editors Thomas Blom Hansen and Finn Stepputat note that as modern forms and practices of governance penetrate and shape human life in unprecedented ways, governance itself becomes more dispersed, diversified, and fraught with inconsistencies.[8] Yet, taking the position that this lack of coherence does not indicate the weakening of the state, Hansen and Stepputat suggest that inconsistency and incoherence not only characterize the modern state, but also make it more powerful.

States may seem omnipotent. Films, television shows, and novels in India, Britain, and the United States, for example, routinely depict the state as all-powerful bureaucratic structures, that are unified, centralized, and riddled with the secret machinations of power. These myths of the state are not limited to popular culture but inform our understandings and confusion of what we mean by "the state" and how we experience it in our lives. Nonetheless, the power and influence of the state is always being contested. (North) American popular culture recognizes challenges to the state in at least two ways: the predictably male vigilante who faces up to the power of the state out of love for his family or country and the renegade band of officials who subvert the authority of the state and its ability to protect ordinary people. Needless to say, the real scenarios are more complicated. For example, the right to bear arms, the right to terminate pregnancy, the medical use of marijuana, are just a few of the areas in which organizations in the United States struggle against state intervention.

On the other hand, various activist groups take the position that the state in question does not do enough to ensure parity of rights and social justice for its residents, given the differences in their racial, class, ethnic, gender, sexual, religious, and national identities. Especially in postcolonial settings, there appear to be two contradictory trends: growing demands for decentralization of the state and greater local autonomy; and an expanding discourse of rights and entitlements for citizens. So the role of the state is paradoxically strengthened as it is simultaneously called upon to confer full-fledged rights on citizens, to recognize more institutions, movements, and organizations, to address developmental issues, and to extend and ensure the rights of citizenship.[9] We may worry about the reach of the state but we also look to state institutions and state apparatuses to protect legal and customary rights and privileges of individuals, communities, and political groups.

In contrast to prevailing myths, the state emerges as a contradictory and fraught set of institutions, structures of governance, and social relations that are neither stable nor uncontested. The overall picture of the state, then, is one of messiness rather than smooth functioning, one of power rather than neutrality, one of tensions between power and resistance rather than outright domination, and one of variability rather than a fixed entity. Hansen and Stepputat show that "myths of state" are cultivated inside bureaucracies and among political figures, and enacted in state spectacles, stamps, architecture, and other symbolic arenas of the state.[10] They are less certain whether these state rituals are meant to enforce the authority of the state over its population or to strengthen the sense of a unified state among its dispersed officials and administrators. Timothy Mitchell, a well-known scholar of state and state theory, pushes this line of reasoning further; he suggests that the coherent and unified state is a myth; this false sense of coherence and unity is the result of how power functions in general, and in particular is the effect of modern governmentality.[11] While we will pursue these arguments more fully below, I anticipate these arguments here, both to unravel prevailing myths surrounding the state and to gesture toward alternative understandings.

Defining the modern state

So, what can we say the modern state is? The French Revolution is heralded as the turning point in the emergence of modern states, and centralized, direct rule and close monitoring of the population are among its key characteristics, according to Charles Tilly, a leading scholar of the state.[12] The gradual differentiation of the economic and political arenas, first witnessed through the sixteenth and seventeenth centuries, is another important characteristic. A number of practices, beginning in the nineteenth century, together constituted the transition to modern states in western Europe. Among them were: a centralized taxation system and bureaucracy, the use of standing armies, the building of social infrastructure, the regulating of economic activity in a planned way, policing and managing potential threats to social order, monitoring industrial conflict, installing systems of national education, organizing aid and social services to the poor, building and maintaining communication networks, and imperial expansion.

Alongside their material aspects, modern states are defined by what Hansen and Stepputat refer to as "imagination of the state,"[13] or, the idea of the state. As they succinctly describe it, the state is characterized by three aspects: the claiming of territorial sovereignty through a monopoly of violence; the gathering and control of knowledge about the population; the generation of resources and ensuring the well-being of the population through developing and managing the national economy. But what is also essential to the existence of the state is to reproduce the idea of the state as a normal and permanent feature. Hansen and Stepputat argue that the

institutionalization of law and legal discourse as the source of state authority, the materialization of the state in permanent signs, rituals, monuments,
letterheads, etc., and the nationalization of the territory and state institutions through the writing of history and notions of a national community
are three ways in which the idea of the state continues to be sustained.

Not surprisingly, the difficulties in identifying the state and its limits
have led scholars to focus upon what the state is not, or to abandon the
concept of the state altogether in favor of the notion of political systems,
matters to which we will return below. The state is not synonymous with
politics, government, or administration. Even though it is hard to separate
politics from the state in contemporary times, politics are not limited to the
state. Especially if we understand politics as more widely present among
social and cultural institutions, then surely politics extends beyond the
scope of the state to non-state groups, associations, and communities.
Similarly, the term "government" may have multiple connotations but
it is recognized as different from the concept of state. "Government" may
refer to the institutional structures and procedures (parliament, three
branches of government, etc.). In other cases, "government" is used
interchangeably with administration; so one can refer to Tony Blair's
government or the Bush administration. "Administration" also has been
used to identify the cadre of persons and bodies who execute policy and
discharge public services under the direction of the government, but this
use is on the decline.[14] In contrast to these terms, "the state" refers to
more enduring structures and ideas.

Two definitions describe states as "coercion-wielding organizations that
are distinct from households and kinship groups and exercise clear priority
in some respects over all other organizations within substantial territories,"[15] or, "as administrative and coercive organizations that are potentially autonomous from, although conditioned by, socio-economic interests
and structures."[16] These two definitions, by Tilly and Theda Skocpol respectively, give some indication of the differences, and also the similarities,
between numerous definitions of the state.

Of all the characteristics associated with the modern state, there is most
emphasis on an identifiable territory. The state lays claim to jurisdiction
over this specified territory and the population within its parameters.
Borders of these territories may change with political developments or
may be disputed, but they are an essential attribute of the state. Building
upon the ideas of Friedrich Ratzel, an earlier German geographer, Anthony Giddens, an important state theorist, usefully distinguishes between
the notion of frontier and that of border.[17] For Giddens, a frontier is an
area on the periphery of a state, although not necessarily adjoining

another state, in which central authority is diffuse or thinly spread. A border, on the other hand, is a "known and geographically drawn line separating and joining two or more states."[18] What is important, according to Giddens, is that, unlike frontiers, borders exist only in the era of modern states.

Within their territory, states claim predominance or supremacy over all other groups and organizations, a claim that is backed by legal institutions and structures. For this reason, states have significant control over such matters as extracting and allocating taxes and overseeing resource centers: business firms, universities, hospitals, etc. Understanding the state as a pre-eminent power container, Giddens sees state control as rooted in four essential aspects.[19] First is state surveillance, involving the accumulation and storage of information about the population, such as births and deaths, income, health, marriage, etc., or the direct and indirect monitoring of institutions (businesses, prisons), groups (religious, non-profit, political), and individuals. Second is the creation of a group of individuals dedicated to the functioning of the state, a group not directly involved with production and one that may not (in theory) use the resources of the state for personal gain. Third is the development of military power, which directly or indirectly backs the administration and existing legal structures with the threat of violence. Fourth is the ability to influence people ideologically through schooling and the mass media. These factors give the state its ability to claim predominance over all other groups within a given territory.

That states have control over the use of violence is an issue that led the arguably most influential scholar of the state, Max Weber, to note that states have monopoly in this matter by mobilizing the police, the army, and other institutionalized forms of violence. By threatening or using both physical and symbolic violence, states have sought to pacify civilians by eliminating non-state-sanctioned violence, such as gang warfare, militant non-state groups, protest movements that use or appear to trigger disorder or bloodshed. Paradoxically, states have introduced new forms of aggression and physical force through increasing emphasis on the military and on war, and on creating compliant and somewhat homogenous populations through educational systems, and state-led stigmatization of some groups (such as "welfare mothers" in the United States). But Tilly and Giddens both disagree with Weber's notion that the state monopolizes violence; for them the issue is that the state claims monopoly over "legitimate" violence.

What gives power and pre-eminence to the modern state is not only the direct or indirect threat of violence, but also law. A central aspect of

modern states is the codification of law, which is the source of its authority. This is hardly an uncomplicated relationship; even though there are
other forms of law – such as customary law – that challenge the state as
the highest legal authority, state formation and the legal codification of
social relations occur simultaneously, thereby pinning the authority of the
state to law. In Pakistan, for example, the tension between state and
customary legal practices is encouraging many activists and international
human rights organizations, such as Amnesty International, to call on the
state to override customary law. Two recently highly publicized cases –
one involving a tribal council's sentence consisting of the rape of a woman
by way of punishing her brother and the other in which a tribal council
saw fit to recompense a family for murder by forcing the family of the
perpetrator to hand over two young girls to the wronged family – highlight conflict between tribal law customarily followed by some communities and the legal authority of the state. Since tribal councils are not part
of the judicial system, do not function under state-recognized guidelines,
and do not have any legal standing, human rights groups in Pakistan and
abroad look to the higher legal authority of the state and its ability to
abolish or modify tribal councils. Just as the legal sphere might be seen as
biased, or as the state's instrument legalizing discrimination and inequality, the state is itself seen as the legal means to institute rights, to interpret
them, and to guarantee them.

Another fundamental aspect of the modern state is the claim to sovereignty. Not only does this claim imply that the state is the ultimate
political authority with pre-eminence over all other groups and organizations within the territory; more importantly, it applies externally with
respect to other states. Sovereignty suggests that each state is recognized
by other states as a separate, territorial unit with a right to self-govern-
ment, and a right to defend its borders against external threat. Each state
can make decisions about the course of its future. The mutual recognition
of individual claims to sovereignty amidst an international system forms
the basis for diplomacy and international law.

Typically, power needs to justify or legitimize its existence; the state is
no different. Weber famously argued that, alongside territory and monopoly over violence, legitimacy was a central aspect of the state. For him,
while state legitimacy could be embedded in traditional or in charismatic
authority, the legitimacy of rational legal authority is most compelling for
its impersonal and disinterested basis; rational legal authority is based on
the position rather than the person, and states that are so organized
appear more legimate. The state as an expression of territorial sovereignty
and authority, capable of protecting and nurturing the population and

economy, and the legitimate representation of the will and interests of its citizens, gained wide currency since the 1940s.[20] Little lends more legitimacy to the state or to the principle of nationalism than the notion of "the people" as the basis for sovereignty – that there exists a unique and unified community identified with a sovereign territory. Today, political leaders who come into power through military coups or rule through repressive measures without the political mandate of the people are likely to attract reproach, not respect, from the United Nations or other states. The vilification of Saddam Hussein after the Gulf War in 1991 and in the aftermath of September 11, 2001 may have been motivated by complex political interests and alliances, but he was broadly condemned for his regime's brutality to its people as well as its threat to other states.

Nationalism, Nation, and State: Which Comes First?

There are broadly two ways of thinking about the intricate relations between nationalisms, nations, and the state. One trajectory of the state in nation-formation can be traced to the second phase of the French Revolution (1789–92). Although some historians, Benedict Anderson in particular, argue that nationalisms and the idea of nations were first conceived in the American colonies, it was the French Revolution that helped crystallize the concept of political or state-based nationhood. The French, American, and British states are associated with political nationalisms; they are politically derived from the concept of common citizenship. What matters is that, in principle, the nation is defined as a civic community of equal citizens, regardless of their social and cultural differences. According to Rogers Brubaker citizenship was formally defined as a result of the French Revolution, civil equality was established, political rights were institutionalized, and legal and ideological distinctions between citizens and foreigners were elaborated.[21] Nations were, therefore, forged out of a shared political affiliation to the state.

What is equally important to note is that nations so defined brought legitimacy to modern states. Key to the modern state is the idea that even though as a centralized, overarching authority a state has recourse to the use of force, what gives it legitimacy is the consent of its people. Rather than residing in king or emperor, sovereign authority is vested in the people, and the role of the state is to represent the people and protect their interests. The modern state is envisioned as a direct relationship between individual citizens as well as a community of consenting citizens unified as a nation. If states are seen as representing the collective will of the people, they are less likely to be seen as coercive and more likely to be seen as neutral administrations. The French Revolution, therefore, re-imagined the cultural and political relations between individuals and the state through the concept of nation. Nationhood is a means to ensure that a unified community of citizens/people is the sovereign authority of the state. This is also what made the idea of nations and nationalisms revolutionary; they challenged the legitimacy of the existing state.

Nonetheless, states become important to nation-formation and notions of national citizenry by making nations logistically possible. Certain key state functions create the conditions for consciousness of the nation: the centralization of administration, (tax collection, means of communication, official languages, infrastructure to connect regions within the territory), militarization, implementation of industrial development, creation of market economies, and establishment of colonial relations. Wars, interstate rivalries, markets, and transportation systems, which are all part of state-making, help forge national consciousness; but national consciousness is neither simply available for modern states to invoke nor is it simply a product of state formation. I think it would be a mistake to understand the rise of nations and nationalisms simply as ideological tools of the state. Rather, nations are facilitated by the mechanisms of modern states in important ways but are not reducible to state formation.

In cases where the nation is forged as a political community, the state also plays a crucial role in fostering national consciousness and managing the tensions between the principle of equality and the reality of differences among its citizens. This is what Tilly refers to as state-led nationalism.[22] State-led nationalisms impose a particular definition of the nation. To this purpose, some forms of culture might be suppressed, and preferred versions of national languages, names, costumes, rituals, museums, and educational programs might be promoted; in extreme cases, nonconforming groups might be expelled or killed. This is perhaps why injecting history textbooks with accounts of national struggle and fortitude, teaching the national anthem, and in some cases teaching the national language in schools, are widely used strategies by the state to transform individuals into members of a national community of citizens.

Hugh Seton-Watson helpfully refers to such state-led nationalisms as "official nationalism."[23] Seton-Watson further describes official nationalism as a move by leaders of nations to strengthen the state by creating within it a single homogenous nation based on impositions of religion, culture, or language. Official nationalisms may be overt, as in the case of India's attempt to foist Hindi on the people as a national language despite the fact that less than 50 percent of them speak it. Or they may be effectively reinforced through images or ideas, such as of Britain as an English-speaking nation. The notions of state-led or official nationalism implicitly acknowledge the possibility of multiple nationalisms within the same territory competing for representation.

The histories of white-unity-based nationalism and African nationalism in South Africa are instructive in examining the differences between official and resistant nationalisms within the same state. Anthony W. Marx notes that official nationalism in South Africa was based on an uneasy alliance between the Dutch-descended Afrikaners and the British-descended English speakers.[24] Given the history of conflict between these two groups (e.g. the Anglo-Boer War, 1899–1902) and the enduring differences, official nationalism vacillated between Afrikaner nationalists and an Afrikaner-English alliance based on white unity. When the Afrikaner Nationalist Party came into power in 1948, it was better able to structure state policies in keeping with their Afrikaner nationalism than with white unity. The party's policy of apartheid was widely institutionalized by categorizing the population into races, forbidding interracial marriage or sex, enforcing Bantustans or black homelands, segregating education, and having separate services for blacks, and generally excluding Africans from South African citizenship. When Africans' and colored peoples' protests exploded into violence in 1960, major anti-apartheid organizations were banned and forced into exile by the state.[25] The African National Congress (ANC), the party that came into power in 1994 after apartheid had ended, had provided a sustained form of resistance to racist state-led nationalism. While the ANC is not the only example of resistant nationalism in South Africa, it garnered the most support in its opposition to state repression and state-led nationalism. In contrast to the white unity of the Afrikaner-English alliance, the ANC initially used black unity to bring together various groups and later sought to include all those marginalized by apartheid. However, Marx notes that since the ANC and its supporters united against apartheid rather than in forming a political program, with the dismantling of apartheid many felt their nationalist identity splinter.

In contrast, the second route to nation formation is described as a cultural or ethnic route. In some cases, nations are based on possibly mythical claims of common origin, or of peoplehood derived from a shared culture. The gradual emergence of an ethnic and culturally based nation in early nineteenth-century Germany, independent of the state, can be seen in contrast to civic nations. Nations may be defined primarily in cultural or ethnic terms and statehood is then seen as an ancillary political extension. Nationalisms, in these cases, are state-seeking, and aim at securing a sovereign state or a territory carved out of an existing state. These nationalist movements challenge the legitimacy of an existing state, especially when they make demands for cultural and political autonomy or sovereignty, and trigger the counter-force of official nationalisms and state institutions, such as the police and the military. This is what initially distinguished nationalism in the ex-colonies. Typically, in the colonies, nations were defined in cultural terms and the political movements against the colonial state precipitated the harsh measures of colonial rule, in the form of massacres, deportation or jailing of leaders, or attempts to fracture the unity of nationalist movements.

Indeed, some scholars make a distinction between cultural and political nationalisms. Political nationalisms are defined in relation to the state. But John Hutchinson, in particular, believes that not all nationalisms seek to become congruent with the state, and may instead be used especially to rally certain groups together.[26] For Hutchinson, cultural nationalism is not narrowly directed at unifying people under the political umbrella of citizenship governed by common laws. Instead, the cultural nationalist sees the state as accidental and focuses on the nation as either the outcome of a common past or through shared traditions and a shared destiny.[27] Hutchinson usefully summarizes the main aspects of cultural nationalism: importance of history; competing definitions of nation; and the importance of cultural symbols.[28]

The overall position taken in this book is that the interplay between nationalisms, nations, and states, between cultural and political nationalisms, and between official and resistant nationalism, is crucial to understanding the roles and meanings of nationalisms. Even though nationalisms are by definition political and expressed in relation to an existing or new state, they are elaborated culturally. Ernest Gellner, a well-known theorist of these ideas, suggests that the meaning of nation is drawn from the concept of nationalism, so that nationalisms occur first and then give rise to the nation. Therefore, nationalism engenders nations, and not the other way around;[29] in other words, principles of nationalism give form to a particular nation, its defining characteristics, its past, and its common destiny. This position may seem easier to explain in the case of political nations, where states foster national consciousness and shape ideas of national identities. But it is no less true when culturally defined nations aspire to independent statehood.

In either case, nations come into existence as the result of active political and cultural intervention, such as writing national histories, defining the national community and its shared culture, creating a national economy, and defining or aspiring to clear territorial boundaries. Even in cases of cultural or ethnic nations, there is no transparent relationship between a people and a nation. A foremost scholar of nationalism, Eric Hobsbawm, notes that despite these putative links, there is no logical way of constituting "a people."[30] Language, religion, ethnicity are important "causes" that define a people, but ironically these commonalties are essentially redefined when filtered through nationalism. They are selectively highlighted, subtly altered to enable a sense of peoplehood associated with a specific nation. In other words, ethnicity, language, or religion may help define the people of a nation, but the framework of nationalism and the role of the state shape how these forms of identity play out in people's lives, which groups flourish as the soul of the nation, and which groups are sidelined. State-seeking nationalisms also suppress some aspects of a people/nation and promote others. Even though anti-colonial nationalisms may have been revolutionary in their challenge to colonial states, they were hardly encompassing; as is well established, specific forms of anti-colonial nationalisms and representations of nations were institutionalized with the formation of postcolonial independent states.

In their article on the politics of Irish nationalism, Breda Gray and Louise Ryan address the ways in which Irish nationalism emerged against British colonialism and the Irish sought independence as a state.[31] They suggest that under colonialism Irish cultural nationalism was what first gave shape to the Irish nation and its demands for independent statehood; it was partly predicated on the definition of women primarily as mothers. Established in the 1920s, the Free State not only drew upon this legacy of cultural nationalism but also politically and legally reinforced it. Endorsing Irish women as mothers, emphasizing common characteristics to make all Irish people a "race," elaborating Irish cultural uniqueness in language, sports, and lifestyle, but also passing censorship laws to protect from foreign corruption, were some of the strategies through which the newly established state formed the Irish nation. Cultural nationalism may forge a nation and lead to demands for political independence, but states, in turn, also institutionalize cultural nationalism.

Nation-states, nation states, and national states: what are the differences?

It is commonplace to use the term "nation-state"; the hyphen indicates a sovereign political territory that is congruent to a single nation, a unified community. This concept invokes the idea that a culturally or ethnically homogenous nation is linked to a state. Despite the seemingly intuitive claims of many nations or states that they are politically and culturally congruent, some scholars have made the crucial point that these claims are well-nigh impossible. Making a distinction between nation-states and national states, Tilly believes that nation-states should include only those examples where people share a strong linguistic, religious, and symbolic identity within the confines of the state,[32] i.e. one people to one state. With this more careful definition of nation-states, Tilly suggests that even though Sweden and Ireland may approximate that ideal, few European states would ever qualify in this category; it is questionable whether even Sweden and Ireland meet the criteria.

National states are defined as those states governing multiple contiguous regions by means of centralized, differentiated, and autonomous structures; this notion uses the concept of state-based or politically forged nations. In these cases, the interlocking of nation and state is more a political and administrative effect rather than the outcome of a singular, cohesive nation with the state as its political organization. These national states first emerged in Europe in the last few centuries, mapped their territories and their colonies, and since World War II have recognized the principle of mutual existence.[33] Thus the contemporary world is mostly made up of national states, characterized by dominant forms of nationalisms and, in many cases, by multiple nations. Rather than seeing the United States as a politically and culturally congruent nation-state, we can better understand it as a national state, constituted as a mostly white, English-speaking, Christian nation, but with coeval resistant nationalisms (black nationalism), and more than one nation (the Navajo nation and others). China, Britain, India, Iraq, Zimbabwe, and any number of other cases do not pass the litmus test of nation-states; they are more appropriately described as national states. From here on, when necessary I will use the term "nation-state" in its narrow sense and more typically use the terms "national states" or "nation states" without the hyphen.

Ironically, the greatest threat faced by national states is the fundamental principle of nationalism, namely that each national community is entitled to its sovereign territory. A significant number of people are making demands for independent statehood, highlighting an inherent problem between the model of nation states and the reality of national states. For example, while numerous colonized nations such as India, Egypt, and Algeria may have deployed the principle of one nation to one state to realize their demands for independent statehood between the 1940s and 1960s, the reality is that these and most other states contain more than one ethnic and nationalist group; in these cases, nations forged out of anti-colonial nationalisms are challenged by the presence of resistant, ethnic nationalist movements. There is concern about the splintering of the existing 190 states recognized by the United Nations into innumerable unviable nation states. Not only do these ethnic and separatist movements tax the legitimacy and scope of existing states, but all too often they precipitate harsh state repression and control under the guise of protecting the common good, the collective will, and national security. That these are often not simply internal but cross-border and volatile international issues is well illustrated in the cases of the Palestinians, the Kashmiris, and the Kurds.

Theories of Nationalism, Nation, and State

In this section, I would like to foreground key theoretical approaches and debates that are implicit in how we describe nationalism and its links to nation and state. As stated in the introduction to this chapter, my purpose is to suggest a "culturalist" understanding of nationalism. Therefore, in this section I propose to explore the meaning and importance of this approach; to locate it *vis-à-vis* key theoretical perspectives on nationalism; and to think through the complexity of the links between nationalism, nation, and state from a culturalist perspective. My underlying aim is not only to introduce readers to the chief theories of nationalism, but also to highlight the importance of studying nationalism as a historical and cultural predicate, and to avoid reinforcing the Euro-American perspectives on nationalism that color most theoretical approaches.

If it is important to link nationalism to the state, the question of how to understand the state is no less relevant. With some exceptions, theories of the state and theories of nationalism have separate trajectories. Apart from theorists such as Giddens and Tilly, most theorists of the state have little to say about questions of nationalism, and while scholars of nationalism are more likely to consider the relevance of the state, as we will see below, this is not always the case. In contrast, if we accept that the logistics of modern state-making foster national consciousness through centralized administration, militarization, economic planning, and inter-state conflict, then how we understand the state bears on our perspectives on nationalism. If we push this a step further and say that modern states seek the legitimacy of nationalism and among the state's key functions is nation-building, then theories of the state and nationalism are not mutually exclusive. I will therefore start with a discussion of the approaches to, and debates about, the state before addressing theories of nationalism. As we shall see, key debates amongst state theorists – on state autonomy, on the role of elites, on the difference between state and society – raise important questions about the nature and role of nationalism. One other important reason for exploring theories of the state here has to do with their limitations. As will become clear shortly, the limitations of dominant state theories mirror the problems found in dominant theories of nationalism.

Theories of the state

Three main theoretical approaches shape studies of the state: Marxist, Weberian/statist, and "political systems." Influenced by the views of Karl Marx and his understanding of the state as an instrument of bourgeois society, Marxist theories tend to see the state as an ideological effect of the ruling class and its need to secure capitalist social relations. Among prominent proponents of the idea that the state is an instrument of domination, because of ties between the capitalist elites and state officials, are Ralph Miliband and Nicos Poulantzas. For Miliband, the state in class societies is the guardian and perpetuator of dominant economic interests; to achieve more democratic and effective government the state should ally with class power from below rather than with the dominant social classes.[34] In contrast, Poulantzas, influenced by Louis Althusser and Michel Foucault, emphasizes the relative autonomy of the state from capitalist elites; instead of positing the state as a monolithic, dominant entity, Althusser had emphasized the multiple, complexly related, social, political, economic, and ideological structures present in a social body; Poulantzas also builds on Foucault's relational and productive approach to power.[35] In what became a well-known debate, Miliband stressed the complex but influential effect of ruling class elites on the state.[36] However, Poulantzas disagreed with Miliband, saying that rather than being dependent on capitalist elites, the state ensures the reproduction of capitalist society and manages the equilibrium of classes in struggle.[37] Therefore, one class or fraction of the dominant social class, according to Poulantzas, cannot manipulate the state.

In contrast to this emphasis on the nature of the links between the state, class elites, and capitalism, Antonio Gramsci's reworking of Marxist theories of the state is important to note here.[38] An especially influential scholar, Gramsci highlighted the intervening role of civil society in state and class domination. Through the concept of hegemony, Gramsci argued that notwithstanding the use of force at times of intense conflict, the state typically maintains its domination through its intellectual and moral influence in civil society; therefore, the state works not just through the threat and use of direct violence, but also solicits the consent of the people through the institutions of education, religion, popular culture, etc. Owing to Gramsci's influence, civil society – private firms, corporations, voluntary organizations of various kinds – along with elites classes and capitalism, became important factors in Marxist analyses of the state. More recent proponents of the Marxist approach, such as Bob Jessop, take a more nuanced approach to the state as an ideological effect of the dominant social classes.

Supporters of both the political systems and the Weberian/statist approaches objected to what they saw as a Marxist overemphasis on the alliances and dependencies between the state, capitalism, and the dominant social classes. In an insightful discussion of the background and nature of these two theories, Mitchell argues that scholars such as Gabriel Almond, David Easton, and Sidney Verba referred to political systems instead of the state because the latter term was vague, with uncertain boundaries, and unable to encompass the complexities of modern politics, and because the scope of American political science expanded after World War II.[39] In his overview of state theories, Roger King notes that the political systems approach concentrated on collecting and evaluating data, utilizing new research techniques to measure political behavior.[40] By abandoning the concept of the state in favor of meticulous examinations of political systems, this approach also developed a pluralistic view of American society, as one that was relatively egalitarian and open to competition between multiple interest groups. Not only did this interpretation end up being overly behavioral, it also made it harder to sustain a pluralistic, competitive view of political systems in the light of institutional abuse of power, such as the Watergate affair. Moreover, it ran the risk of over-stretching the scope of its analysis to every conceivable form of collective expression of demand.[41]

Drawing on the early writings of Weber on state theory, neo-Weberian analyses reacted sharply against the Marxist view of the state as an instrument of capitalism as well as against the turn to political systems in place of the state. What distinguished this approach was its emphasis on the relative autonomy of the state from elites and civil society; it came to be seen as a state-centered or statist analysis. In an excellent discussion of the differences between these Marxist and Weberian/statist theories, Steinmetz argues that state-centered theory effectively addressed gaps in Marxist theory, particularly when there was no easy coincidence between state structures and policies and the interests of the dominant social classes.[42] In their attempt to show that the state was relatively or fully autonomous from these social classes, scholars such as Theda Skocpol posited the state as an actor or institution in its own right. Even though Mitchell is skeptical about this stance, he notes that state-centered theorists rightly argued that the difficulties in theorizing the state should not lead to the abandonment of the concept; rather, the various practices, rituals, and institutions associated with the state have an empirical reality that cannot be denied in favor of a seemingly more neutral concept of political systems.[43] Proposing to "bring the state back in" redressed the problems of Marxist analyses, and also the neglect of the state by the political systems theorists; the Weberian/statist solution was to see the state as a monolith, more or less autonomous from society, and a powerful, policy-making actor.

By now the issues at stake in these approaches and their implications for nationalism must be becoming clear. To underscore two aspects, the issue of state autonomy and the boundaries between state and society are key to the Marxist and Weberian debates. Not surprisingly, Marxist approaches to the state are marked by an inherent skepticism toward nationalism: nationalism hinders the formation of class-consciousness by attempting to build a cross-class community. From this perspective, nationalism is an ideological tool in the hands of social elites; it helps consolidate their power and influence through emphasizing a national community that obscures class inequalities. The importance of the links between social elites, the state, and capitalism is what makes Marxists skeptical about the liberating or resistant role of nationalism. But what about cases where there is a groundswell in nationalism? Surely, these cases are not simply explained by the delusions of the masses. Alternatively, to what extent does nationalism help preserve the relative autonomy, neutrality, and unity of the state, from a Weberian perspective? Does nationalism serve the functions of a centralized and unified state to promote industrialization and standardization? Especially in the case of state-based or civic nations, is nationalism a means to enable the operation of the state? A state-centered analysis also raises the possibility of nationalism as a product and instrument of the state but in a more functional sense. At the other end of the spectrum, if we favor a political systems approach, we are likely to lose sight of nationalism's relationship to state institutions and structures. In effect, how we conceptualize the state (or abandon it), whether we consider the role of power, what weight we place on the part played by social elites and capitalism, and whether we grant culture a place in our understanding of the state, bears on our approach to nationalism.

There are certain limitations common to all three of these accounts of the state, which presage those of the foremost theories of nationalism. First, the three approaches either neglect the effects of culture or grant it only a limited analytical role. Arguing from a culturist perspective on the state, Steinmetz suggests that social objects and practices, such as the state or the economy, are not just culturally shaped, but are fully "cultural."[44] From his point of view, the state does not exist outside of the cultural framework that gives it meaning and power. Taking a similar point of view as Steinmetz's, Philip Corrigan and Derek Sayer argue that English state formation from the eleventh through the nineteenth centuries was a *cultural* revolution.[45] This means seeing the state not only as constructed through cultural practices, but also as a cultural form of regulation. According to Corrigan and Sayer, state formation coincides with "moral regulation," or the attempts to make what is part of the social order appear to be natural and normal; state agencies attempt to unify and homogenize differences among groups within society.[46] Most importantly, states attempt to erase the recognition of existing social differences of gender, race, class, religion, ethnicity, occupation, and age by claiming that people's primary loyalty is to the nation. Yet, Corrigan and Sayer note, state formation ironically also individualizes people as citizens, voters, taxpayers, parents, homeowners, students, etc. They argue that while alternative modes of collective and individual identification are denied legitimacy, state formation is shaped through struggle with oppositional groups. Therefore, to ignore the effects of culture on the state is to miss it as a culturally constructed form, a product of history and cultural context, and an influence on social and moral regulation; it also overlooks its contentiousness. No less, ignoring the role of culture obscures the complex and contradictory relations between state, nation, and nationalism.

Addressing the distinctions between state and society, Mitchell also takes a culturalist approach to the state.[47] He argues that what may be recognized as the line between state and society does not separate two discreet entities but is the line through which social and political order is maintained. Therefore rejecting the position that state and society can be practically or analytically separated, Mitchell argues that the power to regulate and control lies in the appearance of a clearly delineated difference between state and society. In September 2002 a controversy erupted in Britain over Prince Charles's weighing in on political affairs. The concern was that, in acting contrarily to the royal family's public deference to elected officials and other state representatives on political matters, and bringing to bear his influence in matters of state, Prince Charles was muddying the distinction between the nominal authority of the royal family and the political authority of elected officials. Even though the royal family represents the British state in some political matters, it is important to preserve the distinction between political and ceremonial authority, as the controversy illustrated. According to Mitchell, the state is a structural effect: not a real structure, but a powerful and metaphysical effect of practices that sustain the myth of its coherence, unity, and distinction from society. In fact, state institutions and practices are fragmented and incoherent. No less complex, unstable, and varied are the relations between state and private institutions. Thus the culturalist approach to the state also means discarding any notion of the state as a freestanding entity, while taking seriously the politics of the distinction between state and society and its constant affirmation.

The second criticism of the Marxist, Weberian/statist, and political systems theories is related to the neglect of culture: the Eurocentric nature of these theories of the state. If the culturalist approach to the state entails a culturally and historically grounded understanding, then there cannot be a single or universal measure of the state. These three theories are not only developed within a Euro-American perspective but are used to evaluate non-western, Third World states. Notions of "traditional" or pre-modern states in contrast to rational, modern, and superior European states mark Weber's approach to the state and later Weberian theories. Not limited to Weberian/statist theories, putative distinctions between the West and the Third World or between modern and traditional states are based on the idea that development and western cultural modernity are universal standards. Western states are therefore implicitly or explicitly seen as modern, rational, and with functionally differentiated political, and cultural spheres, while non-western states are seen as the reverse: irrational, traditional, perhaps anti-modern, where culture and politics are hopelessly intermingled.[48] Nowhere are contemporary distinctions between western, modern states and non-western, culturally/politically fraught states more evident than in the parceling of Euro-American and Islamic states; this, despite the fact that culture, religion, and politics cannot be easily separated within *most* western and non-western states. Further coinciding with notions of strong versus weak states, democratic versus undemocratic states, and successful versus failed states, these distinctions rest upon Euro-American-centered notions of modernity, participative democracy, and the importance of the separation between religion and the state. Ironically, what are culturally-based notions of state and social organization are objectified as universal understandings of the state.

Critical scholars have responded to the challenges of these flawed, universalized understandings of the modern state in two ways. In the first, historians and anthropologists, in particular, have focused on colonial states in an effort to understand the histories of what eventually became Third World states.[49] This approach paves the way for researchers to look at the *interactions* between the emerging modern western and Third World states. We will explore this scholarship and the links between colonialism and the state in Chapter Two. A second approach has been to focus on studies of state formation in the Third World and the politics of postcolonial states.[50] The breadth of the scholarship and the diversity of cultural settings defy any easy characterization of these studies. However, they have collectively broadened our understandings of the state, challenged the implicit Eurocentrism in much of state theory, and presented alternative approaches to postcolonial, Third World states that avoid the pitfalls of derogatory stereotypes.

Theories of Nationalism

Theories of nationalism raise questions about how to locate its meaning, origins, continued significance, and important aspects. These theories can be organized along three dimensions: whether nationalisms are seen as natural or social occurrences, what their relations to history are, and what underlying notions of power they have. Below, I will briefly explore these differences and address three theoretical perspectives that exemplify them. In so doing, I will also introduce and locate modernist theories, which are by far the most influential and widely prevalent theories of nationalism, and the section will focus on them. Modernist theories have collectively added to our understanding of nationalisms and nations as modern phenomena, and of their links with other structures and practices of modernity, some of which are not limited to the modern state. The differences in emphasis and disagreements between varieties of modernist theories have productively brought out the meanings and contradictions of nationalisms. Nonetheless, not only do the various strands of modernist theories of nationalisms suffer limitations, but, as we shall see, they also share another problem, namely the search for an overarching explanation of nationalisms. Furthermore, modernist theories of nationalism, although significantly different from theories of the modern state, echo the neglect of culture and a Euro-American standpoint.

Among the three groups into which theories of nationalism fall, the first point of difference has to do with whether nations are a natural rather than a social occurrence. Exemplifying the former idea, *primordial* theorists grant nations a primordial or "natural" origin; in other words, nations are intrinsic to human evolution.[51] For primordialists, nations are the foundations of human history, extensions of primitive kinship groups with common ancestry and clear social and territorial boundaries; they can be forged out of a variety of elemental aspects such as language, race, religion, and custom, and nations and their characteristics can be identified from one another. These theories are most sharply criticized for giving biological accounts of nations, which in fact are better seen as cultural and political phenomena.

The second difference lies in the role of history. In contrast to primordialists, other theories see nations and nationalisms as the outcome of social and historical processes. Despite the signal importance of nations in contemporary life and primordialists' attempts to grant them prehistorical status, other theorists understand nations as the products of cultural events and historical circumstances. *Perennialist* theories most closely approximate the foundational emphasis on nations by primordialists but differ in the important respect that nations are not "natural."[52] For perennialists, contemporary nations may trace their roots to antiquity, but are the products of human social organization. While these theories attempt to look at nations as historical creations, they ignore the fact that nations and nationalisms, in their contemporary usage, may be fundamentally dissimilar from earlier expressions of community and collectivity. To ascribe contemporary nations and nationalisms to antiquity would be anachronistic; the same charge can also be levied against the primordialists. What this means is that historical periods are distinct and by importing concepts from the modern period to earlier times, perennialists are looking at "retrospective nationalism."[53] Like primordialists, perennialist theories fail to sufficiently account for the role of history and culture in the emergence of nations and nationalisms or to acknowledge what is unique about the modern concept of nationalism and nations.

The dimension of power constitutes a third difference between theories of nationalism. No doubt, primordialists and perennialists see nations and nationalisms as enduring, indeed powerful, phenomena. The difference is that some theories see a nation as a form of power rather than a powerful entity: a manifestation of the unequally distributed ability to manipulate people and represent them nationalistically. *Instrumentalist* theories sharply differ from the two previous theoretical approaches and say that nationalist beliefs or a sense of a unified community are the result of human manipulation.[54] While instrumentalists would not deny deep and abiding affective ties, they argue that nations are "made up" by social elites in order to serve their interests; nationalism is merely a tool in the hands of interest-maximizing elites. Against this it must be said that although elites undeniably can play a significant role in whipping up or directing nationalism, nationalism is not simply the preserve of the elites. Though the instrumentalists rightly emphasize nationalism as a form of power, they conceive it too narrowly. At best, this approach failed to see the widespread and popular participation in Serbian nationalism by the early 1990s, for example, and in the worst case sees ordinary people as mere dupes of elites. Neither scenario is satisfying.

In comparison to primordialists and perennialists, *modernist* approaches consider nationalisms and nations as historical rather than natural phenomena or the product of early history. As clearly indicated in the title, modernist theories emphasize that nations are modern in the sense that they are historically recent. Modernists would therefore fault perennialists and primordialists for failing to see how nations differ from pre-modern ethnic groups in important and fundamental ways. Modernist theorists, in turn, sit more comfortably with the instrumentalists, but do not simply see nationalism and nations as elite-driven phenomena. For them, the power of nationalism is enforced through the modern state, through the social and political elites, through civil institutions. But it also relies on the participation of the people. So modernist theories are likely to see nations and nationalisms as forms of power but not simply as ideological instruments in the hands of social elites.

Background to modernist theories of nationalism

Modernist theories view nations as modern in one other, equally important respect: that they are born out of the conditions of modernity. These conditions are the result of the social, economic, and political changes of the last few hundred years, which are related to the rise and expansion of industrial capitalism, imperialism, the French and American Revolutions, and the modern bureaucratic state. Principles of democracy, individualism, scientific rationality, widespread changes in the organization of home and work, greater physical mobility, significant technological innovations, demands for equality are but a few expressions of modernity; whether all the mixed and complicated after-effects are beneficial is debatable. In modernist theory, as well as the rise of nations and nationalisms being a fundamental aspect of modernity, the ambivalent effects and ills of modernity make nationalism necessary. Modernists believe that the rapidly changing social context of the eighteenth and nineteenth centuries alienated elites from ordinary people, and widely disrupted traditional forms of support, so that new kinds of communities such as "the nation" had to be promulgated by the elite to win the cooperation of people and bring order into the apparent social chaos. Modernity not only disrupted existing forms of community and civic life, but also sharpened the distinctions between the work and home, between the public and private sphere, and between the state and civil society. Even though many scholars, especially feminist theorists, would question these distinctions, most agree that the appearance of a separation between these spheres is a crucial aspect of modernity. In this historical and cultural context, the nation – as a unified community taking precedence over other aspects of social identity and differences – is considered to mitigate the cleavages of modernization and enable social and political functioning amidst these changes.

Among the early investigations into the meaning of nationalism, which were to be influential to modernist theorists, was Ernest Renan's lecture at the Sorbonne, Paris, in 1882, entitled "Qu'est-ce qu'une nation?" ("What is a Nation?").[55] In this now famous lecture, Renan suggests that a nation is a matter of people's will to be a nation, it is based on their common ancestry, and their present-day desire to live together, which must be continually and routinely affirmed. Despite the flaw in Renan's argument that the nation is based upon the voluntary consent of the people, his reflections on nation are important. First, he tries to show that nations are made under the right historical circumstances; they are not permanent fixtures throughout history due to factors such as language, dynasty, race, or geography. For example, nations such as France, he says, are born out of conquest by the Germans, and more importantly the racial and cultural fusion of the invaders and the local people; in other cases, such as those of Holland, Switzerland, and Belgium, nations are born out of general consciousness. Second, Renan emphasizes that, once formed, nations are contingent on the bonds among people and the will to be a nation. Therefore, for Renan, nations are not simply predestined or necessarily elitist, but come from an act of choice that must be constantly affirmed. His assumption that a nation is built upon people's consent may be too simplistic, but his approach helps us see nation as a historical rather than an inevitable process and one that is not simply dependant on the delusion of ordinary people by the elites.

Through the turn of the nineteenth century and in the interwar period of the twentieth century, issues of nationalism continued to receive sporadic attention. After World War II, defeat of the Nazis in Germany by the allied forces and the subsequent end of formal empires in various parts of the world triggered a spate of new national states, and a renewed interest in the meaning, function, and impact of nationalisms. One such theoretical intervention came from Elie Kedourie in 1960 with the publication of his book, *Nationalism*. Thereafter among the most-cited modernist scholars, Kedourie developed the approach that nationalism is an ideology developed in Europe as a response to the predicament of modernity.[56] Coming upon the heels of the disastrous possibilities revealed in World War II, nationalism is perhaps not surprisingly seen by Kedourie as an ideology – as a kind of false belief system that elicits our agreement; we are led into believing that we will live better only as a collective, as a nation, since at heart we have the same interests. Nationalism was part of the unfortunate ideological style of politics that came to dominate at the time of the French Revolution, according to Kedourie. Later, this style of politics expanded to non-European settings, owing to Europe's ensuing domination in the world.

Why was this style of politics necessary, according to Kedourie? The separation between the government and those governed, the decline of community and the alienation of individuals from one another, and the conflict between reason and feeling are, Kedourie says, some of the conditions that made nationalism a necessary response in the nineteenth century. The unmooring of individuals in modern life is both alienating for them and a threat to social order because the norms and rules of life are no longer as clear or valid. Nationalism is "ideological" because it is a way to impose social order by providing people with a collective social ideal. Central to this social ideal was the principle of self-determination of each individual, but, as Kedourie goes on to say, it was believed that each person could attain this self-determination only in the context of national determination. This means that if the individual cannot be considered apart from the whole, i.e. the nation, then individual self-determination can find its highest expression only in national self-determination. Finally, Kedourie roundly challenges nationalism because, like other ideological politics, it is unable to cure the ills and oppressions of modernity or indeed really help the individual attain self-determination. From his perspective, then, nationalism only deflects attention from the sound and fair social policies that are necessary for a better society.

Following Kedourie and especially since the early 1970s there has been a veritable explosion of modernist theories on nationalism that are not necessarily as cynical. Together, these theorists grapple with three central questions related to nationalism. First, they seek to define the meaning of nationalism in order to explain it as the kind of model of social life that has been widely prevalent since the eighteenth century. They believe that nationalism should be treated as a social concept. Despite the varieties and types of nationalism, there is an overarching meaning and explanation for it. In other words, there may be plural nationalisms – such as

Irish nationalism, Saudi Arabian nationalism, British nationalism, and so on – but they are simply variations of one social concept and phenomenon namely, nationalism, that can be explained through social and historical factors, namely, modernity. Second, they explore the social conditions under which nationalism emerges and remains influential. Since nationalism is held to be humanly constructed over the last two or three hundred years, these theorists look for explanations in the sociological and economic aspects of modernity and, in some cases, in the rise of the modern state. They try to account for both the revolutionary and the reactionary possibilities of nationalism. Third, they attempt to understand the importance of nationalism in contemporary times. If nationalism is related to modernity, then is it conceivable that with the decline of modernity, we will see a parallel decline in nationalism? The theories explored below are not exhaustive, but help highlight the key insights as well as limitations that are broadly characteristic of modernist approaches to nationalisms and nations. We should note that classifications such as those used below are not always unambiguous, but they are helpful in noting patterns and problems.

Nationalism-as-culture approaches: cultural responses to the conditions of modernity

In this category, I include those theories that see nationalism as a cultural phenomenon. Unlike the "culturalist" approach, however, these theories have only a limited understanding of culture. At one end of the spectrum are prominent theorists of nationalism, such as Anthony Smith. To summarize, Smith argues that although nationalisms and nations are modern phenomena, the first influential examples of "nation" have pre-modern origins in ethnic communities. He emphasizes the role of pre-modern ethnicities in the origins of modern nationalisms, attempting to bridge the gap between modernists, who insist on the modernity of nationalisms, and perennialists, who emphasize the long-standing, pre-modern influence of nationalisms and nations. Dwelling on this continuity between pre-modern forms of ethnicities, which he calls "ethnies," and contemporary nationalisms, Smith thus attempts to show how modern nationalisms are forged out of pre-modern forms of ethnicity and their deeply abiding ties.

Clearly, Smith emphasizes the role of culture in the origins of nationalism, although taking "culture" in a limited sense. For him, the "ethno-history" of communities, in the form of myths, rituals, customs, historical memories of territory, heroes, and golden ages, give shape to ethnies and transform them into nations.[57] Equally importantly, Smith points toward the political nature of the transformation of ethnies into nations. With the qualification that not all ethnies evolve into nations and not all nations are rooted in ethnies, Smith cites historical evidence for when ethnies evolve into nations. According to him, there are two primary routes for this development.[58] First, loosely formed, aristocratic ethnies mobilize the middle classes into a territorialized nationalism; the bureaucratic state helps forge the nation in cases that include England, Spain, and France. In its second route, native intellectuals appropriate and remake a selective ethnic identity and past out of popular cultural practices in order to mobilize a nationalist movement. A third route may be one where sections of ethnies emigrate and constitute a national identity in another territory, such as in the United States, Canada, and Australia. Chapter Five, which is focused on the interconnections between nationalism and ethnicity, will reconsider Smith's theory of ethnicity and nationalism.

To anticipate, my major concern is with Smith's notion of culture as potentially continuous and transhistorical. Smith certainly acknowledges that ethnies must be actively transformed into nations, but, at heart, he sees culture in the form of myths, symbols, and historical memory as enduring across time, available for transformation. Culture, then, is seen as transhistorical instead of as practices and beliefs that are continually undergoing change, that may be contested, and that continually have to be created and re-created in order to have meaning. In so far as this view of culture guides Smith's analysis, ironically, he is unable to avoid the "retrospective nationalism" associated with perennialist theories. Since ethnies and nations belong to different social eras and have different meanings, Smith is wrong to put the roots of nationalism in earlier social eras. Secondly, as further explored in Chapter Five, although there is little doubt about the importance of ethnic communities in the rise of nationalisms, there is disagreement which is the cause and which is the effect; put differently, ethnic solidarities may be produced by nationalist sentiments and are projected back into history just as much as ethnic groups may help forge nationalist sentiments.

Another leading scholar of nationalism, Ernest Gellner, also analyzes nationalism through the lens of culture, but in a significantly different way from Smith. Unlike Smith, Gellner firmly believes in the modernity of nationalisms, and is interested in the social and cultural aspects of modernity, such as industrialization and the changing role of culture.[59] In his definitive work, *Nations and Nationalism*, Gellner identifies three phenomena as the basic components of his thesis: industrialization, a society with a single shared culture, and nationalism. According to him, industrialization

creates a society with the following characteristics: high degree of special-
ization of work; standardized forms of education; frequent communications
with strangers, which are made possible with the standardization of meaning; and emergence of a shared, homogenous culture. For Gellner, nationalism is the manifestation of a common, homogenous "high" culture that is
necessary under modern industrialization, and that is characterized by no
basic social inequalities or differences between those who are in power and
ordinary people. It is not that Gellner supports nationalism as much as he
sees it as a necessary form of unity and identity that is desired at higher
levels of industrialization. He defines nationalism as a political principle,
which holds that the political and national unit should be congruent, or
that the political/state and national/societal/cultural unit are congruent.[60]
Thus nationalism is shown to be a sociological response to the exigencies of
industrialization and industrial society, a form of cultural standardization,
and a means of ensuring the smooth political functioning of the sociocultural national unit. Modern mass education, according to Gellner, is crucial
to ensuring cultural standardization and promoting the congruence between the political and national/cultural unit.

As noted earlier, what is compelling about Gellner's approach is that he
is able to show how nationalism effectively creates nations. Equally
notable is his highlighting of the role of culture, albeit one that is homogenous and unified, in economic and political development. But nationalism is reduced to being a function of industrialization. Secondly, as Smith
points out in his criticism of Gellner, the link between industrialization
and nationalism is not causal, nor does industrialization adequately explain the emergence of nationalism. For example, in France and Mexico
nationalism preceded industrialization and in Australia development occurred through the modernization of agriculture rather than industrialization.[61] Gellner's disregard for power and conflict underlying a seemingly
homogenous culture pose significant problems for his approach. Cultural
theorists have widely agreed on the importance of not seeing culture as
unified or homogenous but as fraught, plural, and unequal. Gellner's
neglect of the contested, hierarchical nature of culture, and therefore
nationalism, reduces nationalism to an ideology that serves industrialization and modernization.

Gellner's approach to culture and cultural difference – high or garden
cultures versus low or wild cultures – creates another troubling problem.
He believes that, in contrast to industrialized societies, pre-industrial (pre-
modern) societies are composed of numerous groups and cultures and are
highly unequal in terms of class, clans, caste, etc., so as to be incapable of
nationalism; they are characterized by the presence of low or wild cul-

tures. By analyzing the social transition from agrarian to industrialism, Gellner is able to account for nationalism as a modern phenomenon. But in so doing, he promotes a theory of nationalism that is biased in favor of industrialization and modernization. Non-industrialized, "traditional," and by implication, many non-European societies are incapable of nationalism, according to Gellner's theory. Thus Gellner's emphasis on nationalism as a necessary, unified expression of culture underwrites a hierarchy of nations and culture from a Eurocentric perspective.

Nationalism as political mobilization: political responses to the consequences of capitalism

One of the cornerstones of modernity is the proliferation of capitalism. The precise meaning of capitalism is debatable, but it is largely regarded as an inherently expansionist economic system, based on an unending search for profit. For scholars such as Tom Nairn and Michael Hechter, the key to understanding nationalism lies in the social ills of capitalism. Their views are influenced by the emphasis put by Marx and Friedrich Engels on the national state as the instrument of industrial capitalism and the vested interests of ruling elites in ensuring conditions suitable for its capitalism. As noted above, earlier Marxists have viewed class struggle as the vehicle of change and have therefore been skeptical of nationalism's emancipatory potential; this, despite the many cases where nationalist movements have overcome class differences. Accordingly, more recent proponents have reworked Marxist theories to account for the enduring appeal of nationalism and its bearing on relations between social classes.

Consistent with this reworking, Nairn sees nationalism as the ideological outcome of capitalist social relations. Nairn's point of departure, however, is that nationalism is a form of political mobilization against the social consequences of the uneven development of capitalism. Highlighting the interlinked proliferation of capitalism and imperialism (to be defined in the following chapter), Nairn describes "uneven development" as the process through which development in some areas is contingent upon lack of development in other areas; the phrase also refers to the dependency of the exploited, underdeveloped areas upon the developed areas.[62] Nairn argues that capitalism and imperialism created the phenomenon of uneven development whereby peripheral areas, colonies such as Haiti, Mexico, Nigeria, Egypt, India, became dependent for their development upon the center, colonizing countries such as Britain, France, Italy, Spain, and the United States.

While several scholars note the way this dependency forms relationships across different countries and within them (urban–rural relations, for example), Nairn uses uneven development to explain nationalism as a political response, a way out of exploitation for peripheral or colonized nations. The problem, then, is not the failure to modernize or the lack of industrial development; rather, it is the nature of development. Nationalism is the means through which peripheral areas under the grip of imperialism resist exploitation. For Nairn, the role of elites in the colonies is important in mobilizing the population to rise against domination and exploitation by the center. Therefore, at one level, nationalism is the outcome of the unequal relations between center and periphery and, at another level, it is the outcome of class differences as a result of uneven development. Arguing that nationalism marshals people in the peripheries and, by implication, remains unimportant in the center, Nairn reverses Gellner's logic. For Gellner, modernization needs nationalism as a form of cultural homogeneity and therefore exists in the industrialized areas. In contrast, Nairn sees the uneven, exploitative nature of capitalist industrialization as the problem, and understands nationalism as a political counter-response in the peripheries rather than in industrialized areas. Nonetheless, there are the following four problems with Nairn's account of nationalism. He explains what triggers nationalism but not what it means; uneven development as a result of capitalism also occurred within the so-called developed areas, so that the link between uneven development and the emergence of capitalism remains unproven; he fails to account for nationalisms in the center; and he does not explain the role of culture and ethnicity in forging nationalism.[63] By locating nationalism within the framework of capitalist exploitation, imperialism, and uneven development, he makes it a political tool, this time in the hands of elites in the peripheries, while the center is seen as exempt from its influences.

Nationalism and state formation

While some modernist scholars emphasize nationalism's links to capitalism, theorists such as John Breuilly, Anthony Giddens, Eric Hobsbawm, Michael Mann, and Charles Tilly focus on the role of the state within the framework of capitalist industrialization.[64] Unlike Nairn, these theorists concentrate on the emergence of the modern state in the West and the subsequent surge of nationalism and nation formation. Their theories are shaped by Marxist insights on the influence of industrial capitalism and the cleavages between state and civil society; Weber's emphasis on the modern state as a political organization, with its legitimacy in rational authority and claim to monopoly over violence; the increasing importance attributed to warfare and militarism (traceable to Georg Simmel); and the communications revolutions in modern societies suggested by theorists such as Karl Deutsch.[65] Breuilly, Giddens, and others provide important insights into the role of the modern state and political institutions in understanding the meaning and significance of nationalism, but often at the risk of ignoring the role of equally important factors such as cultural nationalism and the role of non-elite or ordinary people.

Briefly put, Breuilly understands nationalism as a form of politics that arises in the context of the modern state. According to him, nationalism rests upon the following assertions: there exists a nation with an explicit and peculiar character; the interests and values of this nation take priority over all other interests and values; the nation must be as independent as possible and usually requires the attainment of political sovereignty.[66] Breuilly argues that nationalism arises in opposition to the modern state even as opposition to the state gives it shape. He defines the modern state as one that possesses sovereignty over a given territory, and has an elaborate institutional structure that specifies, justifies, and exercises the claim of sovereignty on behalf of a monarchy or parliament. It is seen as the highest form of human existence in that everything else is subordinate to it. Breuilly points out that someone who is excluded from a state more or less becomes a non-person, since it governs people's births, deaths, property, mobility, etc. Externally, the sovereignty is limited by other states and internally by the distinction between the public and private spheres. However, the growth of capitalism creates a split between the state and society (the private, "civil" aspects), between politics and non-politics.

Nationalism emerges as a response to this problem between state and society by elites, collaborators, and political institutions; through nationalism, they seek to reconcile the split between state and society by making them one and the same, according to Breuilly. Yet he says, the modern state shapes nationalism because it shows that possession of a sovereign, territorial state power is necessary and that just as each state has its special characteristics, so must each nation. Also, in either case, the use of power must be in the name of the society. Rather than God, the modern state and then the nation come to derive their power from the people. But nationalist movements (for example that of the Scots) do not always aim for control of the state.

Similarly, Giddens, Mann, and Tilly focus on nationalism's links to the state while taking into account the complicated effects of capitalism and industrial production. Each of them is primarily concerned with the modern state and derives the role of nationalism from it. Militarism and war-making are crucial to their analyses of the modern state and nationalism.

Concentrating on European nationalisms, Giddens argues that any account of nationalism must address its political character, as associated with the state; its relation to industrial capitalism, especially in connection with class inequality; its psychological characteristics, to include sentiments and attitudes; and its particular symbolic content, linked with notions of homeland, reconstructions of history, and culture. Despite his definition of nationalism as primarily a psychological phenomenon, Giddens is wary of seeing nationalism in psychological terms.[67] Nationalism's links to the state and the coordination of administrative power within the boundaries of the nation state make it inherently political, for Giddens. Nonetheless, he rejects nationalism as simply an ideology of dominant social classes or, unlike Nairn, solely as an effect of the world capitalist system. For him, "nation" refers to a collectivity existing within a clearly demarcated territory, administered as a unit, and monitored internally by the state and by other states. Nations and nationalism are the preserve of the modern state and therefore, not unexpectedly, the national state rather than nations or nationalisms are far more important for Giddens.

As mentioned earlier, Giddens sees the nation state as a bordered "power-container" of the modern era. Historically, all states have claimed monopoly over formal violence, but the nation state is more conducive to this purpose. Giddens uses this definition for nation states:

> The nation-state, which exists in a complex of other nation-states, is a set of institutional forms of governance maintaining an administrative monopoly over a territory with demarcated boundaries (borders), its rule being sanctioned by law and direct control of the means of internal and external violence.[68]

What distinguishes the nation state from its precursors is the centralized control over administration and violence, and the wide and intensive forms of control internally and at external borders. Perhaps because of his focus on the nation state, nationalism largely remains, for Giddens, a political phenomenon incidental to state control.

In his focus on the modern state, Tilly takes the view that the organization of coercion and war are central to the dynamics of modern state formation in two ways: states came about primarily as a result of a ruler's efforts to acquire the means of war and extract necessary funding; and they took their form through relations with other states, especially as a result of war and the preparation for war.[69] Tilly argues that the state used direct means of coercion, in the form of navies, armies, police forces, weapons, to extract resources from some areas and indirect means of extraction in more capital-intensive regions, where markets and exchange prevailed. For Tilly, then, dynamic interplay between capitalism, coercion, preparation for war, and position within the international system was crucial in the transition to the modern state.[70] "Nationalism," in Tilly's view, refers to the mobilization of populations that do not have their own state toward political independence, as in Palestinian and Chechnya, or state-seeking nationalism, which was discussed earlier. Nationalism also occurs in an existing state, when a population is mobilized by a strong identification with that state. This is especially evident at times of war, such as the aftermath of September 11, 2001, with (north) American nationalism. Tilly argues that the homogenization of the population and the imposition of direct control under the modern state have facilitated nationalism in the latter form.

Accounting for nationalism in its political form, and making it ancillary to the modern state are concerns running through the above three theories, but none of them sufficiently accounts for the importance of cultural aspects of nationalism, or of nationalisms and nations that are not related to states. There is no doubt of the importance of locating nationalisms within the modern state; Breuilly, Giddens, and Tilly also rightly focus attention on structural factors such as capitalism, industrialization, and the national state as the pillars of modernity. But nationalisms do not always aim for state control or independent statehood, as, for example, do the Scots. Further, the explanations of these theorists are not helpful in understanding the cultural nuances of nationalism, its influence on ordinary citizens, or nationalism as opposition to an existing state. Cultural nationalism can be as important as the political forms of nationalism highlighted by these theorists. But, as in the theories of nationalism criticised above, the problem here goes beyond the failure to include cultural aspects of nationalism or a focus on nationalism only in Western Europe. The problem is an approach to the state or political aspects of nationalism that ignores culturalist understandings of the state and nationalism, the contentiousness of nationalisms, the fragmented aspects of the state, inconsistency between state institutions and dominant nationalisms, and, as we will see, the gendered and racialized inclusions and exclusions of nationalisms.

Nationalism as invented practices: laying the groundwork for culturalist approaches

Modernist scholars agree that nationalisms are entirely modern phenomena, but differ from the above theorists in one important way: they reject the cause-and-effect explanation of the origins and importance of nationalism that underlies the theories so far discussed. In each of those cases, nationalism was the epiphenomenal effect of either the demands of industrialization, or capitalist uneven development, or the modern state.

In contrast, Hobsbawm and Anderson are more concerned with what makes and continues to make nationalism a credible set of practices and beliefs. They are interested in the broad operations of power that make nationalism seem so normal and natural that we are skeptical of claims that nations and nationalisms did not exist in the pre-modern period. The questions raised are: what are the origins and mechanisms of nationalism that make it appear timeless, that reinforce practices ensuring that nations have defined and sovereign territories, and that shape enduring beliefs that nations are forms of community that supercede all other forms of loyalty?

Unlike Smith, the primordialists, or the perennialists, Eric Hobsbawm emphasizes the *discontinuities* of modern nationalisms with the past. Using the concept of "invented traditions," he shows that nations, nationalism, the national state, national symbols and histories are types of recently invented traditions and that any seeming continuity with the past is largely fictitious.[71] He defines invented traditions as those ritual and symbolic practices that seek to inculcate certain values and norms of behavior by repetition, implying continuity with the past. The repetition of symbolically endowed practices – such as flying the national flag, playing the national anthem, and using the national emblem – engenders and maintains the belief in nationalism and nationhood. Hobsbawm does not suggest that invented traditions such as nationalism are fictions and therefore meaningless; rather, he shows how "traditions" such as nationalism, which seem or claim to be old, are recent in origin and actively created. He concedes that although instances of invented traditions can be found throughout history, the rapid transformation of modern society explains why they were likely to be frequently invented in the recent past.

Like the modernists who see state control as a central objective of nationalism, Hobsbawm emphasizes the importance of the nation state as the political outcome of nationalism. He traces the two kinds of trajectories of nations and nationalisms: the revolutionary and democratic nationalism associated with the French Revolution and the "ethno-linguistic" nationalism between 1870 and 1918. In the former case, nations operated on the "threshold principle," which meant that only nations with large territories and populations were able to lay claim to sovereign states.[72] Moreover, a lengthy association with a current or a recent state, a long-established cultural elite, and a proven capacity for conquest were the practical criteria that determined whether a people could be classified as a nation. These nation states were also inherently expansionist in the sense that they were aimed at uniting all of the people who fell within the purview of the nation and extending the reach of the state into the lives of individual citizens. After 1870, the threshold principle was abandoned, ethnicity and language became the decisive criteria for nationhood, and nationalism increasingly became the preserve of the politically conservative. For Hobsbawm, nationalism is based on the role of political elites and political institutions, but also includes popular beliefs and sentiments, as expressed in ethno-linguistic nationalisms. He cautions students of nationalism not to rely on official ideologies of nationalisms and, instead, to understand nationalism from the perspective of ordinary people, i.e. to take the view from below.

The idea that nationalisms and nations are cultural and historical constructs that need to be unraveled is also well represented in Anderson's influential book, *Imagined Communities*. Interestingly, both Anderson's concept of nation as an imagined community and Hobsbawm's concept of invented traditions were published in the same year, 1983. But there are important differences between the two approaches. Anderson defines a nation as an imagined political community that is inherently limited and sovereign.[73] The nation is imagined because even the members of the smaller nations never meet personally and nationalism is a particular way of imagining a community. It is imagined as limited because every nation by definition has finite boundaries beyond which are other nations. And it is imagined as a sovereign entity that is autonomous and self-governing, and as an egalitarian fraternal community of men regardless of their inequalities. Yet, like Hobsbawm, Anderson does not imply that there is anything untrue or fictional about the nation. On the contrary, by looking at nations as a particular way of imagining community that is different from the past, Anderson addresses the question of why nationalisms have such a hold on us despite their problems and limitations.

Anderson argues that three significant changes occurred for the nation to be imagined: the decline of the belief that truth was encoded in sacred languages such as Latin; the decline of the belief that human society was necessarily hierarchically organized and ruled by a monarch, who was fundamentally different from ordinary people and divinely privileged; and the rise of a calendrical conception of time as a steady march toward progress and the belief that human beings and the world have the same origin. In addition to his focus on nation and nationalisms as imagined rather than literally existing, Anderson departs from the above modernist theorists, including Hobsbawm, in one other way: he points out that sentiments of nation-ness seem to have developed among the colonies in the New World of the Americas well before most of Europe. According to Anderson, creole intermediaries, who were either of European descent but born in the colonies or functionaries sent to the colonies by the empire, engendered a new consciousness in the form of nationalism. Away from the heart of the Spanish empire, they were able to imagine separate political provinces that were communities of like-minded creole people. Once the idea of the nation was conceived and created as a kind of module, he believes, it quickly spread to other parts of the world through the spread of standardized languages such as English and French.

Critiques of Modernist Theories

Modernist theories have surely contributed to understandings of nationalism. As was evident especially in the modernist perspectives that focus on sociocultural aspects, or the role of capitalism, or the importance of the state, the theories pivoting around aspects of modernity rest on certain cornerstones: nationalism, the state, industrialization, capitalist expansion, and to some extent imperialism. The central questions that they wrestle with are: how do nationalisms and national states anchor the institutions, socioeconomic networks, beliefs, and practices of modernity; and in what ways are nationalisms and states the outcome of the exigencies of modernity as well as its ill effects? Another important concern debated here is the role of elites. While not all theorists equally emphasize the role of elites, modernist perspectives tend to be wary of the ways in which elites are instrumental in mobilizing nationalism and consolidating the power of the national state.

We briefly considered the limitations of each of the modernist perspectives above but there are also some overarching concerns. These limitations are outlined in the theories that both build upon but also counter the insights of modernist perspectives. The concerns with modernist perspectives can be summed up in five ways. First, modernist theories are at fault for their search for an overarching theory of nationalisms and nations. Despite the changing, unstable, and contradictory nature of nationalisms over the last two to three hundred years, modernist scholars attempt to construct a single, inclusive theory. Notably, the modernist scholars explored above do not see their approaches as partial and limited, but as means to construct an encompassing theory of nationalism and nation. According to critics of modernsit theories, this search proceeds on the assumption that nationalisms are objective and coherent realities that can be explained through the right theoretical model. Therefore, the lack of an encompassing theory of nationalism implies that the right theoretical model remains elusive. Second, modernist theories are to be faulted for being Eurocentric. There is little disagreement between scholars of nationalism that the French Revolution and the American Declaration of Independence mark the visibility of nationalism. But does that mean that nationalism remains a fundamentally European phenomenon that is simply incorporated into non-European contexts? For critics of modernist perspectives, the focus on Euro-American history and context produces partial and biased understandings of the diversity of nationalisms. Third, the dualities that underlie modernist perspectives of European and non-European, East and West, nationalists and patriots, elite-led and ordinary people's nationalisms, and colonizers and the colonized, can be challenged in favor of an approach that looks at the linkages between these groupings. Fourth, in parallel to the criticism of the modernist Eurocentric focus, is the concern that the theories remain elitist in their disregard of nationalisms' links to gender, race, and sexuality. Despite the fact that gender, race, and sexuality are among the primary determinants of equality or otherwise among citizens, these issues receive scant attention in the dominant literature. Finally, modernist theories are at fault for their conceptualization of power. For them, power is located in elite-based nationalisms, in the political institutions, or springs from the inequalities of industrial capitalism. What this ignores is how nationalisms are rooted in the unequal relations between self and other, how nationalisms disappear into the ordinary web of life so as to appear normal and natural, and how nationalisms are constantly invented and imagined through endless repetition and reiteration of its symbols. Contrary to the structural and elite focus of the modernist theorists, it may be more useful to understand nationalisms and nations as lived practices; in this, the critics build upon the work of Hobsbawm and Anderson.

Below, I will identify four theoretical approaches that either foreground the importance of imperialism in the spread and diversity of nationalisms or consider aspects that are largely neglected by the modernist theories of nationalism considered above. These four approaches correct the sidelining of crucial aspects of modernity in these theories, and grant culture a more central and broader role in the formation of nationalism. In that sense, the theories considered below do not clearly fall outside what we may label as modernist theories of nationalism. But what distinguishes them is that they attempt more "culturalist" approaches to nationalism and its modernity. Like the above modernist theories, they express profound skepticism about nationalism as a principle that unifies and homogenizes a group of people. At the same time, the latter approaches overlap with Hobsbawm's and Anderson's insights to argue toward multiple trajectories of nationalism, to avoid Eurocentric accounts of nationalism, and to grant primacy to the dynamics of imperialism, race, gender, and sexuality in theorizing the meanings, roles, and varieties of nationalism in contemporary life.

Nationalism as decentralized power

Critics of the modernist approach locating power in the political institutions or in the hands of elites call instead for wider, decentralized explanations of power. They draw heavily on a productive rather than merely repressive understanding of power. These scholars therefore call attention to not only the myriad institutions, such as the family, media, law, and education that serve to promote nationalisms, but also examine their less institutionalized expressions, such as in literature and poetry, and in the seemingly mundane use of flags, anthems, and other related symbols. Instead of focusing on the repressive and restrictive nature of nationalisms and states, they turn their attention to how nationalisms are lived out in quotidian life, how these become part of the taken-for-granted social environment, how nationalisms produce particular accounts of history and cultural identity, how state policies deny some people equal citizenship not through proscription but through prescription. Billig's notion of "banal nationalism," explored in the Introduction, is in keeping with this approach. Building upon the work of Hobsbawm and especially Anderson, these critics focus attention upon the "imagined" nature of nationalism and national community to examine the institutionalized and non-institutionalized mechanisms through which nationalism retains its hold and normality. Taking this decentralized, productive view of power also emphasizes the importance of looking at the fraught nature of nationalism. The idea is that power is not completely effective or totalizing, but open to conflict and resistance. Thus nationalisms and nations appear to be much more changeable social realities than unalterable structures of modernity.

Exemplifying this approach, Homi Bhabha considers nationalisms as contradictory, fragmented, and hybrid narratives.[74] Why the analogy to narrative? Looking at it as a narrative acknowledges the influence but transitional nature of nationalism. An account of nationalism, like a narrative, can be told, understood, and experienced from more than one perspective, whether of official or counternationalisms. Like narratives, nationalisms must constantly be re-told to be kept alive in living memory and to have influence. At the same time, narratives rarely have any traceable origins; rather, they are hybrid, dynamic versions about some aspect of social life and nationalisms are no different in that way. Lastly, the parallel between narrative and nationalism also draws attention to how language reflects the interaction between social and institutional structures and our deepest emotions and psyches. Disagreeing with the view that nationalism is merely a political instrument, Bhabha emphasizes a more ambivalent approach that looks at the contradictions, ambiguities, missteps, and margins of nationalism. The strategy, here, is to reveal the limitations of the power of nationalism and look for sources of resistance; Bhabha's point is that where there is power, challenges to power and the possibilities of social change are also present. Bhabha and others taking this approach have been influential in the study of nationalism especially since the 1990s. Although there is no inherent reason for this perspective not adequately to consider nationalism in relation to the state, such an analysis is frequently absent and the basis for the chief criticism of it by modernist theorists, among others.

Nationalism as anti-colonial resistance

Bhabha and other scholars are equally critical of the Eurocentric position of modernist theories of nationalism. Loosely identified as postcolonial scholars of nationalism, these investigators fault modernist theorists not only for their Eurocentric approach but also for not sufficiently addressing the role of empire in inciting nationalism. Modernist scholars either ignore the crucial links between colonialism and nationalism, especially in the nineteenth century, or they are likely to suggest that colonialism was the route through which (European) nationalism was exported elsewhere. Even though there is general consensus that nationalism was first actualized in Europe, it is misleading to suggest that this European model was simply exported elsewhere as a result of European domination or that it was automatically welcomed in Europe's colonies. Further, ignoring the role of empire from a critical perspective does not allow us to acknowledge and understand the ways in which nationalisms in Europe and in the colonies were mutually constitutive, from the nineteenth century onwards.

While the second point of criticism will be fully developed in Chapter Two, I wish to briefly dwell on Partha Chatterjee's criticism of the Euro-centrism reflected in modernist theories of nationalism.[75] Chatterjee takes issue with Anderson's argument (which Anderson later modified) that once nations were imagined as modules, they were widely adopted by both colonialists and anti-colonial movements in order to resist colonialism. As his starting point, Chatterjee wonders how, if anti-colonial movements merely adopted colonial modules of nationalisms, they would have been able to differentiate themselves from the colonialists – an ability essential to resistance. To argue that anti-colonial movements simply adopted nationalism as a model implies that anti-colonial elites were incapable of challenging colonialism of their own accord because both the domination and the resistance would have been on European terms. On the contrary, Chatterjee says, anti-colonial movements were based on difference from, not similarity to, the modular nationalisms of Europe. The indigenous elites adopted nationalism, but also resisted colonialism by specifying how their nation was different; this argument is more fully fleshed out in Chapter Two.

Rarely has the work of a single scholar been more influential than that of Frantz Fanon; colonial criticism and black consciousness have been widely inspired by him. Fanon's body of work addressed the nature and strategies of colonialism, the psychology of the colonized, and the path out of oppression for colonized peoples. Writing with respect to colonization and decolonization in Africa, especially in Algeria, Fanon sees nationalism as a means of survival against the violence of colonialism and also as a path toward liberation.[76] For Fanon, national culture registers the awakening of the fighting spirit. But national culture is not merely the turn to precolonial times to discover a nation and a common culture that is elite-led; rather, it is a fight for national liberation that cannot exist apart from the popular struggle of the people. In his words,

> A national culture is not a folklore, nor an abstract populism that believes it can discover the people's true nature. It is not made up of inert dregs of gratuitous actions, that is to say actions which are less and less attached to the ever-present reality of the people. A national culture is the whole body of efforts made by a people in the sphere of thought to describe, justify, and praise the action through which the people has created itself and keeps itself in existence. A national culture in underdeveloped countries should there-

fore take its place at the very heart of the struggle for freedom which these countries are carrying on.[77]

Clearly, national culture is powerful and genuine as a populist revolution against the throes of colonialism. This leads Anne McClintock to note that Fanon saw the inventedness of nationalism long before Anderson.[78] The forging of a national culture is key to national liberation only if it is based on the efforts of the people. Thus, nationalism is not without its pitfalls. In this, Fanon is resoundingly critical of the ways in which national elites hijack nationalism in their personal interests. Instead of serving the interests of the people and the nation, they seek to wrest control of the unfair advantages earlier enjoyed by the colonizers and in doing so they divest nationalism of any uniting potential. While he urges overthrowing the psychological and physical shackles of colonial racism, Fanon is skeptical of racial rather than national unity. He is critical of the search for pan-African or black unity in the struggle for decolonization and nation-building. At heart, each national culture is distinct. No doubt the racialized basis of colonialism fosters transnational black unity, but Fanon argues that ultimately there are distinct national differences and that blacks in the United States, for example, have different concerns from blacks in African nations.

Nationalism as racial resistance

Nonetheless, racial identity can be the wellspring for expressions of nationalism and the forging of a national culture. In the example of South Africa, which was explored earlier, racial identity was clearly used to foster nationalism both as repression and as liberation. The contemporary meaning of race as a means to organize and oppress groups has its roots in the modern epoch, which makes the inadequate attention paid to race in the modernist perspectives on nationalism all the more troubling. To some extent, all anti-colonial nationalisms have had to contend with questions of race that were fundamental to colonial rule. Therefore, theorists focusing on anti-colonialism such as Chatterjee pay careful attention to the race politics of colonialism and anti-colonial nationalist movements. But the turn to race as the chief criterion for mobilizing nationalist movements against an existing colonial or independent state is of a somewhat different ilk.

Briefly exploring theories on black nationalism in the United States gives us some insight into how race can form the basis of a distinctive nationalist resistance. Theorists of (north) American black nationalism, such as Dean Robinson, Rod Bush, and Rodney Carlisle, have noted that black nationalism has been visible since the late eighteenth century.[79] Robinson shows that black nationalism was contingent upon the emergence of an educated group of African Americans in the Northeast who were well aware of Euro-American formulations of nationalism.[80] Responding to American or "white" nationalism, which served the interests of privileged white groups through legislation and social policy, black nationalists led a pragmatic movement to protect black people from the injustices of slavery and other social inequalities. For them, race and nation were nearly identical. Drawing upon the strategies of anti-colonial movements, they looked to ancient African societies, reinforced the moral nature of blacks and the importance of resistance to white domination. But what distinguishes this as nationalism, from more general criticisms of racism and enslavement, is that they believed that blacks had to establish a separate nation in order to achieve political, social, and cultural liberation. Initially Liberia, then Haiti, and then Sierra Leone were considered possible sites for the relocation of American blacks and the establishment of self-rule. Nonetheless, black nationalism had a relatively narrow base in the black upper classes in the Northeast. Marcus Garvey, the charismatic figure most associated with black nationalism, endorsed the importance of racial distinctions, the purity of the black race, and emigration, and by the 1920s had garnered much support for black nationalism.[81]

Nonetheless, theorists urge broader conceptualizations of black nationalism that do not solely rely on emigration and the creation of independent states. Leaders such as William E. B. Du Bois promoted the project of black nationalism in opposition to black integration into white American life, a stance associated with another powerful leader, Booker T. Washington. Du Bois actively participated in the development of black cultural nationalism; his interest in separate black institutions and organizations furthered bolstered the language of nationalism.[82] What defines these contributions as black nationalist is the questioning of race-based inequalities, the emphasis on race-based solidarity and racial pride, and notions of a shared but separate culture and a past in the search for black self-determination. These views on black nationalism and its opposition to integration also influenced the emergence of the "Black Power" movement in the 1960s. Drawing inspiration from the work of Fanon and anti-colonial movements in the Third World at the time, a cross-section of black nationalists promoted notions of a black nation of people with a separate language and culture that was under siege as a colonized territory.[83] Under the auspices of the Nation of Islam, black nationalists further disavowed the Christian traditions of white America. What is also noteworthy about black nationalism since the 1960s is that, compared to its historical roots, it is no longer largely a movement of black elites; its support base is largely the working classes.

Nationalism as gendered and sexualized

The inattention to race by modernist theorists is paralleled by the scant attention given to gender and sexuality with respect to nationalism; this criticism also applies to many of the critics considered above who fail to consider the interplay of gender and sexuality in the meaning, expressions, and salience of nationalism. Since Chapters Two, Three, and Four will examine these links in depth and the contribution of feminist theories of nationalism, here it suffices to outline these links and why it is important to consider them. Taken together, feminist scholars of nationalism make the point that gender and sexuality and nationalisms affect each other; that gender and sexuality are central, not incidental, to the origins, meaning, and implications of nationalism. The influence of these factors on each other can be looked at in three ways. First, women play a central role in nationalism. They can be leaders, the foot soldiers, the inciters, and followers in nationalist movements. The important point is that nationalisms impact women and men differently. So perhaps it took feminist scholars working in the international arena to call attention to the role of gender and sexuality in understandings of nationalisms. Second, definitions of masculinity and femininity shape the meaning of nationalisms, and nationalisms help shape norms of femininity and masculinity. The Miss America pageantry offers insight into how American nationalism and femininity are embodied in women who are attractive but with some displayable talent, assertive but not aggressive, likeable without being too pliant, and competitive but able to rise above it. Third, nationalism impacts how we think about sexuality. When Vanessa Williams, who is black, resigned from her 1984 Miss America post under pressure from those who disapproved of her for appearing nude and sexual with a white woman in *Penthouse* magazine, expectations of "sexual respectability" in American women were symbolically and literally endorsed. That nationalisms are also highly sexualized is equally evident in the eroticized language of "love for one's country" and metaphors such as a nation raped or the nation as bride.

Conclusion

It is surely clear that there is no single story of nationalism and its meanings. I have therefore tried to account for the significant theoretical approaches to nationalism and why they are important. I expect that it is also clear that a chronicle of theories of nationalism is neither continuous nor based on discrete categories. On the one hand, theories inform each other and scholarly work sometimes cuts across theoretical divisions. On the other hand, there are some profound differences between, say, perennialists, modernists, and their critics that are worth noting. The position taken here is that the various approaches contribute to our understanding by highlighting certain questions but ignoring others. Taken together, these approaches to nationalism also tell us much about the importance of pursuing the concept of nationalism, given what is at stake. No single approach is definitive or all-encompassing.

Instead of belaboring the pros and cons of theoretical perspectives, I would like to end this chapter by recapitulating the importance of a culturalist perspective on nationalism. This is less by way of persuading readers how to think about nationalism, than it is to underscore the reasons for my own approach. First, I do believe that nationalisms ought to be considered as modern phenomena. This does not foreclose the possibility of continuity between the past and our present; instead, it acknowledges that the past always figures selectively in our present and how it does so is always contingent on the changes of the present. If perennialists and primordialists do well to remind us about the deep-seated visceral influence of nationalism, then the emphasis on nationalism as an instrument and outcome of modernity is compelling indeed. The contributions of modernist approaches are useful reminders about the power and unpredictability of nationalism. Nationalism is a product of the social, political, and economic changes and disruptions – the rise of the modern state, industrial capitalism, warfare and militarism, distinctions between the public and private and between state and civil society – associated with modernity.

Second, a culturalist approach to nationalisms acknowledges the "invented" nature of nationalisms and the imagined nature of the nation. Yet this does not mean that nationalisms or nations are any less real or reduced in their power. On the contrary, recognizing the "produced" nature of nationalism allows us to see its inconsistencies, its ambivalences, and unstable aspects. Third, these inconsistencies of nationalisms include its revolutionary and repressive potentials, its power to impose unity but also to create longing and desire, its external and internal lines of exclusion structured along dimensions of race, gender, sexuality, and ethnicity.

Fourth, a culturalist approach would be incomplete without consistently positing nationalism's connection to the state, where the state is seen as a set of structures and institutions and a social relation among state institutions. At the same time the connection must be made between state institutions and individuals, groups, and organizations that fall within the loosely defined civil sphere. Fifth, a cultural approach avoids privileging a Euro-American-centered approach to the proliferation of nationalism and challenges the idea of a monolithic theory of nationalism. This also means abandoning dual accounts of western and non-western, official and popular nationalisms, or divisions between nationalists and patriots, in favor of linkages between nationalisms across the colonial divide or the contemporary divides of the "First World" and "Third World," a point explored in Chapter Two.

Sixth, recognizing nationalism's spectacular moments through rituals of celebration or making war and its banal quotidian aspects are equally important. The point is to see nationalism as lived practice. In this sense, nationalism has no predetermined or inevitable existence but must be actively sustained whether by state institutions or through popular culture, thereby exposing it to conflict, dissension, and resistance from numerous directions. Therefore, literature, nationalist rituals, films, the commonplace presence of the national flag, singing the national anthem at sports events, legal decisions on the parameters of citizenship or on matters of sexuality, among other phenomena, are important indicators of how nationalisms are reproduced and represented in everyday life.

Seventh, and finally, we need to recognize how much elites and the intelligentsia give shape to and normalize the meaning and significance of nationalism. While the instrumentalist insight that elites manipulate nationalist sentiments runs the risk of making ordinary people simply instruments rather than participators in the arena of nationalism, it is hard to ignore that in some cases nationalisms do involve political maneuvering and stage-management. But the instrumentalist view overlooks not only the possibility of popular nationalisms, but also the part played by public intellectuals. If we take the approach that nationalisms have to be invented or imagined, the influence of public intellectuals is as striking as outright elitist manipulation in the production of nationalism. Intellectuals have played a crucial role in transforming groups into national communities by selecting, revising, and reframing cultural characteristics. No less, through the nineteenth and twentieth centuries, intellectuals have imagined nationalism as a revolutionary force against the grain of the state. But more often than not, the mobilization of ordinary people, the groundswell of popular nationalisms, has been key to successful nationalist movements. It may be more useful to look at the interactions rather than the neat divisions between elites, intellectuals or ordinary people, or between official and popular nationalisms.

NOTES

1   Partha Chatterjee, *The Nation and its Fragments: Colonial and Postcolonial Histories* (Princeton, NJ: Princeton University Press, 1993), p. 4.
2   For example, see Philip Corrigan and Derek Sayer, *The Great Arch: English State Formation as Cultural Revolution*, with a foreword by G. E. Aylmer (Oxford: Blackwell, 1985); Philip S. Gorski, "Calvinism and state-formation in Early Modern Europe," in George Steinmetz (ed.) *State/Culture: State-formation after the Cultural Turn* (Ithaca, NY and London: Cornell University Press, 1999), pp. 147–81.
3   George Steinmetz, "Introduction: culture and the state," in Steinmetz, *State/Culture*, p. 9.
4   Ibid., p. 8.
5   For example, see Charles Tilly, *Coercion, Capital, and European States, AD 990–1990* (Cambridge, Mass.: Blackwell, 1990).
6   E. J. Graff, *What Is Marriage For?* (Boston: Beacon, 1999), p. 38.
7   On this point, see Thomas Blom Hansen and Finn Stepputat, "Introduction: states of imagination," in Thomas Blom Hansen and Finn Stepputat (eds.) *States of Imagination: Ethnographic Explorations of the Postcolonial State* (Durham, NC and London: Duke University Press), pp. 1–38; see also Steinmetz, "Introduction: culture and the state," esp. pp. 20–3.
8   Hansen and Stepputat, "Introduction: states of imagination," p. 16.
9   Ibid., p. 2.
10 Ibid., pp. 16–17.
11 Timothy Mitchell, "The limits of the state: beyond statist approaches and their critics," *The American Political Science Review*, 85/1 (1991), pp. 77–96.
12 Tilly, *Coercion, Capital, and European States*, esp. pp. 114–17.
13 Hansen and Stepputat, "Introduction: states of imagination," p. 8.
14 Andrew Vincent, *Theories of the State* (Oxford: Blackwell, 1987), p. 30.
15 Tilly, *Coercion, Capital, and European States*, p. 1.
16 Theda Skocpol's definition of the state cited in Roger King, *The State in Modern Society: New Directions in Political Sociology*, with ch. 8 by Graham Gibbs (Chatham, NJ: Chatham House Publications, 1986), p. 47.
17 Anthony Giddens, *A Contemporary Critique of Historical Materialism*, vol. 2: *The Nation-state and Violence* (Berkeley and Los Angeles: University of California Press, 1987), esp. pp. 49–53.
18 Ibid., p. 50.

19 Ibid., p. 120.

20 Hansen and Stepputat, "Introduction: states of imagination," p. 7.

21 Rogers Brubaker, *Citizenship and Nationhood in France and Germany* (Cambridge, Mass. and London: Harvard University Press, 1992).

22 Charles Tilly, "Epilogue: now where?," in Steinmetz, *State/Culture*, pp. 407–19.

23 Hugh Seton-Watson, *Nations and States* (Boulder, Colo.: Westview Press, 1977), p. 148.

24 Anthony W. Marx, *Making Race and Nation: A Comparison of the United States, South Africa, and Brazil* (Cambridge: Cambridge University Press, 1998).

25 Anne McClintock, *Imperial Leather: Race, Gender and Sexuality in the Colonial Contest* (New York and London: Routledge, 1995), esp. pp. 329–51.

26 John Hutchinson, *The Dynamics of Cultural Nationalism: The Gaelic Revival and the Creation of the Irish Nation-State* (London: Allen & Unwin, 1987).

27 Ibid., p. 13.

28 Ibid., pp. 29–30.

29 Ernest Gellner, *Nations and Nationalism* (Ithaca, NY: Cornell University Press, 1983), p. 55.

30 Eric J. Hobsbawm, *Nations and Nationalism since 1780: Programme, Myth, and Reality* (Cambridge: Cambridge University Press, 1990), p. 19.

31 Breda Gray and Louise Ryan, "The politics of Irish identity and the interconnections between feminism, nationhood, and colonialism," in Ruth Roach Pierson and Nupur Chaudhuri (eds.) *Nation, Empire, Colony: Historicizing Gender and Race* (Bloomington and Indianapolis: Indiana University Press, 1998), pp. 121–38.

32 Tilly, *Coercion, Capital, and European States*, p. 3.

33 Ibid.

34 Ralph Miliband, *Class Power and State Power* (London: Verso, 1983), esp. ch. 2.

35 For a helpful discussion on Poulantzas, see Bob Jessop, *Nicos Poulantzas: Marxist Theory and Political Strategy* (New York: St. Martin's Press, 1985).

36 On the debates see King, *The State in Modern Society*, esp. ch. 3.

37 Jessop, *Nicos Poulantzas*, p. 61.

38 David Forgacs (ed.) *An Antonio Gramsci Reader: Selected Writings, 1916–1935*, (New York: Schocken, 1988).

39 Mitchell, "Limits of the state"; Timothy Mitchell, "Society, economy, and the state effect," in Steinmetz, *State/Culture*, pp. 76–97.

40 King, *The State in Modern Society*, esp. ch. 1.

41 See Mitchell, "Limits of the state," pp. 78–81; Steinmetz, "Introduction: culture and the state," pp. 19–20.

42 Steinmetz, "Introduction: culture and the state," p. 17.

43 Mitchell, "Limits of the state," p. 81.

44 Steinmetz, "Introduction: culture and the state," p. 27.

45 Corrigan and Sayer, *The Great Arch*, esp. "Introduction."

46 Ibid., p. 4.

47 Mitchell, "Limits of the state" and "Society, economy, and the state effect."

48 Steinmetz, "Introduction: culture and the state," p. 22.

49 On this point, Crawford Young, *The African Colonial State in Comparative Perspective* (New Haven, Conn.: Yale University Press, 1994).

50 Deniz Kandayoti (ed.) *Women, Islam and the State* (Philadelphia: Temple University Press, 1991); Sita Ranchod-Nilsson and Mary Ann Tétreault (eds.) *Women, States, and Nationalism: At Home in the Nation?* (London and New York: Routledge, 2000); Gilbert M. Joseph and Daniel Nugent (eds.) *Everyday Forms of State Formation: Revolution and Negotiation of Rule in Modern Mexico,* foreword by James C. Scott (Durham, NC and London: Duke University Press, 1994); Hansen and Steppputat (eds.) *States of Imagination.*

51 Anthony D. Smith, *Nationalism and Modernism: A Critical Survey of Recent Theories of Nations and Nationalism* (London and New York: Routledge, 1998), esp. ch. 7.

52 Ibid., p. 159.

53 Anthony D. Smith, *The Nation in History: Historiographical Debates about Ethnicity and Nationalism* (Hanover, NH: University Press of New England, 2000), p. 51.

54 Craig J. Calhoun, *Nationalism* (Minneapolis: University of Minnesota Press, 1997), p. 31; Smith, *Nationalism and Modernism,* pp. 153–9.

55 Ernest Renan, "What is a nation?," in Homi K. Bhabha (ed.) *Nation and Narration* (London and New York: Routledge, 1990), pp. 8–22.

56 Elie Kedourie, *Nationalism,* 4th, expanded, edn. (Cambridge, Mass. and Oxford: Blackwell, 1960).

57 Smith, *The Nation in History,* p. 68.

58 Smith, *Nationalism and Modernism,* pp. 193–5.

59 Gellner, *Nations and Nationalism.*

60 Ibid., p. 1.

61 Smith, *Nationalism and Modernism,* p. 36.

62 Tom Nairn, *The Break-up of Britain: Crisis and Neo-nationalism,* 2nd edn. (London: New Left Books, 1977).

63 Smith, *Nationalism and Modernism,* pp. 49–55.

64 John Breuilly, *Nationalism and the State* (New York: St. Martin's Press, 1982); Giddens, *The Nation-state and Violence;* Hobsbawm, *Nations and Nationalism;* Michael Mann (ed.) *The Rise and Decline of the Nation State* (Oxford: Blackwell, 1990); Tilly, *Coercion, Capital and European States.*

65 Smith, *Nationalism and Modernism,* pp. 70–1.

66 Breuilly, *Nationalism and the State,* p. 3.

67 Giddens, *The Nation-state and Violence,* p. 116.

68 Ibid., p. 121.

69 Tilly, *Coercion, Capital and European States,* p. 14.

70 Ibid.

71 Eric Hobsbawm, "Introduction: inventing traditions," in Eric Hobsbawm and Terence Ranger (eds.) *The Invention of Tradition* (Cambridge: Cambridge University Press, 1983), pp. 1–14.

72 Hobsbawm, *Nations and Nationalism,* p. 31.

73 Benedict Anderson, *Imagined Communities* (London: Verso, 1983), esp. "Introduction."

74 Homi K. Bhabha, "Introduction: narrating the nation," in *Nation and Narration*, pp. 1–7.

75 Chatterjee, *Nation and its Fragments*.

76 Frantz Fanon, *The Wretched of the Earth*, tr. Constance Farrington (New York: Grove Press, 1963), esp. pp. 148–248.

77 Ibid., p. 233.

78 McClintock, *Imperial Leather*, esp. pp. 352–89.

79 Dean E. Robinson, "To forge a nation, to forge an identity: black nationalism in the US 1957–74," Ph.D. thesis, Yale University, 1995; Rod Bush, *We Are Not What We Seem: Black Nationalism and Class Struggle in the American Century* (New York and London: New York University Press, 2000); Rodney Carlisle, *The Roots of Black Nationalism* (Port Washington, NY and London: Kennikat Press, 1975).

80 Robinson, "To forge a nation," esp. ch. 3.

81 Ibid., esp. ch. 5; Carlisle, *Roots of Black Nationalism*, esp. ch. 13.

82 Bush, *We Are Not What We Seem*, esp. ch. 3.

83 Robinson, "To forge a nation," esp. pp. 119–24.

CHAPTER TWO

Fraught Legacies: Nationalism, Colonialism, and Race

Europe is literally the creation of the Third World.[1]

. . . the Orient has helped to define Europe (or the West) as its contrasting image, idea, personality, experience. Yet none of this Orient is merely imaginative. The Orient is an integral part of European material civilization and culture.[2]

Have you ever wondered what colonialism has to do with life in the early twenty-first century? After all, in most cases formal colonialism is at least fifty years in the past. Do you think that colonialism is a matter for historians and not students of contemporary social structures, beliefs, and practices? Do you find yourself sometimes becoming impatient with the turning back to the past in a book on nationalism? Perhaps you concede that colonialism is of some relevance to societies that are ex-colonies and their contemporary nationalisms and not, by implication, to Western Europe and North America. Do you wonder what exactly we mean when we refer to colonialism? Or, maybe, what are the differences between colonialism and imperialism? Perhaps some readers feel differently; you are convinced of the salience of colonialism and its legacies in contemporary life. What are its legacies in your opinion? Maybe the previous chapters helped anticipate the links between colonialism and nationalism for you. What answers did you come up with regarding colonialism's bearings on nationalism?

Broadly speaking, this chapter considers nationalism against the grain of colonialism in order to consider how imperial expansions and nationalisms were tightly connected. As evident in the overview of modernist theories in the previous chapter, nationalism's links to colonialism are either ignored altogether or treated in a limited way; by the same token, scholars of colonialism typically do not address issues of nationalism. For our purposes here, I focus on the links between colonialism and nationalism through the nineteenth and early twentieth centuries at a time when Britain and France were ascendant, thereby limiting the scope of the analysis. Although the USA, Japan, and Germany, among others, entered the fray toward the end of the nineteenth century, in this chapter I focus on the enduring impact of Britain and France. From this partial analysis of nationalisms and colonialisms through the nineteenth and mid-twentieth centuries, there appears to be no summary explanation; the links were varied enough to result in multiple, divergent legacies of nationalism. On the other hand, it turns out that official and anti-colonial nationalisms had everything to do with colonial rule and its eventual ousting.

Specifically, I will start by defining colonialism, its types, its important dimensions, and its links to race and nation. Bringing together the social, political, and cultural aspects of colonialism will help us construct a picture of the broad context of the nineteenth century – the Industrial Revolution, capitalist expansion, empire-building, race and racism – that bears on the gathering momentum of nationalisms at the time. Equally important, starting with a discussion on colonialism allows me to lay the groundwork for a culturalist approach to nationalisms in that historical and cultural context. Not only will this help move us away from Euro-centered formulations of nationalism, but it will also give us a more nuanced perception of the linkages and differences between metropolitan and colonial nationalisms. The underlying approach is to look at colonies and metropoles as two related, different, and internally non-homogenous sites. How metropolitan and colonial nationalisms were linked through colonial encounters, and how these nationalisms differently revealed the revolutionary and repressive potentials of nationalisms in the nineteenth through the mid-twentieth century are the questions of most concern in this chapter.

Therefore, the second and third sections of the chapter respectively focus on the interplay between colonialisms and nationalisms in the metropoles and the colonies. Attention is also given to the importance of metropolitan and colonial states to rising nationalisms. These sections lay the groundwork for looking at race, gender, ethnicity, and sexuality as central rather than tangential aspects of colonial rule and rising nationalisms. While subsequent chapters focus on gender, sexuality, and ethnicity, here we will consider how discourses of race did more than impact on colonial and nationalist politics both in the metropoles and the colonies; they made nationalist and colonialist politics possible and consequential.

Colonialism and Imperialism: Context and Significance

While the initial thrust of European expansion can be dated to the end of the fifteenth century with Spain at the vanguard, the nineteenth century witnessed rapid colonial expansion, a shift in strategies of colonialism, and the ascendancy of Britain, France, and gradually the United States. At the start of the nineteenth century, the European empire, including Europe and its former and current colonies, extended over 35 percent of the earth's land surface, but toward the end of the century it expanded to 76 percent, and further increased to as much as 85 percent by the early twentieth century.[3] The latter period (1889–1914) has been described as a mad scramble of former and relatively new colonial groups to acquire colonies. Between 1876 and 1915, Britain increased its territories by approximately 4 million square miles, France by 3.5 million, Germany by an additional one million, Belgium and Italy by just fewer than one million each; the United States and Japan entered the imperial race during this period.[4]

Defining colonialisms

Though "imperialism" and "colonialism" are terms comparable in meaning, for purposes of clarity, "colonialism" is here taken to mean a specific form of power and domination that involves the direct application of military, political, and socio-economic control.[5] Typically, it involved the destruction and re-organization of social, economic, or political aspects of the society under occupation in order to facilitate control by the colonizing society or nation. Broadly speaking, colonialism has taken two forms: *settlement colonies* that entailed either the marginalization or the removal of people from their lands through coercion or annihilation; and *colonial rule* that triggered the overwhelming transformation of societies. A third type can also be identified, but since it comprises economic and political forms of domination and subjugation that do not involve direct occupation, it is interchangeably referred to as "imperialism" or "informal colonialism."

Cases such as the United States, the West Indies, South Africa, and Australia are examples of the first form, *settler colonialism*. The permanent settlement of large numbers of colonizers, who forced the marginalization of indigenous peoples into reservations or forcibly took over their lands, was its cornerstone. The death of untold indigenous peoples through exposure to foreign diseases and massacres was also typical of settler forms of colonization. Contrary to popular opinion, early European conquest of the Americas, for example, had less to do with technological prowess and more to do with the introduction of diseases foreign to the colonies and the ability to capitalize on local political rivalries. The initial control of land and trade, and plunder of wealth and transportable resources, was followed by the setting up of administrative units that systematized colonial extraction. The emergence of substantial creole communities–persons of European descent who were born in the Americas[6] – was key to the relationship between these colonial provinces and the metropoles.

By the nineteenth century, *colonial rule*, which signaled a partial discontinuity with the earlier pattern of colonialism, was more widely prevalent. Like colonial settlement, colonial rule was typically established through relatively small numbers of conquerors, who relied on a mix of force, negotiations, and strategic alliances. At the Battle of Plassey, which was the watershed of British colonization of India, 950 European infantry and 150 gunners were able to vanquish Nawab Suraj-ud-Daulah's 50,000 foot soldiers and 18,000 horsemen only because one of the Nawab's generals defected with his troops.[7] Like colonial settlement, colonial rule also sought to make extraction and exploitation more systematic by setting up administrative and bureaucratic units after the initial phases of plunder. Colonial administrative policies triggered massive disruptions in the colonies through the widespread political, economic, and social changes. Changes in land and property arrangements or even the introduction of private property in some cases, the creation of direct or indirect sources of labor supply for the metropole, the expansion of money-based economies, and curtailment of productive capacities in the colonies (such as the cotton industry in India) were some of the most obvious and significant of these changes.[8]

In contrast to colonialism, *imperialism* can be defined as "a concept that signifies any relationship of domination and subordination between nations, including the modern form of economic control."[9] Although there is considerable debate on the concept of imperialism, V. I. Lenin's approach to imperialism as a specific stage of capitalism influenced the characterization of the period 1889–1914 as the "Age of Imperialism."[10] For Lenin, imperialism is a stage of capitalism marked by: the development of monopolies; consolidation of financial capital; the export of capital rather than just commodities; increasing control of the world by international capitalist systems; and the territorial division of the world among capitalist powers. A foremost scholar of the history of imperialism, Harry Magdoff, suggests that colonialism existed before imperialism, but imperialism has outlasted colonialism. By the same token, Magdoff also believes that imperialism would not have developed without the base laid by formal colonialism. This approach to imperialism, as economic and political control triggered by monopoly capitalism, which may or may not include formal colonization, captures the ongoing crises of imperialism, and brings within its scope examples ranging from the Atlantic slave trade to contemporary relations between the United States and Haiti.

In her remarks on the typologies of colonialism, an insightful feminist scholar of colonialism, Catherine Hall, notes that there were no neat demarcations.[11] The fundamental difference between colonial settlement and colonial rule consisted in the number of colonizers and the degree to which the colonized people assimilated their culture. While, under colonial settlement, the local groups "assimilated" the hybrid cultures of the settlers, under colonial rule, there were significantly large creole communities undergoing what was seen as foreign occupation. The differences between colonialism and imperialism are not always clear either. For example, Ethiopia was never formally colonized, and although the Ethiopian army defeated advancing Italian troops in 1896 it was at the cost of strengthening the influence of the French, who were able thereafter to stage military expeditions from Ethiopia. Similarly, many Latin American countries became independent nations in the early nineteenth century only to become an informal part of the British empire; at the time, Latin American economies came to be almost completely dependent on British imports. Magdoff observes that Latin America provided the single largest market for British cotton textiles in the first half of the nineteenth century. Conversely, exporting goods to Latin America, providing railway equipment, and constructing public roads and communications in these countries allowed Britain to serve its domestic, industrial needs through informal domination.

Regardless of the type of formal or informal colonialism, conquest was not always easy; frequently, it met with resistance. As Peter Worsley reminds us, the Afghans, the Zulus, and the Ashanti defeated British armies and in other cases rebellions, uprisings, and challenges to colonial authority were not uncommon.[12] Anti-colonial nationalism was one such form of resistance to colonialism that is of special interest here. In the case of settler colonialism in the Americas, anti-colonial nationalism was often led by creole communities who shared descent and language with their European colonizers.[13] Nonetheless, they sought to undo the economic and political harnesses of the colonial relationship. But, in the case of colonial rule that came to dominate by the second half of the nineteenth century and in early twentieth century in Asia and Africa, colonialism was seen as foreign, indeed, alien domination.

Especially after World War I, nationalist independence movements in an array of colonies gathered momentum and eventually resulted in widespread decolonization after World War II. Principles of national self-determination and an international order organized through sovereign national states was most clearly articulated in the aftermath of World War I; the League of Nations, predecessor of the United Nations, was conceived at the time. With the weakening hold of the colonial powers, numerous nationalist movements came to fruition as independent states between the end of World War II and 1960s. This period also witnessed the ascendancy of the United States and the Soviet Union as the dominant national states in world politics. Formal colonialism might have unraveled at the time, but there is ongoing concern that colonial and imperialist relations of domination took on new shapes and forms; terms such as neocolonialism and neo-imperialism are attempts to capture the legacies of colonialism and current shifts in capitalism.

Dimensions of colonial rule

The patterns of nineteenth-century colonialism can be understood along two broad dimensions: economic and cultural. These dimensions are not easily separable, but are useful as a way to explore the nature and scope of colonialism. Economically, colonialism can be more fully understood through the inextricable links between colonial expansion, the Industrial Revolution, and capitalism in the nineteenth century. Dating from the second half of the eighteenth century in Britain, the Industrial Revolution wrought massive social and economic changes, in the organization of work and social life, and workers produced goods on a potentially large scale through machines rather than hand tools. This converted earlier colonial demands for slaves, spices, and sugar to calls for raw materials and food from the colonies, to feed the expanding populations in the metropole. Above all, colonialism facilitated the Industrial Revolution in the metropole by setting up new markets for industrial goods in the colonies.

The industrialization of cotton provides useful insight into the links between the British Industrial Revolution and colonial expansion. In his

The Age of Revolution, Eric Hobsbawm reminds us that the cotton industry was first created through slave labor and later expanded through the export of large quantities of cotton cloth, which had been produced in British factories.[14] But key to the expansion of the cotton industry was the creation and monopolization of markets elsewhere through colonial rule. The deliberate destruction of the then thriving cloth industry in India coupled with the subsidization of British cloth sold in the Indian markets is perhaps the best-known example of the creation and monopolization of markets under colonial rule. The fact that the cotton industry was easily and cheaply mechanized, and colonial rule ensured favorable market conditions, guaranteed large profits to European investors and served further to accelerate colonial expansion and industrialization.

The Industrial Revolution was coterminous with the spread of capitalism. The search for new markets was not only vital for exporting industrial goods but also for meeting the restless need of capital constantly to expand. Driven by the needs of colonialism, a flourishing capitalism helped create a world economy, international monetary markets and international financial institutions, resulting in interdependent but highly unequal economies. An "international division of labor," under which colonial powers extracted raw materials from and then sold produced goods to the colonies was the trademark of this capitalist world market. Entire directly ruled colonies and informal colonies were converted to specialized producers of one or two products: Cuba for sugar and cigars, Malaya for rubber and tin; Egypt was transformed into a cotton plantation and countries in Central America became plantations of bananas and other fruit. This division of labor whereby formal and informal colonial economies were reduced to sources of raw material without sufficient self-producing capacities triggered a lasting dependency of these colonies on the metropole. Distinctions between "industrialized" and "Third World" nations can be traced back to this unequal division of labor in which the latter were unable to adequately develop productive capacities of their own, and became externally dependent for their basic needs, such as food and infrastructure.

That economic considerations provided strong motivations for nineteenth-century colonialism is indisputable; but the economic and cultural dimensions of colonialism cannot be separated. To focus on imperialism or colonialism as entirely economic processes related to a particular stage of capitalism is to miss the point that material considerations in our lives, such as our work and economic survival or the economic system, are fully shaped by cultural considerations, and vice versa. For example, colonial economic policies in the African continent lured male labor to mines and towns but restricted women to rural areas and subsistence production, thereby disrupting gender roles, family units, and women's access to independent livelihood.[15] Because the presence of women in colonial towns aroused suspicion, they were sometimes forcibly deported, with the help of elderly African men. The difficulty in separating economic and cultural aspects of our lives is further reflected in the widespread and devastating effects of introducing a monetary system among the Naga people, who lived in what later became Northeast India. The changeover to money as a means of transaction triggered the practice of child marriage for girls. Earlier, a prospective groom paid the bride's family in the form of rice or cattle over several years, thereby delaying the age of marriage, but as the payments were replaced by a lump sum of money girls were married off at a younger age. Social inequality was another effect of introducing money; some people incurred large debts and became landless, while others consolidated their land holdings.

Approaches to colonialism

Understanding the links between the economic and cultural aspects of colonialism goes beyond merely adding cultural considerations to the economic motivations of colonialism. Appreciating this, Nicholas Dirks argues that colonialism was a cultural project of control that included, but was not limited to, economic motivations.[16] Indeed, there is considerable debate on whether colonialism was primarily an economic force. Critical scholars point out that colonialism can not be reduced to economic interests nor can there be a single overarching explanation for it. In their introduction to the influential collection, *Tensions of Empire*, Ann Stoler and Frederick Cooper say that though there is no doubt that economic motivations played a large part in colonization, it did not make a substantial long-term difference to capital accumulation in Britain or France, the major nineteenth-century colonial nations.[17] Hobsbawm notes that because formal colonization was only one aspect of economic globalization and expansion, none of the colonial powers apart from Britain and the Netherlands was overly economically dependent on its colonies. In fact, he observes, the bulk of the import and export trade in European countries was between themselves and with emerging national economies in countries with populations of European descent: Canada, Australia, South Africa, among others.

It is clear that the cultural dimensions of colonialism need to be broadly defined so as to include the psychological aspects of colonialism, the realm of literature, popular music, etc. Few scholars have furthered the under-standing of the psychological effects of colonialism more than Frantz Fanon and Albert Memmi. Fanon and Memmi separately argued that colonialism had profound effects on the psychology of the colonized and also the colonizers. Memmi suggests that the colonial relationship chained the colonizer and colonized into economic and psychological dependence so as to mold their character and conduct. His work brings troubling attention to how colonizers accepted the privileges and oppressive tasks of their positions, and also how the colonized could simultaneously feel passionate hatred and admiration for the colonizers.[18] In a parallel vein, emphasizing the role of literature for both the colonized and the colonizers, Edward Said and other scholars of literature have explored the deep intertwining of colonialism and literary imagination. Said examines how the work of writers such as Joseph Conrad and Rudyard Kipling reflects and shapes the dominant perspective of colonial rule.[19] But that cultural forms, such as literature, are a space to challenge colonial power is equally well reflected in the writings of Salman Rushdie and Chinua Achebe, he finds.

Drawing upon this far-reaching and critical understanding of colonial-ism, Cooper and Stoler suggest that we explore the contradictory, com-plex, and multiple dimensions of colonialism. What is necessary is to understand colonialism in a complex way: as an economic process that is not limited to economic effects; as a cultural process that has material impact on people's lives; as characterized by patterns and changes over a wide expanse of time and geography, but also by inconsistencies and contradictions; as an expression of power as well as of resistance toward it. As Stoler and Cooper put it, simply and eloquently, colonialism was shaped through struggle.[20]

Furthermore, Dirks argues that colonialism was not so much a process that started in Europe and then extended outward to the colonies as it was a moment when the understanding came about that the world is made of Europe and its colonies.[21] This is precisely the point made by the two quotations opening this chapter, by Fanon and Said: that Europe and its colonies were shaped by their relationship with each another. Seen in this way, colonialism is an *unequal relationship* out of which groupings such as metropole and colonies are created, and through which these societies came into hierarchical contact. An eminent scholar, Mary Louise Pratt, uses the concept of "contact zones" to describe this area of unequal encounter between metropoles and colonies.[22] These contact zones existed not only in the colonies, but also in the metropoles. As another important feminist scholar of colonialism, Inderpal Grewal, notes, Indians have had a continuous presence in Britain for the past three centuries, belying any assumptions that the metropoles or, for that matter, the colonies were internally homogeneous.[23] Thus, if the past colonial relationship shaped what we now know about the world and made this knowledge seem normal and self-evident, then it is useful to take a skeptical attitude to classifications such as metropoles and colonies, Europe and the Third World, or to the belief that they are internally homogenous.

Strategies of colonial rule: the significance of race and nation

Colonial rule was inherently contradictory. The dissemination of reason, progress, science, civilization, culture, citizenship, together with equality under law, were some of the underlying tenets that rationalized the colonial expansion of countries such as Britain and France. These helped mask the violent effects of conquest and colonial rule by justifying them. In fact, in the last twenty-five years of the nineteenth century, European elites justified colonial coercion and brutality on the grounds that this allowed them to build stable governments, establish orderly commerce, and create social order in the colonies.[24] But if creating better societies through the dissemination of universal European principles was the stated premise of colonialism, then colonizers faced a fundamental contradiction in the widespread application of these principles in the colonies: it would make colonial rule redundant. In other words, if the colonies were indeed "Europeanized," then there would be no further need for European colonial presence.

This contradiction within the colonial relationship was partly resolved through the "rule of colonial difference," a term used by Partha Chatterjee.[25] That there were fundamental, and irreconcilable differences of mind, emotion, body, culture, psychology, race, strength, capability, among others, between the colonizers and the colonized was a persisting idea underlying colonial rule. A related aspect of the "rule of colonial difference" was that these perceived differences denoted inequality; so colonized peoples were consistently deemed not only different but also inferior. Colonial powers rationalized the withholding of rights and privileges from people in the colonies on the basis that there were essential differences between the two groups. In this tautological framework, the perceived differences between the colonized people and Europeans proved the supremacy of "universal" European principles, but the differences also justified why so-called universal European principles could not be applied to the colonies. As the British and the French tried to regularize colonialism in places such as India and Algeria in the nineteenth century, they were continually faced with the contradiction of the superiority of European principles as a justification of colonial rule and the reason that these principles could not be equally applied to indigenous peoples in the colonies.

Perhaps no other way of marking differences between groups of people and justifying unequal treatment was as important to the colonial rule of difference as race. Definitions of race, the racialization of Europeans and their colonies, and unabashed forms of racism were central to dominant perceptions of the differences between groups that warranted different rights and responsibilities. Scholars have persuasively demonstrated that racial classifications and racial theories that continue to endure in many ways were first given shape in the nineteenth century under the aegis of colonialism. One such researcher, Robert Young, suggests that ways of thinking about race, its role, and significance were developed at a particular era of British and European colonial expansion that, in turn, justified the western occupation of nine-tenths of the world's land surface.[26] Speaking to the inextricable links between the imperial phase of European expansion and race, Young suggests that after the 1880s the ideology of race became so dominant that racial superiority overtook economic gain or the proselytization of Christianity as the single most important justification for empire; this was succinctly captured in the self-describing English phrase, "imperial race."[27] Until the late 1840s, however, in England public attitudes toward racial difference were comparatively benign; but three events dramatically increased beliefs of racial difference and the racial superiority of the English, namely, the Indian Mutiny (Rebellion) of 1857, the American Civil War (1861–5), and the Jamaican Insurrection of 1865.[28] Gradually thereafter, the concept of race and racial differences between the colonizers and the colonized were ironically invoked not only to justify European colonial domination but also to argue that it was their moral responsibility to so-called inferior races.

An understanding of race as a distinct way of classifying people according to some perceived physical, mental, and psychological characteristics first emerged in the seventeenth century. Although anthropologists have shown that ways of differentiating and justifying the unequal treatment of some groups have long existed, these racial theories are novel in that they had the backing of "scientific proof" and were disseminated through the force of colonial rule. The power of science and colonialism made what was a cultural concept into a biological, seemingly natural, fact. Despite the origin of race and racial classifications in the unequal encounters between the colonized and the colonizers, areas of study such as philology, anatomy, craniometry, physiology, that shaped the fields of biology and natural history, gave credence to ideas of racial differences as natural, provable facts.

That these understandings were by no means uncomplicated or uncontested is clear in the raging debates between those who took the position that human beings were a single species that originated in Adam and Eve and that racial differences between groups could be attributed to culture and climate (monogeneticists) and those who argued in favor of multiple species/races of humans with permanent, inherited physical differences (polygeneticists).[29] But the search for theories to support racial prejudice took an important turn with Darwin's social evolutionism; the debates between single or multiple races gave way to a hierarchical classification with civilization and white Anglo-Saxon Protestants at the top. These ideas were so thoroughly diffused into disciplines such as anthropology, archaeology, history, classics, geography, and in the general approach of Orientalism, that race became the single most powerful principle of academic knowledge. As summed up in 1850 by Robert Knox in *The Race of Men*, "Race is everything: literature, science, art – in a word, civilization – depends on it."[30]

From the 1840s, in Britain, racial groupings were allegedly based on nature and biology and increasingly organized into a cultural hierarchy of superiority and inferiority. Although race was a cultural invention, this attitude fused biology and culture in the interests of defending racial prejudice. Unequal treatment of groups in the colonies as well as within the metropole could be justified through a concept of race that came to be bound up with inequality and incompatible differences between the groups. Rather than degrees of social difference, notions of race were grounded on biological, sharply contrasting characteristics.

A dimension of difference that was equally important to colonial expansion was national identity. In his book with the sobering title, *Who Do We Think We Are?*, Philip Nicholson argues that race and national identity were the twin pillars of colonial domination.[31] While we will explore these interconnections in greater depth below, I want to note here that under colonial rule national cultural identities such as "Britain" and "India" were shorthand ways of representing positive qualities of the self and negative qualities of the other. Characteristics that have racial, gender, and sexual connotations lend fuller meaning to what these different national identities mean; if the British were seen as strong, disciplined, and cerebral, then Indians were deemed by colonizers as childlike, irresponsible, and sensual. In her book *Imperial Leather* Anne McClintock reasons that imperialism, the invention of race, and nationalism are the foundations of the modern, western world. She suggests that concepts such as race, gender, and nation are "articulated categories" in that they make sense only in relation to each other.[32]

To that extent, then, nation or race signal efforts to put fluid and confusing social and political relationships into pigeonholes that are sufficiently simple and static for the purpose of colonial rule. But a critical further look reveals that these concepts and our notions of gender or sexuality are deeply intertwined. Put in a different way, the concept of national identity – whether positive or negative – can only be thought of in words that are drawn from our languages of race and, as we will see in subsequent chapters, of gender and sexuality.

Nationalism, Colonialism, and the State: In the Metropoles

In this section, I start by exploring the links between nationalism, colonialism, and industrial capitalism from the perspective of the metropoles because, compared to the colonies, less attention is paid to these issues in the metropoles. Although some scholars have, since the early 1990s, focused on the links between empire and nationalism from the perspective of metropoles, their approaches are beset by interrelated problems, as Antoinette Burton points out with respect to scholars writing on Britain.[33] For one, the British nation and the British empire are seen as separate rather than interdependent realms. The counter-argument is not that nation and empire were the same, but that they were intricately interrelated. Furthermore, in the above problematic view, the British nation is seen as the source and origin of the British empire, so that Britain would have been a homogenous nation with an unequivocal national identity that led to the formation of its empire. On the contrary, British national identity was riven with differences of gender, class, and race, not to say anything about the presence of Welsh, Irish, and Scottish nationalisms. Therefore, the argument developed below is that nationhood shaped and justified colonial expansion, and colonial expansion gave form and meaning to nationalism. Furthermore, the empire helped secure the role and influence of the national state.

There is little question that in metropoles like Britain and France, nationalism played a crucial role in nineteenth-century colonial expansion. This insight is not limited to recent critical analyses of colonialism or nationalism. In a series of lectures published in 1883, J. R. Seeley, who is held to be the founder of British imperial history, demonstrated that nation, empire, and race were intricately connected.[34] However, as Catherine Hall suggests, Seeley was concerned that the links were not being adequately appreciated, for Britain was in danger of losing its empire. For Seeley, it was essential that the English realize that they were an imperial race and that empire and colonial expansion were necessary to the national life. Though Seeley's position was motivated by a questionable agenda, he captured well an important reason why nationalism was necessary to colonialism. Put bluntly, nationalism provided a purpose for colonialism and colonial expansions. Britishness, Englishness, or Frenchness were variously used to invoke the mission of colonial rule.

By the end of the nineteenth century, imperial expansion also became a status symbol for nations competing to assert their domination. Earlier, I mentioned that despite the seemingly economic rationale of colonial expansion, recent critical scholarship on colonialism suggests that cultural factors may have been just as important as economic concerns. Some territories, such as South Africa or India, doubtlessly held economic importance. However, Hobsbawm argues, regardless of the economic advantages of conquest, once colonialism became associated with hoisting one's national flag over a foreign territory, the acquisition of colonies was in and of itself important.[35] He shows that this national competition for foreign conquest motivated countries such as the United States to assert formal control over territories, and led Italy to fight hard to gain control over economically unimportant stretches of African desert. Although those groups in the metropoles associated with overseas trade and industries pressed for colonial expansion and, in some cases, did well economically, more typically the economic results from most colonies were disappointing.[36] Instead, the imperial pattern that came to dominate toward the end of the nineteenth century consisted of several "national economies" competing against each other and attempting to demonstrate their national superiority through occupation of foreign territories.

In so far as nationalism provided the purpose for colonial expansion, it also helped justify imperial expansions at home. The idiom of nation and nationalism may have helped mask the brutality of colonial control and domination, but colonial expansion needed to win the support of European citizens in the metropoles. Perhaps this is why there was little dissent against colonialism despite the hardships borne by ordinary people in the home countries. Hobsbawm suggests that there is little evidence that colonial conquest had bearing on the employment or incomes of most workers in the metropoles, and emigration to the colonies as a safety valve for local discontent was more an idea than a reality. Instead, in the metropoles, visions of glory based on the conquest of exotic territories and racialized images of dusky races were used to win support for imperial expansion. Provincial newspapers and periodicals were particularly instrumental in this. Kathleen Wilson notes that as early as the mid-eighteenth century provincial newspapers were preoccupied by colonial acquisition and possession, and included current news on "American Affairs" or "British Plantations."[37] Meanwhile, periodicals filled their pages with details about individual colonies and beautiful maps of colonized territories. More importantly, though, Wilson emphasizes that the press effaced the brutalities of empire, colonialism, and "trade" as well as the points of view of people living under British rule. In its place, it presented a "commercial, sanitized, and 'patriotic' vision of the British empire and its apparent destiny of spreading profits throughout the nation while disseminating British goods, rights, and liberties across the globe."[38]

Colonialism also shaped nationalism by providing a base on which to construct national identity. In the case of Britain, Linda Colley argues three points with respect to the formation of the British nation.[39] First, drawing from the work of Peter Sahlins, she suggests that national identity is based on a collective identity in reference to who and what we are not, the others. Second, British nationhood was set into motion by the Act of Union of 1707 that joined England, Wales, and Scotland, and Britishness was built up out of a series of wars from 1689 to 1815 that allowed Britain's citizens, who were separated by class, region, language, gender, and conflict, to focus on what they had in common, primarily in opposition to its greatest imperial rival, France. Third, the possession of a vast and seemingly alien empire over the nineteenth century encouraged Britons to see themselves as a distinct, special and often superior people.[40] After 1873, the heart of the British empire lay in the East and not the West. Therefore, Colley suggests,

> [The British] could contrast their law, their standard of living, their treatment of women, their political stability, and, above all, their collective power against societies that they only imperfectly understood but usually perceived as far less developed. Whatever their own individual ethnic backgrounds, Britons could join together *vis-à-vis* the empire and act out the flattering parts of heroic conqueror, humane judge, and civilizing agent. [41]

As such, the heightening of nationalism did more than justify the hardship and lack of necessary social reforms at home caused by colonial expansion: it provided a means for people, even the restive and discontent, to identity themselves with the imperial state and the nation.[42] As colonies spread, their increasing numbers of citizens could see themselves as "a people" across ethnic, linguistic, or class lines. As they did so the state gained legitimacy as an institution acting on behalf of "a nation" and "its people" – an attribute that was especially valuable when empire-building was not economically advantageous for most people in the metropoles. Patriotism became the expression of loyalty to state, and colonial expansion as a nationalist endeavor, was supported.

If nationalism supported colonial conquest and strengthened the legitimacy of the state, then colonialism, especially by the latter half of the 1800s, also provided for national expansion and a larger role of the state in the metropoles.[43] Craig Calhoun notes that increasing industrial capitalism at the time fueled both nationalism and an expanding state, in three ways.[44] First, the rise of a world economy necessitated larger, more complex social systems than local networks based on interpersonal relationships; national economies, larger corporations, issues of gross national product, the role of education at the national level assumed greater importance and local networks withered as a result. Second, as industrialization and capitalist networks undermined regional community life, the importance of kinship and interpersonal networks were gradually eroded in favor of impersonal and standardized forms of communication and organization. Instead, local activities such as village or town meetings, markets, or social events became mere building blocks for large-scale social organizations, such as the nation, and helped promote nationalism at the grassroots level. Third, capitalism encouraged people to see themselves as relatively autonomous individuals who make choices about where to work or what goods to consume. Nation as community and nationalism acted as the bridge between the apparently autonomous individual and the enormous world system.

To this outline, Charles Tilly adds the importance of the military and war in the nature and greater reach of states in Europe against the backdrop of colonialism. Just as the wars between European states were ending, colonial expansion was gathering momentum. These external empires gave European states some of the means and the impetus to create relatively powerful, centralized, and homogenized national states in Europe, Tilly says. Although he cautions that empire overseas did not have the same effect on building state structures as did war at home, Tilly finds a dual relationship between European states and colonial rule. The character of the European state and the struggles over territorial control in the colonies governed the form of colonial expansion elsewhere, even as the nature of the empire significantly affected the state's functioning at home. He suggests that some states relied mostly on the coercive techniques of enslavement and forcible extraction of resources, thereby

enlarging the central state bureaucracy. Others relied on trade monopolies, which tended to create powerful, essentially private commercial
groups, such as the Dutch East India Company, founded in the seventeenth century. By the nineteenth century, Britain and France effectively
used combinations of these techniques for colonial expansion.

Nationalism, the state, and citizenship: the case of France

That nationalism forged a new relationship between individuals and the
state through the concept of citizenship may seem a commonplace observation by now. However, examining how nationalism shaped what it
meant to be a Briton against the backdrop of empire and its "others"
provides a different perspective. A central function of modern states is to
identify the boundaries between citizens and aliens, thereby defining the
rights and privileges of citizens while excluding others. But, what's different about this form of nationalism is that citizenship so defined asks
diverse inhabitants within the territorial boundaries to see their loyalty
to their nation or country above all other parochial ties.

Undoubtedly, the French Revolution gave shape to nation as a political
and cultural principle based on citizenship, leading Rogers Brubaker to
argue that French nationalism has been state-centered and assimilationist. He suggests that instead of the question "Who is French?", the
question, "Who shall enjoy political rights?" is what determined French
nationalism and citizenship.[45] Underlying this approach was a Franco-
centric bias that, as well as those born in France of French parents, all
those born in France of resident foreigners should be French in all ways
that matter and have a strong attachment to France. Although this
attachment could be expected in those with French parents, children of
foreign parents, and first-generation immigrants in particular, posed a
problem: they might be assumed to have some attachment to French
soil, but there would have to be evidence of this before citizenship was
awarded. This principle of *jus soli* (place of birth) was in contrast to the
affirmation of *jus sanguinis* (blood descent) in other European territories,
such as Germany, and despite repeated challenges, the principle of *jus
soli* was extended in 1889. Frenchness was seen to be acquired, not
inherited.[46]

The principle of *jus soli* was driven by political considerations and relied
heavily on the state to create French citizens. Despite considerable debates
on its advisability from opponents who did not favor the expansion of
citizenship to "foreign" groups, it was extended in the 1880s out of two

considerations. It was a way to eliminate the privilege of being exempt from military service, which foreigners, whatever the length of their residency, had so far enjoyed. It was also a means to cultivate a French national spirit despite the presence of numerous resident foreign groups, such as the Belgians and Italians. State-run institutions, such as schools and the army, were charged with the task of nationalizing French citizens. Schooling was standardized throughout French territory, which meant that all children were reading and learning the same curriculum; and nation was at the heart of the academic and moral curriculum of the schools. As Brubaker puts it succinctly, patriotism was deliberately and strenuously cultivated. The school curriculum was further reinforced by the army, which taught language, literacy, and citizenship. Nationalized schooling and compulsory military service for all residents, French and foreigners alike, were ways to assimilate diverse groups in order to create French citizens.

But if the example of French citizenship reforms in the latter part of the nineteenth century shows how citizenship was actively created in the metropoles, then it also illustrates how it relied on the projections of "others." Brubaker notes that until about 1870, notions of race were linked to class, not to nation, in France.[47] Race was used to explain divisions and weaknesses within the French nation and not to distinguish France from other nations. After 1870, however, race was increasingly associated with nation, and racial categories were based on comparisons with other nations, such as Germany, England, and the United States, rather than on internal divisions. The flip side of the nationalization of race was xenophobia within France. Brubaker persuasively argues that the heightened French nationalism of the 1880s and expansive citizenship policy that assimilated foreigners were, ironically, also expressions of xenophobia. Nationalism and inclusionary citizenship were means to do away with "foreignness" by getting groups to take on the "French", or what was really a Gallic, way of life. It is perhaps because of this that Philip Yale Nicholson notes that nationalism and race arise together and are influential in creating both social cohesion and disunity.[48]

Citizenship, race, gender, class, and sexuality in Britain

The active creation of nationalized citizenship is not limited to the influence of racism. It is also inflected by the interconnected impacts of class, gender, and sexuality. But how were persistent social differences and inequalities such as class diminished in favor of nationalism and patriotism? To return to Kathleen Wilson's discussion of empire and citizenship in Britain: she suggests that the print media produced images of citizenship that worked in tandem with other local, regional, and social identities.[49] More importantly, though, images of patriotic citizenship were based on generalized ideals calling for an overarching allegiance to the nation. But the generalized ideal of citizenship was not so general after all. According to Wilson, despite the participation of women, slaves and free Africans, Catholics and Jews, in the life of nation and empire, national identity promoted by newspapers was focused on urban, middle- and upper-class, white males. Literacy, typically limited to middle- and upper-class men, was a particularly important aspect of how citizenship was implicitly a factor of social privilege. The intrinsic paradox of citizenship was that though it seemed to be general and inclusive of social differences between its citizens, social privileges of class, region, ethnic origin, and race gave citizenship its particular contours. But the empire and the consequent emphasis on national identity encouraged commonality rather than social differences.

Gender and gender differences were no less implicated in the attempts to produce ideal patriotic citizens against the backdrop of empire. In her exemplary article, "Imperialism and motherhood," Anna Davin argues that by the late nineteenth century motherhood became a matter of imperial and national importance.[50] Proponents of British imperialism and national superiority were concerned about the falling birth rates and infant mortality rates, fearing that they would be outstripped by other imperial races. To protect their national interests, state laws attempted to regulate childbirth, provide meals to needy children, and organize the medical inspection of children in school. Women as mothers were key to this eugenicist project of fortifying the so-called British race with more, and healthier, children. The education of mothers, making childrearing a matter of national duty for women, and improving the health of mothers in order to improve the "racial stock" were all matters of primary state and national concern in the late nineteenth century, Davin shows. Moreover, the focus on motherhood as the key to improving the national population in order to fare successfully in the imperial competition was a means to avoid undertaking much needed social reforms – reforms that would increase social and medical services, reduce poverty, and significantly improve the dismal conditions of working-class life.

If the role of women as mothers was heightened amid Britain's imperial projects, then the difference between British women at home and women in the colonies was equally significant in reshaping notions of British womanhood. Inderpal Grewal points out that some English feminists used images of what they saw as their victimized "sisters" in order to demand equal rights as citizens, as British women.[51] In their efforts to secure the right to vote and to representation, many suffragists argued for equality with Englishmen, but saw themselves as superior to "native" women and men in the colonies. Pro- and anti-suffragists both supported imperialism as an admirable and necessary venture. Even among Englishwomen who were against the subordination of women in England and "native" women in the colonies there was support for the empire. Indeed, Englishwomen's rights were seen as conferred by their nationality, the empire, and their race; in contrast, the inferiority and subordination of women in the colonies was taken for granted. In sum, despite the seemingly neutral and nonfigurative nature of citizenship in this case, gender and racial differences are crucial to specifying nationhood.

But as historians such as Ronald Hyam remind us, sexuality is no less connected to matters of citizenship, nationalism, and empire in the metropoles than race, gender, or class.[52] As a result of the wide prevalence of prostitution in early Victorian England despite attempts to curb it, a Purity Campaign was waged toward the latter half of the nineteenth century. Imperial historians agree that this campaign was a war on prostitution and middle-class male sexuality, the easy-going sexual attitudes of the working classes, and was an effort to suppress adolescent sexuality. The endorsing of "sexual respectability" was in part a means to allay fears of imperial decline and the degeneration of the imperial race. State laws raised the minimum age of sexual consent for girls to 13 and a legal amendment made illegal all sorts of sexual activity between men in order to ensure sexual respectability and sexual purity. Hyam maintains that the Boy Scout movement inaugurated in 1908 was preoccupied not only with fashioning masculinity, but also with purity and empire. Its founder, Sir Robert Baden-Powell, aimed to make generations of boys "into good citizens and useful colonists."[53] And the repudiation of sexuality outside marriage was seen as essential to raising upright men and women in the interests of the nation and the empire.

Earlier, I made the point that it is useful to consider how metropoles and colonies were forged in relation to each other and to question the idea that they were internally homogenous. Metropoles such as Britain included a broad array of people who were considered part of the British empire and Britain, but were not accorded the same rights and privileges as middle- and upper-class Englishmen. As noted in the earlier sections of this chapter, British nationalism was built on attempts to maintain clear differences between Britons and the "native" peoples in its colonies. At the same time, as Colley's work shows, nationalism could not ensure equal rights for Britons since they were not all seen as equal. This was also true within England. Whether white English women of various social classes, who were socially restricted and marginalized, can be thought of as colonizers in the same way as their male counterparts is an important question. Neither the label of colonizer nor that of the colonized easily captures the fact that middle-class English women were both emblems of the nation and, as mothers in the imperial race, its foot soldiers; they also were denied equal social and political status. To the extent groups of English women challenged their marginalization through the suffragist and other movements, they posed a problem for nationalism, for despite nationalism's claims, the English were not homogenous.

England was also a destination for immigrant groups, including the Irish, Scots, West Indians, Chinese, Africans, and East Indians.[54] Wilson argues that the presence of immigrant communities who were frequently part of the poor and the disadvantaged confounded efforts at creating and maintaining a unifying national identity. Their presence and periodic racial discrimination in the form of harassment and forced exile made a myth of the idea that England or Britain was a cohesive nation. In this context, blacks (Africans, Asians, and others) and "people of color" were seen as irredeemably different from the ideal citizen as personified by the middle- or upper-class Englishman. But these black, Irish, Jewish, and other poor immigrants, being to some extent acculturated in the "mother country," even while debarred from certain of its rights and privileges, challenged their exclusion from British nationalism. So as Wilson argues, the idiom of nationalism paradoxically revealed the gaps between privileged citizens and those excluded on the basis of their race, gender, religion, and class. At the same time, the idiom of nationalism was the basis upon which these groups could challenge their social and legal exclusions. The language of nationalism, of who counts as citizen and who is an outsider, was the paramount way to exclude some groups; but, marginalized groups sought the expansion of the scope of British nationalism to demand full social and legal inclusion as British citizens.

In the metropole, the framework of nationalism continued to have its limitations and its possibilities. Although the French Revolution may have triggered the revolutionary force of nationalism against the state in the metropole, by the latter half of the nineteenth century there is little doubt that this force was blunted. As was later evident in France, nationalisms do not simply take root, they have to be actively and creatively implanted through state intervention. Benedict Anderson notes the rise of official nationalisms at the time, in which elite groups attempted to make their own entrenched power part of the nation's power.[55] These official nationalisms, he says, were the reactionary responses of elite groups threatened by the democratic potential of popular nationalism. Nationalisms in Britain and France were also blunted through institutional attempts to justify and facilitate colonial expansion. Moreover, identifying the inequalities of citizenship and belonging reveals nationalism's inconsistencies and exclusionary nature. There is perhaps no greater indication of its contrariness than the fact that it can also be used to challenge the inequalities of citizenship and re-draw the lines of inclusion and exclusion.

Nationalism and the Colonial State: In the Colonies

What about the colonies? By now, the assertion that the links between nationalism and colonialism were significant in the colonies will not come as a revelation. But what additional insights would be revealed if we examine these links from the vantage point of the colonies? In other words, how were these links between nationalism and colonialism different in the colonies from the metropoles? From the perspective of the colonies, there are four discernible themes that I would like to consider below. The first is the way colonialism heightened national cultural differences for colonizers and the colonized. The second is related to the role and contradictions of the colonial state. The third has to do with the extent to which anti-colonial nationalism was both revolutionary and limiting. The last is about how the "rule of unequal difference" laid the groundwork for a fundamentally different sort of nationalism in the colonies.

Illustrating the first theme, about heightened national and racial differences between colonizers and colonized, is Chatterjee's discussion of the Ilbert Bill (1883), introduced in colonial India.[56] The Ilbert Bill proposed to allow Indian judges to adjudicate Europeans. By then, Indians were trained in British law, to help shore up the number of European judges who served in colonial India. But the exceptionalism of colonial rule became crystal clear as many Europeans civilians angrily contended that Indian judges were neither capable of reason nor possibly objective enough to arbitrate in the case of European defendants. European judges were capable of judging all defendants but Indian judges were capable only of judging other Indians, according to this logic. The language of nationalism was used to argue that Indians were incapable of judging Europeans and to consider otherwise was to bring the downfall of the British empire. And any doubts that national and racial differences were not essential to colonial domination are dispelled by George Couper, then lieutenant governor of the Northwest Provinces. He stated, "That there should be one law alike for the European and the Native is an excellent thing in theory, but if it were really introduced in practice we should have no business in the country."[57]

Despite the normative importance of national and racial differences between the colonizers and the colonized, the distinctions were confusing and frequently had to be invented and clarified. Mixed-race children often posed particular challenges to the national or racial boundaries between colonizers and the colonized. In her article, Ann Stoler addresses the raging discussions on whether to classify children of indigenous and European parents in French Indochina and the Dutch East Indies as Europeans or as a distinct category.[58] Underlying these debates, Stoler compellingly argues, were fears that European men living with native women would become morally and physically contaminated, lose their Dutch or French national identities, and waver in their allegiances to Europe's rule as they compromised the distinctions between the colonizers and the colonized. European women who chose to marry native men, and native women who preferred concubinage to marriage to European men, were an affront to middle-class European sexual respectability and racial boundaries. Their children complicated the question of respectable upbringing and acculturation to Europeanness, and made it difficult to distinguish between true nationals and pseudo-compatriots. She points out that this problem of determining true European nationals amidst colonized people resonated in the colonies but also informed and shaped the discussions about what it meant to be French or Dutch that took place in the metropoles.

The colonial state

The second theme, related to the fundamental differences between colonial and metropolitan states, is well developed by Crawford Young in his discussion of colonial states, especially in Africa. Young identifies three significant aspects: the denial of sovereignty; nationhood; and the lack of autonomy in the international arena.[59] Denied sovereignty, colonial states were adjuncts of European administrative, military, and economic interests and the battlegrounds of European nationalisms, especially in the second half of the nineteenth century. Disassembling the monolithic notion of the colonial state, Young identifies four types: the Portuguese maritime empire bent on increasing revenues; the Spanish conquest state aimed at bringing new territories under the jurisdiction of the Spanish state and the Church; the Anglo-Dutch quasi-private mercantile corporation with its underlying logic of expansion and territorial control; and chartered colonial plantations with their relative autonomy from the colonizing state. Young notes that the Dutch, for example, established a fiscal system in Indonesia that designated 40 percent of the rice lands for tax payments to the rulers. Between 1830 and 1870, villages were required to allocate 20 percent of the land to commercial crops, and each male subject had to labor for sixty-six days on state plantations. It is estimated that during these years 189 million guilders accrued to Dutch revenues even as the Indies remained self-supporting.

By the time European powers exploded in Africa toward the latter part of the nineteenth century, colonial rule was rationalized and far-reaching. A systematic but contested partitioning of land and communities into separate territories, ruthless extraction, forced labor of natives, paternalistic treatment of them, and (by the twentieth century) the use of more advanced technologies – motor vehicles, radio, weapons – were all part of the effort to institutionalize and rationalize colonial rule. The colonial state in Africa was further marked by the rise of virulent racism, in which the attempt was made to reconstruct local cultures purportedly to "civilize" colonized peoples. This meant an expanded reach and increased autonomy of the colonial state, in order for it to monitor and manage its subjects, to do away with indigenous structures of rule and political culture, to ensure internal and external security, to regulate revenue, and to accumulate capital by investing in infrastructure, such as railroads. Unlike the metropole, the colonies used two legal systems. Criminal and civil codes drawn from the metropole governed relationships between Europeans and between Europeans and Africans, thereby ensuring protection for the Europeans. In disputes or relations between Africans, the colonial state tolerated "customary law," as long as it did not subvert European law or its moral authority.[60]

In contrast to Mitchell's argument about the inextricability of the state and civil society (see Chapter One), Young notes that a defining characteristic of the colonial state is the wedge between state and society. Yet this is not to say that civil society was not immune from the jurisdiction of the colonial state. Undoubtedly, modern states aim to produce moralized, civilized, rational, sensible, patriotic, productive, responsible, obedient, and law-abiding citizens.[61] No less was true of the colonial state. Central to the reaches of the state in the lives of the polity and the lives of individual citizens are the extensive documentation projects in the form of statistics on finance, trade, health, demography, crime, education, transportation, agriculture, and industry that was carried out in the nineteenth and twentieth centuries, both in the metropoles and in the colonies. Indeed, Bernard Cohn and others have noted how some of these state technologies, which are widely considered the preserve of the modern West, were first invented in the colonies. For example, finger-printing, a basic technique used by the police, was first developed by the colonial state in Bengal, India.[62]

Education and social reforms were especially important in harnessing civil society and natives to colonial projects; in this, the colonial state was instrumental. Analyzing the spread of French colonial education in Algeria toward the last part of the nineteenth century, Fanny Colonna argues that it was motivated by the need to replace the shattered traditional systems of education and promote middle-class values.[63] Skeptical of any neutrality in the French colonial system of education in Algeria, Colonna suggests that it was instrumental in providing knowledge, changing attitudes, introducing Christian ways of life, and preventing violent opposition to the dominant colonial culture and rule.

Equally relevant were the ways in which the colonial state created new lines of social division, namely of class and ethnicity. Western-educated middle classes who manned the colonial bureaucracy, pre-colonial ruling classes who allied with the colonial state, urban, often-migrant workers, and peasants were among the new social classes created through the colonial state. Colonial states could extract revenue and aid in capital accumulation only by creating a peasantry, and a migrant workforce for the mines and plantations, as Young shows.[64] The perceived gulfs between ethnic groups were equally important. Ethnicity is surely socially constructed and therefore subject to change. But the influence of the colonial state on ethnic classifications both heightened and politicized them. Young notes that the British and the Belgians in particular compulsively categorized groups in Africa and, in so doing, imposed ethnic classifications.[65] For example, as we shall see in Chapter Five, the distinctions between Hutus and the Tutsis were historically fluid, and only assumed importance *vis-à-vis* the state. Under the aegis of the Belgians, overlapping class and racial characteristics of the two groups hardened into divisions with enduring political consequences.

In these ways, then, the colonial state was neither simply an effect of the ruling classes in the metropoles nor a relatively autonomous body independent of the forces of civil society in the colonies. In the words of sociologist Jack Wayne, "It was, rather, a political bureaucracy, a form of rule in which bureaucrats are politicians and in which political actors outside the bureaucracy are suppressed or given a minimal role."[66]

The presence of the colonial state fueled the emergence of anti-colonial nationalism in the colonies. It was no spontaneous eruption, but to some extent a consequence of being colonized. For when a people had become unified and somewhat homogenous it was easier for the indigenous elite to claim statehood and independence on its behalf, as a nation. And it was clearer what made this nation different from a European state. As nationalisms burgeoned, states and and the people that they governed began to be at odds. Calhoun suggests that, rather than attempting to merge nation and state, imperial rule aimed to prevent unity.[67] Seen against the background of the colonial state, the spirit of nationalism points to how colonized peoples are denied their own sovereign administrative territory. The point here is not that nationalisms in the colonies preceded colonial rule in most places; rather it is that the disjuncture between an emerging sense of nation and the colonial state became the rallying point for anti-colonial nationalisms.

The role of native elites

The third theme that I introduced at the beginning of this section on nationalism and the colonial state has to do with the contradictory force of nationalism in the colonies: it was simultaneously revolutionary and elitist. Frequently, the language of nationalism and national identity was used by urban and rural middle classes to argue against foreign colonial domination. The native middle classes were themselves the creation of the colonial state, which needed native people to fill the vast number of lower-to middle-level bureaucratic positions and meet the needs of an expanding sector of doctors, lawyers, and teachers, among others. In colonial India, for example, the educational system aimed at creating a literate class that was educated not only in the English language but in an English system of education and thought. Betwixt and between the British administrators and indigenous groups, these bureaucrats and professionals were frustrated by two contradictions of colonial rule: that the British did not fully extend European principles of modernity, liberty, or equality to the colonies and that despite equal education Indian middle classes were denied the same opportunities and privileges as their European counterparts. The idea of nationalism, as "a people" unified by history and territory, provided political legitimacy to these disgruntled middle classes. It allowed them to speak politically on behalf of a wide range of groups and argue that they were all Indians despite differences of region, language, religion, class, customs, and caste, among others. Protest movements of the working poor in various parts of the country, of peasant women, of non-Hindus, which called into question colonial domination as well as domination by the indigenous landed and urban elite, were sidelined at first and then gradually co-opted by this official nationalism. In the process, these middle classes helped create "India" as a nation, with a distinct national identity and history, and a diverse but united people; nationalism was an effective strategy in showing that the colonial state did not represent the people of India, and to call for "Indians" to mobilize against the colonial oppressors.

Anti-colonial nationalisms: of a different ilk

Turning to the fourth theme, about the fundamental differences between anti-colonial and colonial nationalisms, the overarching issue is that nationalism could not simply be imported from Europe by the indigenous middle classes in their struggle against colonial rule. Postcolonial scholars point out that the civil and professional classes in the colonies were faced with another paradox in their turn to nationalism: how to present their similarity and equality to the colonizers while also highlighting their differences. These middle classes could not have blindly imitated the Europeans in their search for national identity for this would eliminate differences between themselves and the colonizers and, therefore, would remove a valid platform for independence. Anti-colonial nationalist middle classes had to prove their orientations toward modernity, progress, and scientific rationalism, all of the criteria by which colonial rule was justified. Yet, they had to also define what was essentially Indian and different about Indians from the British in order to show why colonial rule was unacceptable. Scholars such as Chatterjee are thus convincing in saying that the rise of nationalism in the colonies was no mere European importation. Instead, the dual task of mobilizing diverse groups as "a people" and specifying how this "people" was different from the ruling colonizers, made nationalism in the colonies something of a fundamentally different ilk.

Basing his analysis on colonial India, Chatterjee argues that the elite nationalists invoked divisions of public/private or material/spiritual in their search for a national identity that would straddle the need to modernize while retaining a distinct cultural identity.[68] Through this distinction, nationalist elites were able to imitate and endorse modernization, scientific rationalism, and technological progress in the public sphere; in fact, middle- and upper-class political leaders criticized the British for their failure sufficiently to modernize India. The private sphere, on the other hand, was the space where nationalist elites attempted to specify what was essentially Indian; this included the family, indigenous schools, literature, and religion. These nationalists forged a distinct national identity out of this cultural domain so that India itself was seen as spiritual, with time-honored traditions, and family-oriented in contrast to the material, changing, technologically driven character of Britain. In this way, they used the private, "inner" cultural domain to reverse the hierarchy of the colonial "rule of difference." By selectively embracing and altering pejorative colonial stereotypes of India as traditional or spiritual rather than rational, nationalists reversed the colonial differences of "us" and "them." But their ideas about what defined India or the "us" were specified at the cost of the needs and experiences of marginal groups. In that sense, nationalisms in the colonies and the metropoles were no different. In either case, nationalism centered on some groups while it marginalized others; it could be simultaneously revolutionary and repressive.

The Role of History

I would like to end this chapter by exploring a crucial aspect of nationalism that was hinted at in the Introduction and Chapter One, namely the role of history in expressions of nationalism. Of all of the paradoxes that make up the beliefs and practices of nationalism, its relation to history is perhaps most striking. Depictions of history continue to shape contemporary and past expressions of nationalisms. Despite the fact that nationalisms and nation states are at least in some sense modern, nationalisms claim to be essentially unchanging and, in some cases, to have thousands of years of history. Although the nation of India came into existence only in the nineteenth century out of its contact with British colonialism, "Indian" history is traced as far back as 6,000 BCE and it is taken for granted that there is something essentially "Indian" about it (any attempt to specify what that is quickly runs into trouble).

What is it about the modern nature of nationalisms that they must hearken to antiquity and a lasting national essence? National states such as Canada, Australia, and the United States are exceptions because their national history is based on relatively recent conquest and occupation. If anything, their search for a deeper history is confounded because tracing the history of the nation prior to conquest would only highlight the discontinuities between the past and the present and would put under the spotlight the ongoing impact of colonialism. Given the differences in colonial rule, it has been far easier for Indian nationalists to invent a national history and argue that it was interrupted by colonialism than it has been for the United States to link its national past with Native American histories. This perhaps also explains a widespread nostalgia in the United States about the colonial past and the turn to Europe to trace its history (example, western civilization courses are a foundational requirement of most of its universities).

While the role of history in creating a sense of nation was as important to nationalisms in the metropoles as it was in the colonies, I chose to explore an example of anti-colonial nationalism because it effectively illustrates the inventiveness of history, the imagined nature of nationalisms, and the enduring legacy of colonial rule. In India, as in other similar cases, the nation was imagined and invented under colonial rule in the nineteenth century. But the claim that India had long existed as a nation was paradoxically crucial to this imagination. This paradox was the result of an inadvertent collusion between colonial writers and historians and nationalist groups.[69] European historians and writers in the latter half of the nineteenth century turned their attention to "ancient India." "Ancient India" was of tremendous interest to these Europeans because it allowed them to indulge their fascination with India without disrupting the reality of nineteenth-century colonialism. They focused on the social and religious texts of upper-caste Hindu groups (to the exclusion of other groups) and described "ancient India" as a golden age of great prosperity, cultural vitality, civilization, spirituality, in which women had high status. These projections allowed them to create a romanticized alternative to what they perceived as the social chaos of industrializing Europe and its overemphasis on materiality and technology. But how to explain the fact that India was being colonized? To do this, they suggested that the ancient, glorious civilization had gradually degenerated; it had become mired in retrograde traditions and subjugated its women.

Faced with the dual challenge of creating positive depictions of themselves under the onslaught of colonialism while having to explain their colonization, nationalist elites also contributed to notions of India as a once-superior civilization that had gradually degenerated. Out of these images nationalists constructed a cultural nationalism that harkened back to the glorious, civilized, spiritual, nonmaterial nation that India once was and combined it with the demands of modernization and progress. In sum, European writers and Indian nationalists colluded in their invention of India as a nation and in producing the differences between Europe and India. But in the hands of nationalists, this cultural nationalism provided a platform to challenge colonialism, and to demand political rights and a sovereign nation state.

Conclusion

Nationalism flourished alongside imperial expansion, both in the heart of the empire and in the colonies. In that, Hall reminds us that the mutuality between nation and empire was well recognized by proponents of colonial rule in the last quarter of the nineteenth century – that, for example, there were deep bonds between England and her global territories, nation and empire were one and the same, and expansion was necessary to the national well-being.[70] In the 1880s the leaders of the Third Republic in France simultaneously pursued policies of nationalism and imperialism. In the metropole, they tried to drum up nationalism and produce "French citizens" out of culturally different groups through the school system and other public institutions. At the same time, their imperial pursuits in parts of Africa, in Vietnam and Cambodia helped shape what it meant to be French and why it was necessary to colonize some of these countries. In Britain and Holland, argue Stoler and Cooper, "empire building" and "nation building" were also mutually related projects.[71]

Surely, thinking about the history of imperialism means connecting issues of race, nation, and empire. Fundamental to imperial rule were racialized and nationalized differences between "us" and "them." As Edward Said has argued, stereotypical and pejorative portrayals of "African," "Irish," or "Jamaican" people as inferior and barbaric recurred to enable and justify imperialism as the obligation of the "British" or the "French" to civilize "these peoples": "we" should rule "them" because "they" are different and inferior to "us."[72] The reiteration of the national cultural differences between self and other in the metropole led to a widely shared commitment that distant peoples and their territories should be subjugated and that empires had an obligation to do this.[73]

In the colonies, if national cultural differences were important to justifying imperial domination, then they were also a platform to mount anti-colonial programs, including the dismantling of the colonial state in favor of self-rule. Where the colonizers used the rhetoric of difference between "us" and "them" to justify unequal treatment, anti-colonial nationalists used the differences between "self" and the dominating "other" to justify independence and self-rule. While nationalism was not the only form of anti-colonial movement and not all nationalisms in the colonies were anti-imperialist, nationalism was the key to calls to end imperial rule and to form a sovereign nation state.

Seen through the lens of colonialism, the origins and trajectories of nationalisms in the metropoles and the colonies are different though interrelated. Clearly, there can be no single account of the origins and ascendancy of nationalisms when considered in relation to capitalism, industrialization, and colonialism. Looking at the various courses of nationalism, therefore, helps move us away from Eurocentric conceptualizations. What is also more visible through this approach is how nationalisms have to be actively constructed and reiterated in order to have relevance. Writing national histories, not only in the colonies but also in the metropoles, is an important instrument of nationalisms and national identities. What is further striking is how quickly the traces of the production of these histories are obscured, and how they become incorporated in official national memory and psyche.

Looking at the encounters between disparate nationalisms against the backdrop of colonialism is more fruitful than treating metropoles and colonies as separate and irreconcilably different. Even though this chapter is organized around the two categories of nationalisms and the state in the metropole and the colonies, I hope this strategy effectively points to the looseness of these categories: their links as well as their differences.

The two quotations used at the beginning of this chapter speak of the connections between empires, colonies, and nations; Fanon and Said separately address how Europe and its colonies in Asia and Africa mutually fashioned imperial, national, and racial identities. This is not to suggest that nationalisms in the metropole and the colonies were solely expressed in terms of each other; on the contrary, there is evidence that British and French nationalisms were sometimes mutually constitutive. However, the focus on metropoles and colonies tells us much about the impact of colonial expansion on nationalisms in both western and non-western contexts in ways that show how their meanings are created out of their unequal encounter with each other; their seeming differences are mutually constitutive.

These encounters between nations and races occurred both in the colonies and in the metropole. The mission and motivations of colonial rule, the differences between colonial and metropolitan law, the interaction between colonial agents and native elites, the differences in citizenship, among others, collectively spurred notions of what it meant to be British, Nigerian, or Jamaican in the colonies as well as in the metropole.

Looking at nationalism across the divisions of empires also lays bare the myth of nations as homogenous. In metropoles such as England, the presence of immigrants from the colonies point out the hierarchies within citizenship of race, gender, and sexuality. In the colonies, diverse and unequal ethnic and class groups united under the umbrella of anti-colonial nationalism, motivated by the need to oust an alien ruler more than by a shared sense of a common past and a common destiny. The position taken here is that the inequalities and differences that liberal notions of national citizenship seek to overcome are not merely obstacles but inherent to the discourse of nationalism and citizenship. These fissures of nationalism are clearly evident in the trajectories of empires and colonies in the nineteenth century.

On a final note, I would like to call attention to the enduring influence of colonialism and nationalism in shaping our modern world. Indeed, what more profound evidence of the cultural power of colonialism could there be than its effect on how we know and pigeonhole the world under labels of "Europe," "the East," "the West," and "the Third World." These labels seem to give meaning to our world to the point that it is almost impossible to imagine and think about the world without notions such as "Europe" or "the East." That "Europe" widely connotes industrialization, development, higher levels of education, higher status for women, and democracy, and the East generally connotes relative lack of industrialization, underdeveopment, lower levels of education, lower status of women, and relative absence of democracy, illustrates four points. First, constructs such as the East or the West are shorthand representations of cultural, economic, and political understandings of the world. Second, these constructs are interlinked and oppositional in that the so-called West can have no meaning outside of the so-called East or what the West is not. Third, given the inequality between concepts of East and West, the East is typically talked about as a lack: of industrialization or development or education, or as an absence of positively regarded attributes. Lastly, to the extent that the West seems to be a representation of what the East is not, at heart these representations are of the West and not the East. Notions of Europe and the East were produced from the perspectives of Europeans and out of the inequalities of colonial rule.

NOTES

1   Frantz Fanon, *The Wretched of the Earth*, tr. Constance Farrington (New York: Grove Press, 1963), p. 102.
2   Edward W. Said, *Orientalism* (New York: Vintage Books, 1978), pp. 1–2.

3   Harry Magdoff, *Imperialism: From the Colonial Age to the Present* (New York: Monthly Review Press, 1978).

4   E. J. Hobsbawm, *The Age of Empire: 1875–1914* (New York: Pantheon Books, 1987).

5   Magdoff, *Imperialism*, p. 139.

6   Benedict Anderson, *Imagined Communities: Reflections on the Origin and Spread of Nationalism*, revised edition (London and New York: Verso, 1991), p. 47.

7   Peter Worseley, *The Three Worlds: Culture and World Development* (Chicago: University of Chicago Press, 1984), p. 5.

8   Magdoff, *Imperialism*, esp. ch. 1.

9   Nupur Chaudhuri and Margaret Strobel, "Introduction," in Nupur Chaudhuri and Margaret Strobel (eds.) *Western Women and Imperialism: Complicity and Resistance* (Bloomington and Indianapolis: University of Indiana Press, 1992), pp. 1–15, esp. p. 2.

10 See V. I. Lenin, *Imperialism: The Highest Stage of Capitalism* (New York: International Publishers, 1939, 2000).

11 Catherine Hall, "Introduction: thinking the postcolonial, thinking the empire," in Catherine Hall (ed.) *Cultures of Empire: Colonizers in Britain and the Empire in the Nineteenth and Twentieth Centuries* (New York: Routledge, 2000), pp. 1–33.

12 Worseley, *The Three Worlds*, p. 4.

13 Anderson, *Imagined Communities*, p. 47.

14 E. J. Hobsbawm, *The Age of Revolution: 1789–1848* (Cleveland and New York: World Publishing Company, 1962), esp. ch. 2.

15 Amina Mama, "Sheroes and villains: conceptualizing colonial and contemporary violence against women in Africa," in M. Jacqui Alexander and Chandra Talpade Mohanty (eds.) *Feminist Genealogies, Colonial Legacies, and Democratic Futures* (New York and London: Routledge, 1997), pp. 46–62.

16 Nicholas B. Dirks, "Introduction: colonialism and culture," in Nicholas B. Dirks (ed.) *Colonialism and Culture* (Ann Arbor: University of Michigan Press, 1992), pp. 1–25.

17 Ann Laura Stoler and Frederick Cooper, "Between metropole and colony: rethinking a research agenda," in Frederick Cooper and Ann Laura Stoler (eds.) *Tensions of Empire: Colonial Cultures in a Bourgeois World* (Berkeley, Los Angeles, and London: University of California Press, 1997), pp. 1–56.

18 Albert Memmi, *The Colonizer and the Colonized* (Boston: Beacon Press, 1967).

19 Edward W. Said, *Culture and Imperialism* (New York: Vintage Books, 1994).

20 Stoler and Cooper, "Preface," in Cooper and Stoler, *Tensions of Empire*, pp. vii–x, esp. p. ix.

21 Dirks, "Introduction," p. 6.

22 Mary Louise Pratt, *Imperial Eyes: Travel Writing and Transculturation* (New York: Routledge, 1992), p. 6.

23 Inderpal Grewal, *Home and Harem: Nation, Gender, Empire, and the Cultures of Travel* (Durham, NC and London: Duke University Press, 1996), p. 3.

24 Stoler and Cooper, "Between metropole and colony," p. 31.

25 Partha Chatterjee, *The Nation and its Fragments: Colonial and Postcolonial Histories* (Princeton, NJ: Princeton University Press, 1993), p. 10.

26 Robert C. Young, *Colonial Desire: Hybridity in Theory, Culture and Race* (London and New York: Routledge, 1995).

27 Ibid., p. 92.

28 Ibid., pp. 118–19.

29 Ibid., pp. 101–3.

30 Ibid., p. 93.

31 Philip Yale Nicholson, *Who Do We Think We Are? Race and Nation in the Modern World* (Armonk, NY and London: M. E. Sharpe, 2001).

32 Anne McClintock, *Imperial Leather: Race, Gender, Sexuality in the Colonial Contest* (New York: Routledge, 1995), p. 5.

33 Antoinette Burton, "Who needs the nation? Interrogating 'British' history," in Hall, *Cultures of Empire*, pp. 137–53.

34 Quoted in Hall, "Introduction," p. 2.

35 Hobsbawm, *Age of Empire*, p. 67

36 Ibid., p. 76.

37 Kathleen Wilson, "Citizenship, empire, and modernity in the English provinces, c.1720–90," in Hall, *Cultures of Empire*, pp. 157–86, esp. pp. 160–1.

38 Ibid., p. 161.

39 Linda Colley, "Britishness and otherness: an argument," *Journal of British Studies* 31 (October 1992), esp. pp. 311–16.

40 Ibid., p. 324.

41 Ibid., pp. 324–5.

42 Hobsbawm, *Age of Empire*, p. 70.

43 Ibid., p. 59.

44 Craig J. Calhoun, *Nationalism* (Minneapolis: University of Minnesota Press, 1997), p. 116.

45 Rogers Brubaker, *Citizenship and Nationhood in France and Germany* (London and Cambridge, Mass.: Harvard University Press, 1992), p. 87.

46 Ibid., p. 109.

47 Ibid., pp. 101–2.

48 Nicholson, *Who Do We Think We Are?*, p. 93.

49 Wilson, "Citizenship, empire, and modernity," pp. 161–2.

50 Anna Davin, "Imperialism and motherhood," in Cooper and Stoler, *Tensions of Empire*, pp. 87–151.

51 Grewal, *Home and Harem*, p. 11.

52 Ronald Hyam, *Empire and Sexuality: The British Experience* (Manchester and New York: Manchester University Press, 1990).

53 Ibid., p. 73.

54 Wilson, "Citizenship, empire, and modernity," p. 169.

55 Anderson, *Imagined Communities*, pp. 109–10.

56 Chatterjee, *The Nation and its Fragments*, pp. 20–2.

57 Quoted in Chatterjee, *The Nation and its Fragments*, p. 21.

58   Ann Laura Stoler, "Sexual affronts and racial frontiers: European identities
     and the cultural politics of exclusion in colonial Southeast Asia," in Cooper
     and Stoler, *Tensions of Empire*, pp. 198–237.
59   Crawford Young, *The African Colonial State in Comparative Perspective* (New
     Haven, Conn.: Yale University Press, 1994), esp. ch. 3.
60   Ibid., pp. 114–15.
61   Bernard Cohn and Nicholas B. Dirks, "Beyond the fringe: the nation state,
     colonialism, and the technologies of power," *Journal of Historical Sociology* 1/2
     (1988), pp. 224–9, esp. p. 225.
62   Ibid., p. 226.
63   Fanny Colonna, "Educating conformity in French colonial Algeria," in
     Cooper and Stoler, *Tensions of Empire*, pp. 346–70.
64   Young, *The African Colonial State*, esp. pp. 228–36.
65   Ibid., p. 232.
66   Quoted in Young, *The African Colonial State*, p. 180.
67   Calhoun, *Nationalism*, p. 104.
68   Chatterjee, *The Nation and its Fragments*, esp. ch. 1.
69   Uma Chakravarty, "Whatever happened to the Vedic Dasi? Orientalism,
     nationalism and a script for the past," in Kumkum Sangari and Sudesh
     Vaid (eds.) *Recasting Women: Essays in Colonial History* (New Delhi: Kali for
     Women, 1989), pp. 27–87; Kumari Jayawardena, *Feminism and Nationalism
     in the Third World* (New Delhi: Kali for Women, 1986).
70   Hall, "Introduction," p. 2.
71   Stoler and Cooper, "Between metropole and colony," p. 22.
72   Said, *Culture and Imperialism*, p. xi.
73   Ibid., p. 10.

CHAPTER THREE

Redoubtable Essences: Nationalisms and Genders

Miss America Organization is an essential chapter in the history of women in the twentieth century. Its national scope and longevity alone has had an effect on our nation's conception of womanhood, providing an important register of significant social and cultural trends in American society. Since its beginnings in 1921, it has reflected ideas about national identity, community, and moral standards, as well as beauty, femininity, and the roles of women.[1]

[Televised] representations of Miss World were thus viewed as possessing the power to distinguish India as a modern nation; as similar to ultra-metropolitan spaces in the Western World and newer, modernizing "tourist" nations like Thailand, but different from other Islamic states like Pakistan that are often vilified in mainstream Indian and global media.[2]

Beauty pageants such as Miss America, Miss World, and Miss Universe attract wide audience interest as well as fervent protest. These organizations stage competitions to settle on idealized notions of feminine beauty, and social norms of how women should carry, conduct, and present themselves. As such, feminist groups in various parts of the world question the glorification and objectification of women's bodies and the promotion of dubious ideals of feminine conduct, which are unattainable for the vast majority of women.

More recently, though, feminist scholars make the point that nationalisms are also implicated in these beauty pageants. Nowhere is the inextricability of nationalism from beauty pageants better reflected than the history of the Miss America pageant. As indicated in the first quotation above, beauty pageants are a way to track significant social trends of womanhood, including ideals of beauty, femininity, and women's roles in

American society. The official statement of the organization also makes clear that national identity, community, and moral standards are no less important to the evolution of the Miss America beauty pageant.

The Miss America pageant first started in Atlantic City as part of the week-long festivities, including parades, fireworks, and dances that were aimed at promoting business after the official end of the summer season.[3] This carnivalesque aspect of the beauty pageants continued for the next twenty years or so, when it was held at carnivals and fairs as a sideshow. Although the pageant had started gradually to cater to middle-class sensibilities, it was World War II that marked its transition to a respectable and national spectacle. For the first time, the competition included contestants from each state and, against the backdrop of war, Miss America was transformed into an emblem of patriotism and national pride. At the time, Miss America sold more war bonds than any other public figure and the emphasis shifted to education and career, alongside definitions of beauty. As the official statement of the organization asserts, "In these years, the image of Miss America, with her small-town persona, youth and energy, was becoming enshrined in the nation's imagination as America's ideal woman."[4] The chosen woman visited and entertained troops stationed abroad and came to embody the nation itself. Through the years, although there have been significant changes in the beauty pageant, the link between ideal womanhood and nationalism has endured, as was obvious in the competition held within weeks after the September 11, 2001 events; after initial hesitation about its timing, the organizers proceeded with the event as a patriotic spectacle that, incongruously, had few direct references to the recent tragedy.

But saying that the Miss America beauty pageant is about ideal womanhood and national identity presents only a partial picture. What is not reflected in this account of the competition is that the competition promotes heterosexual, class- and race-based ideals of femininity in the national imagination. Partly in response to widespread feminist criticism against the pageant, first expressed in 1968, the pageant organizers tout images of middle-class respectability by continually emphasizing its links to education and the balance between career and family for young women. Ironically, moments of crisis expose the race- and heterosexual bias in images of ideal American womanhood.

In 1983, Vanessa Williams, the now well-known singer, actress, and model, became the first African-American woman to win the title, for the year 1984.[5] Her victory was heralded as a break through the beauty pageant color bar even though many African Americans were skeptical about what the victory of a light-skinned, straight-haired, and "European-looking" black woman represented. However, ten months into her reign, the pornographic magazine, *Penthouse*, published nude photographs of Williams, which had been taken in 1981. What provoked angry and intense controversy was not only that she was nude in the photographs, but also that she was depicted with a white woman in sexual positions. Despite the fact that the photographs were taken before her victory, the violation of norms of sexual propriety for women and of the implicit taboo against non-heterosexual women in the pageant were more than enough to counteract the stellar role for Williams as a model for American womanhood. Amidst the controversy and debate between the pageant officials, feminist organizations, the NAACP (National Association for the Advancement of Colored People), and other groups, Williams renounced her title.[6] The controversy was reignited when one of her songs was played at the 1993 Miss America competition.

International beauty pageants implicate the links between women and nations no less. These events are competitions not only between young women, but also between nations, thereby further exacerbating controversies about ideals of beauty and womanly conduct. Hollywood films and newsreels may have helped spread the ideas of beauty contests to different countries.[7] Interestingly, beauty pageants proliferated in the Third World at the same time as many of these colonies were emerging as independent national states. India, Belize, Tibet, Sri Lanka and Nicaragua have long-standing beauty pageants. The period after World War II witnessed the internationalization of these competitions even though they were held in Western Europe and the United States. Miss World had been launched in 1951 by Eric and Julia Morley and was held in the United Kingdom for the first thirty-nine years.[8] Miss Universe was created in 1952 as a result of a dispute over photographic rights. For a number of years it was jointly owned by Donald Trump and the CBS Corporation, and from 2002 by Trump and NBC.[9] Since the 1990s in particular the Miss Universe and Miss World competitions have traveled to the non-western world and have been held in places such as Peru, Thailand, Mexico, India, and South Africa.

On one such occasion, the Miss World competition was hosted in the city of Bangalore, India, in 1996, the first time that such an event was held in South Asia. The intense controversy that surrounded the competition uncovered how women are seen as the symbols of culture and modernity and as the means of marking differences between "self" and "others," as reflected in the second quotation above. In a particularly interesting and detailed exposition, Radhika Parameswaran takes the position that Miss World was a site for contests over beauty, gender, and nation.[10] The pageant was endorsed by commercial groups and city officials for its potential to boost tourism and foreign investments, thereby connecting local economies to the international, globalizing realm. But more, the pageant was heralded as a crucial opportunity for India to gain the attention of an international audience and to present modern images of the nation to offset the widely pervasive images of poverty, abject women, and the ill effects of population growth. These groups supported the hosting of Miss World 1996 on the premise that it would serve as a stage for selective images of India and Indian women at a time when globalization was threatening to erode the distinctiveness of national cultures.

Supporters of Miss World 1996 celebrated Indian women as emissaries of nations and national pride. In the words of one such person, "People are bored with seeing only white faces and Western locations."[11] Another supporter further expressed the racial and national differences between Indian women and their western counterparts as: "Our girls sparkle. On camera, they have the most beautiful and expressive eyes, the best smiles, and when they speak, they sound so cultured and intelligent. We have no dumb blondes."[12] In contrast, protests against the pageant included an unlikely grouping of feminists and conservative religious activists. These groups protested several months before the scheduled event, questioning – albeit from different ends of the political spectrum – the objectification of women's bodies and the whittling away of Indian culture by western cultural expansion. Judging by Parameswaran's analysis, such international beauty contests are not only a means to reach across national boundaries and participate within the global arena, but also the sites where material questions of national identity are shaped.

This chapter is based on the position that nationalisms are thoroughly gendered. Rather than seeing gender as one of the myriad aspects of nationalism, the argument makes gender a constitutive part of the beliefs and practices of nationalism. Understanding nationalism as gendered means recognizing its varied impact on women and men of different social groupings. The first part of this chapter therefore focuses on these questions of (select) women's identities, their roles, and their respectability as key to matters of national identity and pride. The attention to nationalism and gender is relatively recent in the literature on nationalism, and the emphasis is mostly on women. The second part of this chapter examines the links between men and nationalism in an effort to correct the skew. Otherwise, understanding gender only as salient to women ignores men as gendered beings; the troubling implication is that women are recognized as women and men as human. The intervening role of the state in institutionalizing some of these aspects of nationalism – promoting or constricting women's reproductive capacities or making mandatory the draft of eligible men as soldiers – threads through the chapter. It also takes a broader approach in which gender is not reducible to women, men, or transgendered people. In the last section, we will explore the ways in which nationalisms and nations are thought through idioms of femininity and masculinity.

Defining Gender

The concept of gender is routinely used in two ways: it refers to women, men, and transgendered peoples; and it considers descriptions of what are widely considered feminine qualities, such as the emotional, spiritual and resilient, or apparently masculine qualities such as the powerful, aggressive, and rational. To argue that the inequalities between women and men are the result of culture and not due to immutable differences that we are born with, western feminists first introduced the concept of gender. By showing that differences between women and men are socially produced, feminists sought to change the inequalities between the lives of women and men in most cultures. A part of this effort toward gender equality is to also challenge how most cultures allow people only two possibilities – of being either women or men– and to conceive of a wider range of personhood.

Typically, western feminists maintain that the social categories of woman and man contain two concepts: sex and gender. With this purpose, feminists use the concept of sex to show how, particularly in western contexts, female bodies and male bodies are seen as fundamentally different so that these sexual differences can be used to separate people into two categories of female and male. There is no denying that most people with female bodies have different primary and secondary reproductive characteristics from those with male bodies. But what's more intriguing to feminists is that rather than the vast similarities between females and males, these differences are used to justify women or men's behaviors, emotions, attitudes, desires, career choices, how much people earn, among other things. Feminist anthropologists and feminist historians have argued against the widespread view that women and men are biologically irreconcilably different, pointing out that it has not been held across cultures or even across the history of western societies. The implication of this feminist scholarship is that widely held beliefs of male and female bodies, and about our biologies, are at least partly the outcome of culture, not nature.

Similarly, feminists use the concept of gender to highlight the range of social characteristics and roles that are culturally assigned to females and males, such as being emotional, rational, strong, fragile, being nurturing or being the provider. This approach questions the division of a broad range of human characteristics and roles into feminine and masculine qualities that are respectively assigned to women and men. Women are therefore expected to be feminine and men to be masculine. Equally importantly, feminists note how in numerous social contexts power is assigned to masculinity; this is called gender hierarchy. As a result, even though women are expected to be feminine they are less likely to be socially sanctioned for being masculine, but men who violate social norms by seeming feminine are more harshly treated. This attitude ignores the presence of a range of non-conforming and transgendered peoples in the West. In contrast, anthropological evidence from a wide variety of cultures suggests that the western two-gender system – in which males, masculinity, and men constitute one category and females, femininity, and women another – is a cultural artifact. Furthermore, anthropologists have pointed out that cultures are known to have three, four, and seven genders, thereby showing that even though the two-gender system may appear normal to some, it is not inevitable.

Concepts of sex and gender, then, are the foundations of feminist critiques of the inequalities between women and men. The concept of gender in particular has become commonplace as a result of feminist scholarship, although it is not always used in a critical sense. But sex is no less important because what we believe about female and male bodies may not be any less the result of cultural beliefs than gender; in other words, our beliefs about the biology of women and men are no less influenced by culture. Furthermore, feminists in western contexts are especially interested in pursuing examples that show us how both sex and gender are culturally produced. The examples they find help bolster the belief that women and men should be treated equally and that society need not be organized around the two-sex/gender system of females/women and males/men, and feminine and masculine qualities. Feminists suggest we may be able to conceive of a much wider spectrum of possibilities that may include a variety of ways of being women, men, transgendered people, and where masculine and feminine attributes are not mutually exclusive.

Although concepts of sex and gender are foundational to feminist challenges of the inequalities that face women in numerous cultures, they are inadequate unless they take into account the differences between women springing from race, class, nationality, and sexuality. Needless to say, differences and inequalities do not simply exist between women and men, but among women and among men, in most cultures. As was implicit in the previous chapter, under colonial rule differences of nationality, race, and class were more important than similarities in women across Europe and in native women in the colonies. Not only this, these differences would also sometimes pit European women against native women, upper-class native women against European women and lower-class native women, "respectable" native and European women against those who are seen as outside acceptable social boundaries, and so on. Nationalism, race, and class thus have to be of as much concern to feminist scholars as sex and gender when challenging the inequalities in the lives of women and men.

Women, Men, National States, and Nationalism

The positioning of women in order to define national identity is pervasive and striking. This is what makes the omission of issues of gender in the bulk of writings on nationalism so puzzling. As we shall see in the following sections, even though scholarship would later expand beyond women and nation to include men and broader issues of gender, early feminist scholarship was primarily focused on unraveling the interconnections between women and nation. This scholarship on gender and nationalism came largely from scholars who were working on issues related to the Third World, to settler societies, and to questions of colonialism. Feminist scholars such as Nira Yuval-Davis and Floya Anthias, Kumari Jayawardena, Deniz Kandayoti, Cynthia Enloe, Anne McClintock, broke new ground by calling attention to the fact that national states and nationalisms do not treat women as equal to their male counterparts and that women are frequently used to further the causes of national states and nationalisms. What matters in this exploration of women and nationalism is that more often than not these connections are not interpretable when class, racial, ethnic, or religious differences are ignored.

Women as symbols of nationalism

If I were to summarize the crux of the concerns regarding the links between women and nation, then it would be that women are seen as symbols of nations but are not equally represented within the idiom of nationalism, and are not treated as equal citizens of a national state.

Indeed, women's importance to definitions of national identity is the flip side of the state's attempt to regulate and control women, particularly in the interests of official nationalisms. In an insightful observation about the parallels between gender and nation, Tamar Mayer notes that beliefs of an enduring, unchangeable "essence" mark both concepts.[13] But precisely because each nation has to define its unique essence, national identity is based on claims about history, about cultural difference from other nations, and almost always on the distinctiveness of its women. By the same token, the essences of womanhood or manhood can exist only in relation to each other, thereby voiding the possibility that these categories have a quintessential meaning. Anthias and Yuval-Davis summarize the links between women and nations in five ways: as biological reproducers of members of ethnic collectivities; as reproducers of the boundaries of ethnic/national groups; as participators in the ideological reproduction of the collectivity and the transmitters of culture; as signifiers of ethnic/national groups; and as participants in national, economic, political, and military struggles.[14]

Below, I synthesize these links between women and nation into three main aspects: women as reproducers of nations, women as vessels of cultural nationalism, and women as markers of internal and external boundaries of nations/ethnic groups. I will focus on discourses of the veil and violence against women at times of conflict to help illustrate these points.

Reproducers of nations: Women are widely recognized as the symbolic and literal mothers of the nation's citizens; frequently, women are more literally seen as the bearers of additional national citizens. Women may be encouraged to have large families as a service to the nation and, in some cases, the state might provide benefits as incentive. In the former Yugoslavia and in Indonesia women's fertility was encouraged as a sign of national prosperity and vitality.[15] In her discussion of Indonesian nationalism, Leslie Dwyer notes that the ideal of nationhood was centered upon ideal women, who restricted their fertility for the sake of the nation, were modest, and committed to the model of the nuclear family.[16] Nations and societies in conflict in particular might actively solicit women to bear more children in the interests of the nation or the "race." Anthias and Yuval-Davis remind readers of the Palestinian saying that the Israelis may prevail at the borders, but Palestinians will prevail through the bedroom![17] Julie Mostov suggests that in the former Yugoslavia claims of nationhood were replete with images of the nation as mother, wife, and maiden.[18] At the same time, images of women as heroines and symbols of virtue and fertility, of strength and continuity helped shape what counted as national identity.

The other side of the symbolic importance of women to nationalism and the national state is that women are the targets of state-based regulation and social control in the service of national interests. As noted in Chapter Two, Anna Davin argues that women as mothers were the targets of state control in early twentieth-century England as part of the effort to increase the size and quality of the population when there was fear of losing pre-eminence in imperial expansion.[19] On the class-based assumption that the family was the right environment for the child, and the person most responsible was the mother, motherhood came under severe scrutiny and regulation by the state. A powerful ideology of motherhood, that it was women's task to serve their race, was bolstered by state legislation to enhance the birth rate and scapegoat mothers for infant mortality and the ill health of their children. Also in connection with the scapegoating of women in the former Yugoslavia, Mostov writes that women who refused to bear children or bore children with foreign men were seen as national traitors.[20] As she notes, women may well have been revered as mothers and they may be protected as symbols of nation, but that also means that women must be closely monitored; their bodies, behaviors, and roles are objects of national concern.

Indeed, strategies to encourage childbearing and to control reproduction can be simultaneously directed toward different groups of women in the same nation. In her remarkable study of the reproductive control of women in various parts of the world, Betsy Hartmann describes how under apartheid the South African state attempted to contain the African population but increase the numbers of whites by targeting almost exclusively black and mixed-race women.[21] At the time, family planning was the only free health service available to blacks and sometimes women who worked in white-owned factories were forced to use Depo-Provera, a form of contraception, in order to keep their jobs. Especially since the 1970s, concerns with a too-rapidly expanding world population has led to the curtailing of women's reproductive rights, especially in many Third World nations. With the support of international aid agencies, national states such as Bangladesh, India, Kenya, and Indonesia have targeted poor and rural women in the interests of national development. In countries such as the United States, poor white women and women of color have borne the brunt of reproductive control. What gets lost in all of this is that population increase may be a symptom of unequal distribution of re-sources, that indigent and marginal women are differently targeted than middle-class, more privileged women, and that family planning without overall health care can hardly be seen as serving the interests of women in a nation.

Women as vessels of cultural nationalism: Related to the assumption that the primary definition of a woman is her capacity to bear children is the perception that women are cultural transmitters, in the service of the nation. In so far as women are generally accorded the role of raising children, they are also seen as the "cultural carriers."[22] Passing on love for the nation to children, teaching them the importance of national symbols such as the national anthem, transmitting a way of life, instructing them in the national language, and communicating the history of the nation, are some of the tasks often accorded to women in their roles as mothers, wives, and teachers. Jeanne Marecek describes how the colonial legacy of Sri Lankan identity – coalesced around a single ethnic group, the Sinhala people, around Buddhism, and around righteous womanhood – was imprinted on contemporary nationalism. Sinhalese women who conformed to the ideals of womanhood were extolled as custodians of national cultural heritage while those who did not conform were attacked and discredited.[23]

It is hardly surprising, then, that women of particular class, ethnic, or racial groups are at the heart of images of official cultural nationalisms, whether as mothers, wives, or maidens. More specifically, women are often at the heart of the dilemmas of modernity faced by nations. For most nations generally, but for postcolonial nations in particular, the questions of tradition and modernity can be especially fraught, and ideal womanhood is often a way to resolve these difficult questions. In the nineteenth and twentieth centuries, countries undergoing formal or informal European colonialism had to contend with problems such as social change, westernization, and the meaning of national traditions; what is now called the "woman question" was salient to the debates that raged at the time.

Writing about the "woman question" from the perspective of mid-nineteenth-century Iranian nationalism, Joanna De Groot confirms that questions about women and images of women were central to Iranians in their encounter with Europeans.[24] The "modernists" and the "traditionalists" may have disagreed on the particulars but both groups focused on the ideals and roles of women as markers of an emergent Iranian nationalism. Debates on the education, veiling, and social reform of women raged less in the outright interests of women and more as indicators of an emergent Iranian nationalism. There was hardly a unified position; De Groot argues the "woman question" was a complicated and contradictory set of questions that contributed to the policies of modernization, of definitions of cultural nationalism, and the defense of religion as a core of Iranian identity. Thereby, Iranian women became symbolic figures of cultural authenticity and national self-esteem, a legacy that became vividly clear with the 1979 overthrow of the second Pahlavi Shah's regime and the subsequent re-imposition of the veil and other Islamic values on women as the repositories of national culture and religion.

Women as markers of internal and external boundaries: By now, undoubtedly, the use of women as the markers of external and internal boundaries of nations is becoming clear. Earlier discussions on international and national beauty pageants have illustrated how women are often positioned to symbolize the nation to the external world. The language of nationhood is thus liberally sprinkled with descriptions of how "our" women are different from "their" women. But women of particular groups are also significant in marking the internal boundaries of the nations, or differences between privileged and marginalized groups within the nation. Especially for colonized groups, the role and status of women were key aspects of an emergent oppositional national identity. There are important parallels between nineteenth-century Iran and colonial India, where the coeval "social reform" of women was partly an attempt to clarify the difference and the boundaries between European colonialists and Indian nationalists. However, what was especially suspect in this reform movement was not just that women's status was seen as a gauge of the Indian nation and Indian nationalism; it was that the movement was concerned mainly with middle-class, urban, Hindu and to some extent Muslim women, and not to all women across social classes and ethnic groups. In this way this group of "respectable" Indian women were used to mark the internal boundaries of the nation. These middle-class, urban, mostly Hindu women were also positioned as the authentic representatives of Indianness while working-class, tribal, peasant, non-Hindu women, and the communities that they represented, were pushed to the sidelines.

Tradition, modernity, and the veil

Currently, for national cultures that are already seen as modern, others who are thought to be on the path to modernity, and still others who aspire to modern conditions of life, questions of what is culturally appropriate or what is the role of tradition and the past in the face of rapidly changing modern life are not easy to determine. This is perhaps why the veiling of women in parts of the world invokes much discussion at the national level and draws attention at the international level. Regardless of the wide variety of ways in which women are expected to veil themselves, this issue is a lightning rod for national debates on modernity versus tradition, on the past versus the future, on the suppression versus the freedom of women, and, equally importantly, for the future of the nation. Colonialism and nineteenth-century nationalisms are not simply part of history, but influence the way nationalism is expressed today.

The use of women's bodies to settle debates between national cultural ideals and the nation's present and future is far more complicated than it may seem. Scholars who have analyzed the preoccupation with the veil in numerous national contexts comment on the difficulty of using the veil to make distinctions between modernity and tradition, despite appearances. Feminist sociologist Fatima Mernissi captures the three connotations of *hijab* or the veil: in its visual dimension, as hiding someone from view; in its spatial dimension, as a means to separate, establish a boundary or threshold; and in its ethical dimension, as a matter of prohibition.[25] In many countries, the practice of veiling is fraught by numerous political considerations. Understanding the veil as a retrograde practice, European colonizers encouraged the de-veiling of indigenous women. Not surprisingly, then, veiling became more widespread in countries such as Afghanistan in reaction to the British. Frequently, European women also participated in indicting the veil, partly out of ethnocentrism and partly as a political strategy to argue for more rights for themselves at home and abroad, by emphasizing their capability in contrast to abject veiled women. Contemporary, relatively simplistic criticisms of the veil by Christian women and men in western countries further fuel the political and cultural significance of the veil, including its appropriation by nationalists in countries where the practice prevails.

Historically and currently, nationalists in countries such as Morocco and Egypt are at odds about which women best represent the nation: the veiled or the unveiled. Today, proponents of modernity and an expanded role of the state in Egypt and Morocco see the practice of veiling as retrogressive and, more importantly, as an obstacle to modernization and development. The partial or complete seclusion of women stalls their education, their health and capabilities as mothers, and as labor in national development projects, according to this view. For conservative nationalist groups, however, the veil is seen as a necessary symbol and implement of modest womanhood, a restraint on female sexuality, and a matter of religious and national tradition, particularly against the onslaught of western modernity. Remarking on the compulsory veiling of women within the Islamist state of Iran, Nayereh Tohidi notes that it signaled the redefinition of gender roles and the anti-western stance of a changing Iranian society.[26] That the veil, the *Hijab-e Islami* in this case, was creatively adopted by women over the recommended *chador* belies claims that this was simply a return to "tradition": this consisted of a scarf covering the hair, a long tunic over a long-sleeved shirt, loose pants or stockings, and flat shoes in a dark or neutral color.[27]

From a critical perspective, both these positions on the veil and the symbolic representation of women can be untenable. If the veil as a means to restrict the perceived threat of female sexuality is questioned, then so are state attempts to force women to unveil in order to include them as objects of modernizing efforts. The use of the veil to prevent women from wider participation in public life or to protect men from women competing for the jobs is no less problematic for feminist groups; the Taliban regime in Afghanistan was criticized by feminist groups for these reasons. The point is not the presence or absence of the veil, but to see the changing and varied meanings of the veil in different social and historical contexts.

Tohidi documents that the veil came to be actively politicized in Iran between 1934 and 1936 when Reza Shah Pahlavi mandated the unveiling of women and the parallel Europeanization of Iranian men.[28] Forty years later, Iranian women were forced to re-adopt the veil by the revolutionary leader, Khomeini, as a challenge to the corrupt effects of the West on Iran. What is striking, however, is that many women voluntarily donned the *hijab* in opposition not only to westernization but also to the repressive nature of the Shah's regime and widespread socioeconomic inequalities. Indeed, the case of Iran reflects how a conservative position on the veil does not necessarily extend to the complete seclusion of women or their inability to participate in public life. On the contrary, veiled women in Iran have been able to secure important professional and political gains. When considered from women-centered perspectives, the veil has both revolutionary and repressive connotations. It has enabled women to participate in political, nationalist movements and to challenge the politics of an existing state and, in some cases, subvert dominant social mores about gender and sexual behavior that might otherwise apply; reportedly, for example, veiled women in Jordan – paradoxically – are better able to fraternize with their male peers than unveiled women.

Among the most compelling feminist critiques of the veil are those on unveiling when it is used to forestall more crucial social reforms. The example of Turkey is particularly helpful here. Kumari Jayawardena and Deniz Kandayoti separately argue that the Turkish Kemalist regime's attempt to modernize women through formal education, through westernization of their dress, including eliminating the veil, was a means to avoid more far-reaching and necessary reform in women's lives.[29] In the 1920s and 1930s, mostly urban, middle-class women discarded the veil and adopted more European garb, but at the same time, Kandayoti notes, women's emancipation under Kemalism was part of the broader efforts of nation-building and secularization. What the harnessing of this "new woman" did was to abort the possibility of women's autonomous movements and the need for more thorough social reform.

Taking all this into account, it is surely clear why the veiling of women assumes such political and national significance. It is easy to rally people around matters of cultural nationalism, including the veil, the politics of pro-life/pro-choice, female "circumcision," because women's bodies and sexualities represent national identity, and the nation's past and future. What these preoccupations also cover up are more complicated questions about nationalism, the national state, and masculinity, as well as necessary and more profound social changes for women, including freedom from poverty and violence, and access to social and cultural resources.

Women as means to an assault on the nation

Precisely because women represent the external and internal boundaries of nations and national identities, they are especially vulnerable to violence. In these cases, violence toward women is an attack on the nation or ethnic group that they represent. Indeed, the use of rape as a means to simultaneously violate women of enemy groups and the group itself led feminists to call rape a war crime. Cynthia Enloe identifies three scenarios under which rape is "militarized," in the sense that it is a part of soldiering and not simply individual or random.[30] The first is recreational rape, occurring where soldiers are seen as having inadequate access to prostitutes, so that soldiers are provided with the sexual services of other women. The provision of what were tragically called "comfort women" for Japanese soldiers presents an especially disturbing glimpse into the vulnerability of working-class and peasant women from Korea, China, and the Philippines to sexual slavery at the time of World War II. What compounds this case is that Japanese military officials forced these women into prostitution in order to reduce the likelihood of rapes of other Korean, Chinese, and Filipino local women, to maintain soldiers' morale, and to reduce venereal disease among them.[31] These institutionalized forms of rape continued through the 1980s and involved American and British soldiers stationed in a variety of places, including Korea, the Philippines, and Okinawa, Japan. What distinguishes these forms of militarized and related forms of recreational rape is that women of different national groups are forced into the sexual servitude of foreign soldiers.

Enloe describes the second form of militarized rape as an instrument of national security. A long list of nations – including, Chile and Argentina in the 1970s, Guatemala in the 1970s and 1980s, and Haiti, China, and Turkey in the 1980s and 1990s – have used rape to maintain internal national security.[32] Sexual assault is used to protect the interests of national authoritarian regimes, and to quell dissenting and insurgent groups by intimidation. Enloe notes that a Canadian survey of 28 former women prisoners who fled the Latin American countries of Chile, Argentina, Uruguay, Brazil, El Salvador, among others, found that 64 percent had been sexually abused during detention and 44 percent had been violently raped.[33] Under the Pinochet dictatorship in Chile, the rape of women was authorized in order to push women back into the private sphere: women of the poorer social classes and those with mixed European and Indian features were more violently treated than lighter-skinned, upper-class women. When the use of rape as national security is seen alongside ongoing police sexual brutality toward women, as in what is called "custodial rape" in India, the scope of the violence and women's vulnerabilities are starkly obvious.

The third type of militarized rape involves systematic mass rape as an instrument of warfare.[34] This form is probably the most recognized as a result of international attention to the systematic rape of Bosnian women by Serb soldiers. As a result of the sustained international feminist lobbying, a United Nations investigation into rapes in Bosnia was commissioned. The report confirmed what Bosnian Muslim refugees and human rights groups had already reported, that local Serb policemen, especially paramilitary militiamen, officers of the Serb-controlled army, and local male politicians who joined the military effort, were responsible. By 1995, it was estimated that a staggering 30,000 to 50,000 women from all communities had endured wartime rape, of which 20,000 Bosnian Muslim women had been targeted by Bosnian Serb men.[35] Rape was seen as a larger pattern of "ethnic cleansing" of Bosnian Muslims by violating the honor of the community and by Serb men forcibly impregnating Muslim Bosnian women. Without an understanding of women as the gatekeepers of a nation or ethnic group's sanctity, or as bearers of a nation's population, perhaps this form of systematic rape of women and girls would have been unthinkable.

Women as unequal citizens of national states

The cruel irony in the intertwining of nationalism and representations of respectable womanhood is that women are frequently denied equal status as citizens. Women are pressed into the service of the nation through the obligations of expanding literacy, taking low-paid work outside the home, bearing and raising children more efficiently in the home, or serving as soldiers. But as McClintock shows, despite the fact that women's work serves national interests, no nation extends equal privileges to its women and men.[36]

As citizens, in some cases women are often the foot soldiers in nationalist movements. At times of nationalist struggles, such as independence movements or times of war and conflict, women are called upon to support the nation as nurses, workers to substitute for the men at war, and as soldiers, freedom fighters, and political leaders. Israel is one of the few national states where military service is compulsory for women citizens. But, as Edna Levy persuasively argues, women's military service does not reap the same benefits, as does that of men.[37] Levy attributes this difference to the ways in which women's integration in the military mirrors their roles in civic life. Women are prohibited from combat but expected to facilitate men's actions through the roles of social workers, instructors, teachers, and secretaries. This is further supported by consistent portrayals of neatly coiffed, attractive, sometimes even sexually alluring women soldiers, which contrast with those of male soldiers, who are depicted as active and engaged in the serious business of national defense. The irony, in a nutshell, is that though women are crucial to the militarization of Israel, they are not on a par with male soldiers.

Not just as citizen-soldiers, in their broader roles as citizens women are often denied equality with men. In Israel and the United States, which are often seen as exemplars of women's equality, significant institutional discriminations belie claims of equality. In both countries, women earn significantly less than men, women are concentrated in lower-paying jobs, women are overwhelmingly responsible for child care, and there is far less representation of women in politics. Israel has a better record on this account; as yet there is little expectation that the United States will have a woman President or Vice-President in the near future. Exemplifying another form of inequality between female and male citizens, Mary Ann Tétreault and Haya al-Mughnini note that though Kuwaiti women enjoy many social and civil rights on par with men, they are denied full political rights.[38] Kuwaiti women cannot run for the national legislature or vote for its members. Tétreault and al-Mughnini argue that extending full citizenship status to women would make them entitled to a range of welfare benefits that are accorded to men and make them less vulnerable to male domination in the family, and possibly make marriage a choice rather than a necessity for women.

National development and women's labor

Since the 1950s, women of various social groups in various parts of the world have been more closely connected than they were to the politics of nationalism in at least two ways: as instruments and indicators of national development. Typically, women of the working, indigent, and peasant classes are targeted as instruments of national development. Particularly instructive is the role of urban and migrant women working in garment factories in places such as Mexico, the Philippines, and Indonesia as part of their nation's development strategies and the international division of labor. Since the 1980s or 1990s the phenomenon of sweatshops has gradually come into the international limelight. The crux of the concern is that hundreds of countries are producing for a small number of importing nations and, increasingly, for the domestic elites. This reorganization of production and consumption is part of the well-documented relocation of the so-called light industries, including garment-making, electronics, and toy-manufacturing, from western national states to the Third World, beginning in the 1970s. This trend is supported by the rising costs of labor, constraints against pollution, consumer demands, and increased competition in first world countries, and the dependency of countries such as Mexico and the Philippines on foreign investment, foreign exchange, and job opportunities for its labor.

By its nature, the garment industry paved the way for the increasing relocation of heavy industries such as auto manufacturing. According to Andrew Ross, editor of the compelling book, *No Sweat*, textile and apparel industries allow underdeveloped countries to begin the industrialization process, since little capital investment is required.[39] On the other hand, raw materials and cheap labor are abundantly available. Especially given the volatility of apparel fashion trends and the market, cheap and flexible labor, which can be easily laid off, is crucial to keeping the costs down for the importing nations. Central to this international division of labor are the Export Processing Zones (EPZs) in the exporting nations. Enloe and other scholars note how these states compete for the investment by offering the retail giants tax incentives, police protection, and cheap but educated labor.[40] In effect, the competition between national states can drive down the wages for labor in an entire geographical region. Increasingly though, the garment industry relies on sweatshops. Ross defines "sweating" as a system of subcontracting which, unlike the coordinated factory system, relies on farming out work by competing manufacturers to competing contractors.[41] The US General Accounting Office describes a sweatshop as one run by "an employer that violates more than one federal or state labor law governing minimum wage and overtime, child labor, industrial homework, occupational safety and health, workers compensation, or industry regulation."[42] Hundreds of thousands of sweatshops exist in nations around the world, and by Ross's estimate several thousand of these are in the United States.

What is the link between national development, garment exports, and women? Enloe and other feminists such as Barbara Ehrenreich and Patricia Fernandez-Kelly first documented the systematic reliance of these light industries upon the labor of young, mostly single and childless, relatively educated women. National states and corporate interests collude to recruit these women for several questionable reasons: widespread beliefs that women can be paid lower wages than men; that they are better suited to tedious, repetitive work; that they are more tractable as labor; and that they are less likely to unionize. The promotion of development through export and free trade zones in Third World and underdeveloped nations is bolstered by claims that such strategies would integrate women in national development; that national development would be enhanced through women's work in these export industries; and that women's increased access to work and income would lead to enhanced development status.

At what cost! Feminist scholars and garment labor activists, including women working at these sweatshops, have pointed out that in some cases women report higher degrees of financial independence and autonomy for a few years, but at the risk of forced pregnancy tests, routine layoffs to avoid paying women employment benefits, and the detriment of their long-term health. There is a high incidence of lung-related problems, partial or total blindness, and inability to work after prolonged exposure to conditions of high physical stress. The problem is not the integration of women into the national economy, but how it is done.

Women's movements, nationalism, and the state

If the connection between nationalisms, national states, and women are clear by now, it will come as no surprise that women's movements have a complicated relationship with nationalisms and the state. Contrary to beliefs that women's movements are a Euro-American phenomenon of the 1970s, women-centered movements have a longer history than that both in the West and in nations elsewhere. Indeed, women's movements in the ex-colonial world are closely tied to the emergence of nationalist movements, and date approximately from the late nineteenth and early twentieth centuries in Korea, the Philippines, Turkey, India, Egypt, Japan, China, Iran, Indonesia, to name a few.

In a ground-breaking overview, *Feminism and Nationalism in the Third World*, Jayawardena captures the intricately related histories of feminist and anti-colonial nationalist movements. Women across social classes participated in the struggle against colonialism and for the right to self-rule. They demonstrated in the streets, actively participated in industrial union agitation, and served as freedom fighters, often suffering the harsh retaliation by the colonial power. Anti-colonial cultural nationalism set the stage for the emergence of women's movements in the colonies. That the status of women was the litmus test of societies was the result of the encounter between the colonial state and official anti-colonial nationalism. At heart, the modernizing efforts in the colonies, especially through women's education and social reform (of age of marriage, property rights, polygamy, treatment of widows, foot-binding, etc.), were aimed at improving women's lives without altering their subordination within and outside the family. This is why women were as galvanized by the need to resist indigenous patriarchal structures as they were by the need to resist imperialism; they frequently had an ambivalent relationship to nationalist movements. Women's groups took male nationalist leaders to task for not carrying social reforms far enough, and for continuing to protect male power. In India, Turkey, Iran, and elsewhere, women fought for the right to vote, to own and control property, and the right to enter professions and politics.

An important point is that anti-colonial struggles and women's reform enabled the emergence of parallel women's movements, which were related to official nationalisms, but also were at odds with them. The gulf between nationalist and women's movements often widened after independence from colonial rule. In Europe and (north) America, however, women's suffrage was, by the late nineteenth century, the predominant political issue for women's movements. In some cases, western feminists and their concerns partly shaped women's movements in the colonies; an example, according to Jayawardena, is Dutch socialist feminists' attempt to engender feminist consciousness in Indonesia.[43] In other cases, suffragists in Britain and the United States made their claims for the vote without including women in the colonies or women of color at home. These suffragists emphasized differences of nation and race in order to justify their own claims to citizenship.

A second point, therefore, is that national and racial identity affected how, or whether, women's movements in the metropoles forged alliances or created irreconcilable differences with their counterparts in the colonies. Furthermore, in the colonies and the metropoles, most reforms had little relevance for the large majority of indigenous women, nor did they alter the basic subordination of women within the family or society. The third point, then, is that women's movements may have used the rhetoric of national identity for the social reform of women but, in many cases, middle-class women's movements eclipsed the causes and concerns for peasant, indigent, or ethnically or racially different women.

Today, women continue to play a significant role in national liberation movements as soldiers, supporters, martyrs, and organizers, as in the case of Palestine and Chechnya. At the same time, women also play a role in right-wing nationalist movements, as demonstrated by their participation in Hindu right-wing movements. More broadly, women's movements tend to have an ambivalent relation with nationalism. Jill Benderly's discussion of feminist oppositions to the nationalism-driven "ethnic cleansing" in the former Yugoslavia since 1991 speaks of the complexities of women's movements at times of ethnic and national conflicts.[44] Benderly says that before 1991 Yugoslav feminism, cobbled out of alliances between Bosnian, Croat, and Serb feminists, was a beacon of opposition to nationalism. But after the outbreak of war in 1991 and the ensuing killing, torture, rape, and displacement of people, she notes, Croat feminists were split into two factions: those who identified with the Croat nation when victimized by the Serbs, and implicated Serb feminists for their silent participation in the genocide; and those who remained staunchly anti-nationalist against the Croat nation despite their outrage at the Serb onslaught. In this time of bitter crisis, one group of Croat feminists allied with Croat nationalism while another group, although continuing to challenge Serbian nationalism, also criticized Croatian nationalism and its marginalization of women.

Women's groups may also appropriate nationalist movements to further their causes. Examining just this possibility, Lois West uses the term "feminist nationalism" to describe movements that see nationalism and feminism from a women-centered viewpoint.[45] "Feminist nationalism," therefore, describes the character of women-centered movements that are attempting to redefine nationalism. In an instructive analysis of the links between nationalism and feminism in Palestine, Frances Hasso shows how two organizations, a leftist-nationalist party in which women became powerful and its nationalist-feminist affiliate, successfully pushed both nationalist and feminist aspirations in the 1980s.[46] Hasso attributes this fruitful appropriation of nationalism by feminists to two things: their commitment to grassroots organizing rather than military mobilization, and their strategic recourse to Palestinian women's status, which figured prominently in Palestinian nationalist representations. In this way, feminists in the two organizations used dominant concerns about the status of women as markers of Palestinian nationalism to point out that nationalist liberation and women's liberation are intricately tied.

More typically, women's groups have a profoundly ambivalent relation to the nationalist state. If, on the one hand, women's movements express concern about the encroaching role of the state in women's lives, then, on the other hand, women's movements often have no other choice but to look to the state to extend and protect their rights. Feminist organizations in the US battle with pro-life groups on the issue of an individual woman's inalienable right to abortion on the grounds that it concerns her body and should be her choice; the state or opposing groups cannot impose a choice on her. In contrast, feminist organizations in China and India have attempted to lobby the state to prevent the abortion of female fetuses by individual women either voluntarily or because of pressure from family members. Not only can feminisms take on different meanings, but they can also relate differently to the state for different issues. The underlying concern can be summarized as: whether state policies adequately protect women citizens of various social classes or whether it is complicit in the violence, oppression, or exploitation experienced by women.

What is also important here is to note the social location of women's movements – whether middle-class based, urban, or grassroots – also shapes their encounter with the national state. To take an illustrative case, Hak-Soon Kim, a 67-year-old Korean woman spoke out against her sexual enslavement by the Japanese imperial army during the 1940s.[47] Kim was one of a group of women who called attention to the role of the Japanese government in the sexual enslavement of foreign women. Another activist, Kim Yŏn-ja indicted the role of the United States military and the complicity of the Korean national state in organizing and promoting militarized prostitution.[48] In her compelling and nuanced article, feminist scholar Hyun Sook Kim notes how these women activists are spearheading protest against military prostitution and Korean patriarchy in a nation where such criticisms encounter resistance.[49] Despite the fact that military prostitution does not receive the kind of attention and redress that is to be expected, Kim argues that these women's resistance is instructive in its refusal to succomb to sexual, imperialist, militarized, and national domination. But Kim also questions how the issue of militarized prostitution has become a battleground for middle-class feminists and nationalists; together, these groups treat women such as Hak-Soon Kim and Kim Yŏn-ja as victims who are to be pitied for their sexual exploitation, while according them second-class or marginal status as citizens. Kim notes that middle-class Korean feminists become inadvertently complicit in reinforcing the links between nationalism and class-based respectable womanhood.

Men and nationalism

If women and nationalisms and national states are connected in complex ways, then how do we understand nationalism in relation to men? All too often when we refer to gender, we concentrate on women. In so doing, we ignore the role of men in the nation and in the framework of nationalism. Men are overwhelmingly the soldiers, heroes, visionaries, political leaders, inciters, and myth-makers of nations and nationalisms. In preserving national interests, men's roles are important, and clearly different from women's.

More than any other modernist scholar of nationalism, Benedict Anderson has pointed out that nationalism is inherently imagined as a community of men.[50] As explored in Chapter Two, one of the key aspects of nationalism is that it is understood as a form of community based on citizenship. In this framework, citizens are seen as inherently equal; each citizen has the equal rights and responsibilities. Anderson argues that this community of citizens is specifically imagined as a brotherhood of men; the nation is conceived as a fraternal community of male citizens. But because of the differences among men, such as those of race, class, and sexuality, hierarchies of citizenship do exist among men. It is arguable that men of color are granted the same privileges as white middle- and upper-class men in the United States. But one has to only consider the pervasive disparities in wealth, education, and civil liberties to note that despite appearances some citizens are "more equal" than others. Regardless of internal inequalities, Anderson believes that the community of the nation is seen as a "deep horizontal comradeship;"[51] it is a comradeship of particular groups of men and the nation largely remains the domain of these groups.

Perhaps then, it is not surprising that frequently efforts are made to protect the homosocialness (same-sex social relations) and social privileges of male citizens. The military, the political arena, educational institutions, the public sphere are some of the spaces that may be protected as male preserves against women and sometimes against groups of men who are part of the political minority. The military can be a particularly important national symbol of male citizenship and privilege. Writing about the military in the United States, Holly Allen argues that opposition to the full integration of women and gay people in the military is a means to preserve the military as a bastion of male heterosexual citizenship in the national community.[52] Allen suggests that military service is especially important to full membership in the national community. One only has to remember the widespread media concern about whether candidates in the presidential election have done military service to appreciate its significance to citizenship in the United States. Indeed, the debates about full inclusion of women and gays in the military in the United States mirror earlier debates about the inclusion of African Americans.

What is clear, then, is that the nation is the domain of men but also the nation is itself represented through male perspectives that are based in race, ethnic, sexual differences. The parameters of national identity, and the past and future of the nation, are based on elite male perspectives of dominant racial or ethnic groups. In their article on right-wing nationalism in the United States, Andrew Light and William Chaloupka argue that this form of nationalism, in reaction to the pluralist versions, privileges the perspectives of white men.[53] Drawing upon notions of white exclusivity and supremacy, this right-wing nationalism maintains that the American nation should be based on white rights – rights that have gradually eroded. According to Light and Chaloupka, right-wing nationalist groups seek to retrieve what they see as a white-based exclusionary national culture from the threat of minority rights and a liberal, intrusive government. This right-wing version of white, male, working-class nationalism in the United States defends the bombing of the federal building in Oklahoma as a justifiable response of a nationalist trying to protect the American nation from its liberal government.

Representations of the nation through male perspectives depend on the marginalization of particular groups of men but also on specific representations of women. Maleness comes to entail preserving women's respectability and defining what respectable womanhood means to the national identity. This is the striking paradox of gender and nationalism: the relation between men and nation is mediated through women. If women are seen as the reproducers of the nation's internal or external boundaries, then men are seen as protectors of internal or external boundaries and of women. Because women represent the inviolable sanctity of the nation and men are seen as the guardians of women and the nation, acts of aggression are seen as attacks on the nation's men. Men are called upon to protect their women and children and the territory of the nation from the external enemy, particularly from rape.

Calling into question this predictable representation of the violated woman as the violation of the motherland that is to be defended by men, Mary Layoun points to how these representations of women, men, and nation obscure the restrictions imposed by men upon the women of their community.[54] In the summer of 1974 Turkey invaded Cyprus, and Layoun notes that the rape of Cypriot women by Turkish soldiers and resulting pregnancies were high enough for the Cypriot Orthodox Church to permit abortions in the fall and winter of 1974. In stark contrast, a short story tells about what might be unthinkable: a sexual relationship and love between a Greek Cypriot woman and a soldier who is either Turkish or Turkish Cypriot. In so doing, the short story challenges the foregrounding of rape as the "national story," and the casting of the Turks as the brutal invaders and the Greek Cypriots as the innocent victims. The story of rape is more than the "rape of woman," Layoun believes. For her, the story does not minimize the experiences of rape or invasion, but shifts attention to how "the rape of woman" conceals the national, religious, cultural and linguistic boundaries between Greek and Turkish Cypriots, between Christians and Muslims, between Greece and Turkey, and between women and men. At stake in all of this is the sexual, political, and national agency of women, women's control over their own bodies, and their ability to choose, which is denied them by the men of their national and religious community.

Men frequently have the role of arbiters and defenders of cultural nationalism. With women tolerating it, men attempt to impose "tradition" on them while they themselves may embrace modernity. In the negotiations over tradition and modernity for national cultural identity, if women are seen as the custodians of tradition, then men are typically seen as the harbingers of modernity. It is not that women are not expected to be modern in some ways. In fact, Turkish nationalism sought to modernize its women through allowing them education, work outside of the home, and western styles of dress. Yet women are expected not to be "too modern," to retain the traditional qualities of Turkish national identity. In contrast, men are more unequivocally associated with modernity. That the Europeanization and modernization of men is less problematic is vividly reflected in the widespread adoption of western clothes, especially in contexts where women are expected to wear traditional dress or balance it with western clothes.

Finally, men also represent the vitality and vigor of the nation. Male athletes are a particularly potent symbol of national prowess. The summer Olympic games, international soccer and cricket matches, and international baseball competitions are spaces where athletes do not simply compete with each other. They also compete as representatives of nations. There was much international criticism of the United States after the 1996 Olympics in Atlanta. Too much nationalism in the form of "USA" chants through the events, flag-waving, in the television and newspaper coverage that was outrightly partial to (north) American athletes, and too little appreciation of athletes from around the world were the predominant and justifiable criticisms. That this was then repeated in Australia four years later perhaps indicates the inextricable links between the Olympics and nationalisms, particularly when the hosting nations feel that they have much to cheer about.[55]

In his exploration of nationalism and sexuality in France and Germany (to be more carefully considered in Chapter Four), George Mosse notes how sports have been seen as a masculine preserve and a way to register the health, vigor, and beauty of the athletes as well as the nation.[56] When female athletes have been present, they have been represented in the image of men. Therefore, it is hardly surprising that not only do international athletic competitions foster nationalism, but also that the ones that seem to arouse more intense expressions of nationalism are the men's sports. Describing the 1998 soccer World Cup, journalist Lowell Sutherland noted that the competition has evolved into earth's greatest tournament, now involving 32 nations.[57] Identifying competition and nationalism as the main attraction for spectators, he points out that players can compete only for their countries. Ironically, Yasuhiko Shibata's remarks on the performance of Japanese female athletes at the Sydney Olympics indicate that athletic competition and nationalism are largely a male preserve.[58] Noting how nationalist leaders have long used world sports festivals to encourage nationalism and glorify the nation, Shibata bemoans Japanese male athletes as "weak" and lacking energy. To his credit, Shibata celebrates the power of Japanese women not only for their athletic ability, but also for being rebuilders of a nation "dominated and ruined by men."[59] Though motivated by admiration for the women and by concern for the men, Shibata inadvertently points to the pervasive links between maleness, athletics, and nationalism – although this is a relationship that might be undergoing change.

Femininity, Masculinity, and Nationalism

Writing in the wake of the September 11 terrorist attacks in New York City, Washington DC, and the Pittsburgh area, news commentator Jonathan Alter disparaged feminist and leftwing groups who were not in favor of the ensuing bombing of Afghanistan by the United States. Targeting his comments to feminists, Alter wrote: "The same people who have urged us not to blame the victim in cases of rape are now saying that Uncle Sam wore a short skirt and asked for it."[60]

This analogy between the sexual assault of women and the terrorist attacks of September 11 is objectionable and not particularly useful. It is not useful because the sexual assault of a woman is not analogous to the terrorist attacks; there are no direct parallels between the sexual assault of one woman by one or more men and attacks by terrorist groups against key symbols of national and international power, i.e. the World Trade Center and the Pentagon. The power relations between aggressor and victim in rape cases do not parallel the power relations between the United States as victim and the terrorists as aggressors. In fact, a complex, historical approach to September 11 and its aftermath suggests the inadequacy of categorizing people as victims or perpetrators. The analogy is objectionable because it is being used to quell feminist criticism of the United States' bombing of Afghanistan. Alter is discrediting those who do not agree with American retaliation against Afghanistan. Instead of allowing for difference and disagreement from various sections of the American citizenry, Alter alleges that disagreement is akin to saying that the United States "asked for" this tragedy and is thereby defending the acts of the terrorists. The use of this analogy is offensive because it takes a serious issue such as sexual assault to silence disagreement on a matter of national and international importance.

I refer to Alter's analogy not only to show its sleight of hand, but also to make one additional point. Unwittingly, Alter draws our attention to the ways in which gender and nationalism are profoundly linked. By this, I do not simply refer to the links between women or men and nationalism, as explored above. Gender and nationalism also means taking seriously how the nation is seen as womanlike or as feminine. Earlier, I identified gender not only in terms of women, men, and transgendered peoples, but also with respect to qualities that are largely seen as either masculine or feminine. The separations between women and men and femininity and masculinity are somewhat artificial but important to make. They are artificial because of the significant overlap between women and femininity and men and masculinity and because our realities are rarely simple. At the same time, these separations are useful in order to help analyze how we think of gender, of nationalisms, and of the links between them.

Regardless of whether we agree or disagree with Alter's analogy, we can follow his argument – of Uncle Sam with a short skirt – because we often see the nation as feminine. We talk about nations as mother and the motherland, as kind and gentle, as spiritual, or as being raped, invaded, and violated. At other times, we speak of nations in masculine terms, as nation as fatherland, as strong, protective, powerful, or as aggressor and attacker. In the United States, press coverage of the 1991 Gulf War frequently described Kuwait as being raped, and the need for the United States to act as protector of Kuwait and Saudi Arabia. The lines between the feminine and masculine, however, were blurred, since Iraq was reported to be "sodomizing" Kuwait. Sometimes positive and at other times brutal, these metaphors indicate and complicate the links between gender and nationalism in our contemporary lives.

Gender, home, and family

"I am not a violent man, but when someone comes into my house, attacks me in my house, I have to strike back."[61]

This was the response of an unknown man who was interviewed on CNN about his reactions to the attacks of September 11. His words capture at least three aspects of the links between gender and nationalism. To begin with, these words draw our attention to an important aspect of nationalism, namely its equivalence to home and family. Anne McClintock notes that the Latin for "nation" and "to be born" have the same root. Just as we are born within families, so we are born within nations.[62] Just as we speak of belonging to nation, we also speak of belonging to family. McClintock says that our understanding of nations as families is important for two reasons. First, the metaphor of nation as family reinforces the beliefs that much like members of a family, members of a nation have common interests even though they are not equals. The subordination of women of various races, classes, or ethnic groups to men in the nation therefore seems less troublesome than it might. The equivalence of nation and family also strengthens the perception that women are less citizens in their own rights and more dependents of the head of the family. Second, the metaphor of nation as family adds force to the beliefs that the nation, like the family, has a single point of origin. Instead of complicated even contradictory histories of how groups separated by important cultural and political differences come to identify or are made to identify as "a people," diverse groups are seen as having a common national past.

This metaphor of nation as family is profoundly gendered. We locate the family within the domestic or the private rather than the public spheres. But there is an imbalance between the public and the private/domestic.

The public is not only seen as more important but also the sphere of men and masculinity. If the state, the military, and the corporate world are seen as part of the public sphere, where typically men are dominant, then these are the institutions which favor "masculine" qualities, such as competitiveness, a kill-or-be-killed attitude, hard-headedness, rationality, etc. In contrast, the private or the domestic realm is the space where women are thought to occupy a larger role as care-takers of the family, as custodians of family morality; there, feminine qualities such as nurturance, love, and emotion are more appropriate, whether expressed by women or by men.

The larger point being argued here is that when we expand our definitions of gender beyond women, men, or transgendered peoples to qualities and attributes associated with femininity and masculinity, we can see how the language of gender shapes just about every aspect of our social world. We make sense of institutions, public and private spheres, and the domestic through a language of gender. The more specific point is that in so far as the family is seen as a metaphor of nation, the nation is profoundly gendered. It is gendered in the sense that women are symbols of both family and nation; both family and nation are seen as matters of internal sovereignty and therefore private; nation as family does not fail to inspire romantic longings for belonging and shelter from a harsh outside world; "feminine" qualities of love, nurturance, and protectiveness are attributed to nation just as to family; we speak of nations as motherlands and fatherlands. Needless to say, the reality is far more complicated than the easy divisions of masculine and feminine, the public and the private, or notions of nation as family, but the framework has considerable consequences in making the nation seem like a normal, natural place of belonging, inspiring devotion and commanding the utmost loyalty as the motherland that – like the dearest family – needs defending.

Gendered colonialisms and nationalisms

One way to understand the unstable, complicated masculinization or feminization of nations is to examine the intersection of colonialism and nationalism more carefully. The previous chapter focused on the links between nationalism and colonialism, but re-examining that link from the perspective of gender would be useful. McClintock persuasively argues that colonial intervention and exploitation was always profoundly gendered.[63] Conquest and occupation of "virgin lands" is particularly indicative of how colonialism was gendered. Seeing land as virgin not only suggested that land was empty and therefore ready for occupation, but it also feminized it and therefore justified the occupation. In this feminized and sexualized idiom, virgin land is the earth ready to be discovered, occupied, entered, and laid claim to. The colonial project, by contrast, takes on a more masculine significance through an emphasis on adventure, conquest, discovery, and ownership of land.

Yet, McClintock cautions us, the gendering of colonialism was never the same for all colonies. Some were never imagined as virgin territory but as a place to domesticate.[64] What is notable is that one of the connotations of the verb "domesticate" until the 1960s was "civilize." Women in North Africa, the Middle East, and in parts of Asia were to be civilized through their undressing or de-veiling, while women in sub-Saharan Africa were to be civilized by being clothed.[65] The civilizing, domesticating colonial missions of the nineteenth century relied on feminizing the colonized societies. Characterizing these societies as barbaric, savage, exotic, uncivilized, backward, and traditional did more than justify colonial projects; by feminizing them they made their subordination seem natural. Depictions of colonized peoples as closer to nature, childlike, emotional, and impulsive were rife and had important consequences for the psychology of colonized peoples – and also the colonizers.

Re-examined within this gendered framework Partha Chatterjee's argument about the premises of anti-colonial nationalism becomes equally important. In the previous chapter, I explored Chatterjee's argument that anti-colonial nationalism could not simply derive from the European model of nationalism that was gathering strength in the nineteenth and early twentieth centuries. Rather, nationalist elites in India endorsed modernization, scientific rationalism, and technological progress in the public sphere, as a means to demonstrate their abilities and capabilities. But the private sphere, which included the family, indigenous schools, literature, and religion, was the basis upon which nationalist elites attempted to specify what was essentially Indian. So India was cast as a spiritual land, with time-honored traditions, and as family-oriented, in contrast to the material, changing, technologically driven character of Britain. What is now strikingly obvious in Chatterjee's argument about anti-colonial nationalism is that it is also working within and through a gendered idiom. If colonial intervention relied on the feminization of India, then anti-colonial nationalists successfully took on the mantle of European, masculine qualities in the public sphere. But they developed and valorized a more feminized form of national identity that was based on family, tradition, and spirituality to challenge what could be seen as not only European but also masculine domination. This anti-colonial stance was coupled with efforts at re-invigorating masculinity in colonial India, efforts that have profoundly shaped post-independence Indian nationalism since 1947.

Contemporary nationalisms as male-centered and masculinist

The legacies of gendered nationalisms endure to this day. Speaking to such legacies and their contemporary influences, Linden Lewis wonders about the blatantly masculinist terms of Anglophone Caribbean nationalism.[66] Lewis suggests that an important factor to understand in this nationalism is the effort of national elite men to affirm their status as adult, mature men, and as capable of governing themselves. At the same time, these nationalist elites did not question the colonial gender order, since they were able to acquire leadership roles and important resources while women were largely excluded. Lewis argues that both the threat to Caribbean men and their privileges as men help us understand how post-colonial nationalism remained as largely male-centered projects. Focused on responding to and challenging European colonialism, Caribbean nationalism was forged out of male experience and remained male-centered. Men – and women, in many cases – supported this masculinist vision of Caribbean nationalism. This is perhaps why Cynthia Enloe has maintained that "nationalism typically has sprung from masculinized memory, masculinized humiliation and masculinized hope."[67]

Writing about masculinity and nationalism among Jews, Mayer also finds that the phenomenon is a reaction to being feminized. Mayer believes that Zionism, the wellspring of Jewish nationalism, was always a masculine project. This masculine nationalism was based on the rejection of caricatures of Jews in Europe and their transformation into a "New Jew," a "Muscle Jew."[68] This physically fit, militarized, heroic person was the Zionist response to the effeminization of Jewish men and Jewish identities in Europe. This new male citizen was expected to take up arms to protect himself, his community, and defend what he saw as his land. Mayer argues that because Jewish history in Palestine has been burdened by a continuous struggle for survival, a masculine, militarized version of Jewish nationalism has continued to predominate. Furthermore, she believes, the homosocial experiences among men that are possible amidst this history of conflict and in the military, in particular, continue to support the ties between Jewish nationalism and masculinity in Israel.

Perhaps nowhere are the uneasy tensions between nationalism, femininity, and masculinity more evident in our contemporary lives than in times of war and conflict. Highlighting just these connections, Michael Rogin questions the policies and politics that led and justified the United States-led war against Iraq in 1991.[69] Rogin argues that the Bush administration of that time effectively demonized Saddam to help justify United States' imperialist policies. Using gendered and sexualized metaphors, President Bush alleged that "Saddam Hussein systematically raped, pillaged, and plundered a tiny nation" and "is going to get his ass kicked."[70] The Kuwaiti nation was feminized through metaphors of rape and sodomy, America was masculinized as protector and defender of the weak, and Saddam Hussein and Iraq embodied deviant, criminal, out-of-control masculinity. What this masculinized American nationalism did was to obscure its complicity with, and the complexities of, Saddam Hussein's dictatorship. Rogin reminds us that the Bush administration was secretly selling arms and supplying intelligence to Iraq while ignoring the threat it posed to Kuwait. This casting of the Gulf War in gendered and sexualized idioms and making Saddam Hussein a monster of colossal proportions justified the recourse to war in the United States and the victimization of thousands of Iraqi citizens through sanctions, despite international pressure to the contrary.

Conclusion

The primary argument in this chapter is twofold: that we ought to consider nationalism from a gender perspective; this means recognizing nationalism as beliefs and practices that are organized through a language of femininity and masculinity, and have significant but dissimilar impact on the lives of women and men. Parallel to Chapter Two's position that race and colonialism were key to making sense of the proliferation and meanings of nationalism, this chapter argues that nationalisms take shape through socially constructed understandings of gender.

More specifically, I argued that women and men are differently hailed in nationalist projects and differently targeted by state policies. Mediated by racial, ethnic, or class-based differences, nationalisms and state policies grant citizenship to women and men unequally. One outcome of this exploration is the importance of undoing expectations around ideal, respectable womanhood or differences between "our" women and "theirs." No less, this chapter challenges the possibility that gender-equal citizenship can be achieved through the mere inclusion of women in what remains a male-centered national community. Rather, this chapter hints at the importance of changing notions of nationalism and state policies to grant full rights of citizenship to a broad range of gender identities. Transgender activist Leslie Feinberg notes that she is unable to travel outside of the United States because she will not check off either "male" or "female" on the passport application.[71] Ultimately, then, this chapter is about the faultlines of citizenship and the importance of its fundamental reconfiguration.

Another point explored in this chapter is that nationalisms take on gendered characteristics. After all, notions of gender are so deeply seated that they shape how we make sense of the world around us. The gendered effect of nationalism is nowhere more effective than in the ways we think about nation as home, as our place of belonging, and as an extension of our family. As cohesive and normalizing as these metaphors of nationalism can be, they can also be ways of excluding other residents and citizens or treating them unequally. The underlying question is: who really belongs to the nation? At moments of war and conflict, the gendering of nationalisms becomes especially complex, and depends largely upon the nationalism and the perspective adopted. The gendered idioms of rape and brutality can be used to justify violence – by prolonging sanctions against the people of Iraq as a result of Saddam Hussein's policies – or to mobilize anti-colonial nationalism by elevating selective notions of femininity. The revolutionary force of the latter type of gendered nationalism is blunted by distinctions between acceptable and marginal femininity. Moreover, as Amrita Basu has had the insight to note, where a nation is feminized as motherland, the state is often represented in masculinist language.

I also want to draw attention to another aspect of this chapter, namely the complex relations between nationalist and feminist movements. This chapter explored the coeval rise of feminist movements and the heightening of nationalist movements in the ex-colonies and the metropoles. Currently, women's movements appear to have a complex relation with nationalisms and states. If, in some cases, women's movements have promoted cultural nationalisms, then, in other cases, they have also opposed them. In numerous cases, women's movements may seek to appropriate nationalist movements. What's more pervasive, however, is the ambivalent relation between women's movements and the national state: women may seek to restrict the encroachment of the state upon their bodies and their lives, even as they are compelled to turn to the state to protect their rights as individuals and citizens.

NOTES

1   www.misamerica.org/main.html
2   Radhika Parameswaran, "Global media events in India: contests over beauty, gender, nation," in *Global Media Events in India: Contests over Beauty, Gender,*

Nation 3/2 (Columbia, SC: Association for Education in Journalism and Mass Communication, 2001), pp. 53–105, esp. p. 70.

3 www.misamerica.org/main.html

4 Ibid.

5 Sarah Banet-Weiser, *Most Beautiful Woman in the World* (Berkeley, Los Angeles, and London: University of California Press, 1999, esp. ch. 4.

6 www.misamerica.org/main.html

7 Colleen Ballerino Cohen, Richard Wilk, and Beverly Stoeltje, *Beauty Queen on the Global Stage: Gender, Contests, and Power* (New York and London: Routledge, 1996), p. 5.

8 Ibid.

9 Parameswaran, *Global Media Events in India*, pp. 53–4.

10 Ibid., p. esp. 53.

11 Ibid., p. 80.

12 Ibid.

13 Tamar Mayer, "Gender ironies of nationalism: setting the stage," in Tamar Mayer (ed.) *Gender Ironies of Nationalism: Sexing the Nation* (London and New York: Routledge, 2000), p. 2.

14 Floya Anthias and Nira Yuval-Davis, "Introduction," in Nira Yuval-Davis and Floya Anthias (eds.) *Woman-Nation-State* (New York: St. Martin's Press, 1989), pp. 1–15, esp. p. 7.

15 Mayer, "Gender ironies of nationalism," p. 7.

16 Leslie Dwyer, "Spectacular sexuality: nationalism, development and the politics of family planning in Indonesia," in Mayer, *Gender Ironies of Nationalism*, pp. 25–62.

17 Anthias and Yuval-Davis, "Introduction," p. 8.

18 Julie Mostov, "Sexing the nation/desexing the body: politics of national identity in the former Yugoslavia," in Mayer, *Gender Ironies of Nationalism*, pp. 89–110, esp. p. 89.

19 Anna Davin, "Imperialism and motherhood," in Frederick Cooper and Ann Laura Stoler (eds.) *Tensions of Empire: Colonial Cultures in a Bourgeois World* (Berkeley, Los Angeles, and London: University of California Press, 1997), esp. pp. 93–7.

20 Mostov, "Sexing the nation/desexing the body," p. 91.

21 Betsy Hartmann, *Reproductive Rights and Wrongs: The Global Politics of Population Control*, rev. edn., foreword by Helen Rodriguez-Trias (Boston, Mass.: South End Press, 1995), p. 206.

22 Anthias and Yuval-Davis, "Introduction," p. 9.

23 Jeanne Marecek, " 'Am I a woman in these matters?': notes on Sinhala nationalism and gender in Sri Lanka," in Mayer, *Gender Ironies of Nationalism*, pp. 139–60, esp. 157.

24 Joanna De Groot, "Coexisting and conflicting identities: women and nationalisms in twentieth-century Iran," in Ruth Roach Pierson and Nupur Chaudhuri (eds.), with assistance from Beth McAuley, *Nation, Empire, Colony: Historicizing Gender and Race* (Bloomington and Indianapolis: Indiana University Press, 1998), pp. 139–65.

25 Fatima Mernissi, *Women's Rebellion and Islamic Memory* (London and Atlantic Highlands, NJ: Zed Books, 1996), pp. 51–2.

26 Nayareh Tohidi, "Modernity, Islamization, and women in Iran," in Valentine M. Moghadam (ed.) *Gender and National Identity: Women and Politics in Muslim Societies* (London and Atlantic Highlands, NJ: Zed Press and Karachi: Oxford University Press, 1994), pp. 110–47, esp. pp. 124–6.

27 Ibid., p. 122.

28 Ibid., p. 125.

29 Kumari Jayawardena, *Feminism and Nationalism* (New Delhi: Kali for Women, 1986), esp. ch. 1; Deniz Kandayoti, "End of empire: Islam, nationalism and women in Turkey," in Deniz Kandayoti (ed.) *Women, Islam and the State* (Philadelphia: Temple University Press, 1991), pp. 22–47.

30 Cynthia Enloe, *Maneuvers: The International Politics of Militarizing Women's Lives* (Berkeley, Los Angeles, and London: University of California Press, 2000), esp. pp. 111–23.

31 Ibid., pp. 79–89.

32 Ibid., pp. 123–32.

33 Ibid., p. 129.

34 Ibid., pp. 132–51.

35 Ibid., p. 140.

36 Anne McClintock, *Imperial Leather: Race, Gender, Sexuality in the Colonial Contest* (New York: Routledge, 1995), p. 353.

37 Edna Levy, "Women warriors: the paradox and politics of Israeli women in uniform," in Sita Ranchod-Nilsson and Mary Ann Tétreault (eds.) *Women, States, and Nationalism* (London and New York: Routledge, 2000), pp. 196–214.

38 Mary Ann Tétreault and Haya al-Mughini, "From subjects to citizens: women and the nation in Kuwait," in Ranchod-Nilsson and Tétreault, *Women, States, and Nationalism*, pp. 143–63.

39 Andrew Ross, "Introduction," in Andrew Ross (ed.) *No Sweat: Fashion, Free Trade, and the Rights of Garment Workers* (New York and London: Verso, 1997), p. 10.

40 Cynthia Enloe, *Bananas, Beaches and Bases: Making Feminist Sense of International Politics* (Berkeley and Los Angeles: University of California Press, 1989), p. 159.

41 Ross, *No Sweat*, p. 13.

42 Ibid., p. 12.

43 Jayawardena, *Feminism and Nationalism*, esp. ch. 8.

44 Jill Benderly, "Balkans: rape, feminism, and nationalism in the war in Yugoslav successor states," in Lois A. West (ed.) *Feminist Nationalism* (New York and London: Routledge, 1997), pp. 59–72.

45 Lois A. West, "Introduction: feminism constructs nationalism," in West, *Feminist Nationalism*, pp. xi–xxxvi, esp. p. xiii.

46 Frances Hasso, "The 'Women's Front' nationalism, feminism, and modernity in Palestine," *Gender & Society* 12/4 (1998), pp. 444–65.

47 Enloe, *Maneuvers*, p. 80.

48 Hyun Sook Kim, "Yanggongju as an allegory of the nation: the representation of working-class women in popular and radical texts," in Elaine H. Kim and Chungmoo Choi (eds.) *Dangerous Women: Gender and Korean Nationalism* (New York and London: Routledge, 1998), pp. 175–99, esp. p. 176.
49 Ibid., pp. 192–6.
50 Benedict Anderson, *Imagined Communities* (London: Verso, 1983), p. 7.
51 Ibid.
52 Holly Allen, "Gender, sexuality and the military model of the U.S. national community," in Mayer, *Gender Ironies of Nationalism*, pp. 309–27, esp. p. 310.
53 Andrew Light and William Chaloupka, "Angry white men: right exclusionary nationalism and left identity politics," in Mayer, *Gender Ironies of Nationalism*, pp. 329–50.
54 Mary Layoun, *Wedded to the Land? Gender, Boundaries, and Nationalism in Crisis* (Durham, NC and London: Duke University Press, 2001), esp. ch. 2.
55 Michael Wilbon, "Whether it's America or Australia, cheering at Olympics finds a Homer," *Washington Post*, September 20, 2000, p. D01.
56 George L. Mosse, *Nationalism and Sexuality: Respectability and Abnormal Sexuality in Modern Europe* (New York: Howard Fertig, 1985), esp. p. 101.
57 Lowell Sutherland, "As a draw, World Cup is without parallel; 32-nation tournament gets under way," *Baltimore Sun*, June 10, 1998, p. 1D.
58 Yasuhiko Shibata, "Women can get nation back on track," *Daily Yomiuri*, October 4, 2000, p. 6.
59 Ibid.
60 Jonathan Alter, "Blame America at your peril," *Newsweek*, October 15, 2001.
61 Unknown man, CNN, October 8, 2001.
62 McClintock, *Imperial Leather*, p. 357.
63 Ibid., esp. ch. 1.
64 Ibid., pp. 30–6.
65 Ibid., p. 31.
66 Linden Lewis, "Nationalism and Caribbean masculinity," in Mayer, *Gender Ironies of Nationalism*, pp. 261–81.
67 Enloe, *Bananas, Beaches and Bases*, p. 44.
68 Mayer, "Gender ironies of nationalism," p. 15.
69 Michael Rogin, " 'Make my day!': spectacle as amnesia in imperial politics [and] the sequel," in Amy Kaplan and Donald E. Pease (eds.) *Cultures of United States Imperialism* (Durham, NC and London: Duke University Press, 1993), pp. 499–534.
70 Ibid., p. 524.
71 Leslie Feinberg, *TransLiberation: Beyond Pink or Blue* (Boston: Beacon Press, 1998), p. 21.

CHAPTER FOUR

Checking (Homo)Sexualities at the Nation's Door: Nationalisms and Sexualities

Surely, if there is one question about nationalism that does not typically get asked, then it is whether nationalisms have sexualities. How can nationalisms have sexualities? The question may seem strange at first glance and so perhaps does not get posed frequently. But I would contend that if we don't dismiss this question out of hand, and instead consider it more carefully, it points us toward significant social issues. Idioms of virility and strength, of "colonial penetration," of rape and plunder of one nation by another, and of beauty pageants and sexual respectability routinely sexualize our language of nationalism. We use these sexualized idioms in order to imagine and give meaning to nationalisms. In the past, Iraq and Serbia have been described as rapacious nations. Other nationalisms, such as India and Korea, have been described with words like "chastity" and "modesty." In that sense the sexualization of nationalisms is no aberration but is the way we ascribe characteristics to nations and imagine nationalisms.

What of the other side of the equation? Can and do nationalisms exert influence on sexualities? The answer lies in the role that nationalisms play in shaping sexuality and the state's role in enforcing it. Whether widows can remarry, whether homosexuality is disallowed, whether HIV-positive visitors are allowed to enter a country, and the presence and significance of sex tourism in some countries are a few of the questions in which the state is active in defining and enforcing sexualities in our lives. Contrary to popular assumptions, then, sexuality is not simply a private part of our lives. We also think of the family, religion, and, especially in Euro-American countries, of the media as the central institutions that weigh in on our sexualities. The nation and state are no less important. Sometimes working in conjunction with these institutions and at other times in conflict with them, nations and states are equally important in shaping our sexualities.

While there seem to be compelling reasons for paying attention to the interconnections of nationalisms and sexualities, the issues have received comparatively little attention thus far. Scholars working in the area of sexualities often do not consider the importance of nationalism and the reverse is equally true; typically, sexuality research is conducted on national contexts but does not directly address questions of nationalisms or the role of the national state. Those who work in the area of nationalism, across disciplines such as political science, international relations, and sociology tend to ignore issues of sexuality altogether, perhaps out of a sense of discomfort in studying sexuality. It is only in the last few years that the subject has gradually gained acceptance; until now it has been the preserve of feminist and lesbian and gay studies scholars. As a result, the relatively small but insightful research on nationalisms and sexualities is based on their particular studies. If I were to summarize these scholars' primary motivations for studying nationalisms and sexualities, I would say that they are threefold: that nationalisms and states regulate the most seemingly private and personal aspects of our sexualities; that nationalisms and states promote what are considered respectable sexualities; and that how we organize our lives according to national and sexual identities are problematic and, often, woefully inadequate.

There is something awkward about separating out issues of sexualities and nationalisms from issues related to gender and nationalisms (see Chapter Three). Many feminist scholars, in particular, would strongly argue for a more integrative approach to understandings of sexuality, one that recognizes the inextricability of gender and sexuality. A valid argument, indeed. As readers may have noted in the previous chapter, in any discussion of nationalisms and genders, questions of sexuality are never far behind. In a parallel manner, exploring issues of sexuality without some discussion of gender would be virtually impossible. This, because social meanings of sexuality are profoundly gendered and gender is profoundly sexualized. But the field of gay and lesbian studies departs from this position in one important way: that though gender and sexuality might be profoundly linked, they are not synonymous. To summarize Eve Sedgwick's theme, the study of sexuality is not coextensive with the study of gender.[1] The previous chapter and this one are therefore meant to focus on two related but not exactly similar issues. These chapters complement each other while providing an opportunity to look at issues relevant to understanding the concept of nationalism and its pervasive effects in our lives today.

To revisit the questions posed above: do nationalisms have sexualities and do nationalisms and the state enforce sexualities? The short answer is "yes." Of course, the thoughtful answer is always more complicated and demands more detailed consideration.

Defining Sexuality

In 1999, the US was in the throes of an internationally publicized sexual scandal, involving the President, Bill Clinton. After charges that he had sexual relations with a young White House intern, Monica Lewinsky, and had lied about this liaison at a previous deposition, the US Senate considered whether the President should be impeached. In the Clinton–Lewinsky crisis, it was remarkable how the details of their sexual contact – the nature, frequency, products, and location – were linked with matters of national concern. There was endless speculation about the legal, ethical, moral, and social implications of Clinton's sexual liaison and, equally, about his attempt to cover up and lie about his behavior. No less important were questions whether Clinton had compromised his tasks as a president, whether the US looked weak as a nation, and whether the US was the subject of international ridicule as a result of either the President's behavior or the partisan political process that helped transform it into an international sexual and political spectacle.

A year earlier, the deputy Prime Minister of Malaysia, Anwar Ibrahim, was charged with, and later convicted for, sex crimes, including sodomy, which allegedly occurred between December 1993 and April 1998. It was widely believed that Prime Minister Mahathir trumped up these charges in a bid to damage the reputation of his political opponent. Earlier that year, a book was published in which graphic sexual allegations and accusations of corruption were made against Deputy Prime Minister Ibrahim. By September, he was arrested, as were two of his close associates, who later recanted their testimonies that they had engaged in "unnatural sex" and allowed Anwar Ibrahim to sodomize them. When he first appeared in public after his arrest, Anwar Ibrahim had bruises on his face and body, for which he blamed his captors. Similarly to the prosecution of President Clinton, Anwar Ibrahim's supporters challenged the partisan process aimed at politically discrediting him. However, where President Clinton was able to retain his political office, Anwar Ibrahim fell victim to a political power struggle. Both of these events generated much national and international speculation. What is of particular interest here is how each of these events brought national interests into the "bedroom," or, as the case suggested, into the Oval Office.

By turning our attention to these highly publicized national sexual matters, my intention is to think through how national interests and the functions of the state can relate to the most intricate and explicit details of people's sexual lives. Needless to say, both these events involved the prosecution of prominent public officials. As a qualifier, I would add that for the most part the reaches of the national state into our sexual lives are hardly this spectacular. But these events are useful as a starting point in two ways. For one, they help us acknowledge that nations and sexualities are not far removed from one another and are part of our social terrain. Secondly, when the more mundane aspects of our lives are considered in contrast with these spectacular events, the importance of considering the pervasive, commonplace aspects of nationalisms and sexualities should be thrown into sharp relief.

Sexuality is a notoriously difficult concept to define. In many ways it seems so obvious so as to not require any formal definition. It can be thought of as a set of practices that encompass pleasures, desires, feelings, attitudes, behaviors, norms, and taboos that are related to sexual activity. We consider sexuality a "natural" aspect of our lives and a private matter that requires little outside intervention as long as we are not in danger of harming others or ourselves, or breaking a significant social taboo. An example of such a sanction was a highly publicized case in the United States, in which a woman schoolteacher was convicted after pleading guilty to second-degree rape of a 13-year-old boy. The boy was young enough to be harmed and too young to give consent, thereby triggering her arrest. Contrast this with anecdotal and research-based reports on youth sexual behavior where boys and girls report having their first "voluntary" sexual experience with someone from their peer group when they were as young as 9 years old. While this is seen as cause for social concern, early sexual activity between adolescents (of sorts) is not seen as a prosecutable offense.

We also recognize sexuality as a matter of personal identity that is based on the object of one's desires, whether one is homosexual or heterosexual. According to this view, we are either one or the other, on the basis of our gender and the gender of the person that we desire. Sedgwick and others have noted how these sexual identities first emerged in the nineteenth century, where the term "homosexual" predated the word "heterosexual." What was new about these Euro-American developments in the last part of the nineteenth century, Sedgwick insists, was that every person was considered to have an assignable sexual identity.[2] Sexual identities were limited to two possibilities – either homosexual or heterosexual – and had implications for even the least sexual aspects of a person's existence. This homo/heterosexual dichotomy was crystallized and reinforced by the medical, legal, literary, and psychological institutions, according to Sedgwick. Despite a range of possibilities that can help determine a taxonomy of sexuality, such as age, power, frequency, preferences for certain acts, the remarkable aspect of these pervasive sexual identities is that they are based on the gender of the object of a person's desires. Exacerbated by widely prevalent inequalities between women and men and femininity and masculinity, these sexual identities became a site of intensive social regulation.

Whether these specific or parallel sexual identities of heterosexuality and homosexuality exist beyond the Euro-American pale has been a source of intense discussion in lesbian and gay studies. Writing about same-sex love and eroticism within the Indian context, scholar Ruth Vanita takes the position that sexual categories and identities have long existed in South Asia even though they may not operate in ways similar to Euro-American cultures.[3] For example, in India, where marriage overwhelmingly remains a social obligation for women and men, same-sex sexual relationships often exist alongside the privileges and obligations of marriage. It is not rare to find advertisements in gay and lesbian magazines circulated in India whereby a gay man solicits a lesbian for a marriage of convenience. Vanita and others have argued that even though sexual identities such as heterosexuality and homosexuality may not have the same connotations or the same currency everywhere, the concept of sexual identity is not simply a Euro-American invention with little relevance elsewhere.

One implication of the above observations is that little, if anything, may be natural about sexuality; a critical examination suggests that there is virtually no aspect of sexuality that is not societally shaped. Who can be sexually active and under what circumstances, where people can buy protection against sexually transmitted diseases, whether people can sell or buy sexual services, what are the punishments for sexual transgressions, and what is considered normal are issues that give pause to the belief that sexuality is a private matter.

On the contrary, whether in its most personal and intimate or most public expressions, sexuality has meaning only within the context of culture and in relation to power. By power, I refer to institutional mechanisms for social control, such as what is seen as normal and what is seen as deviant, and institutional mechanisms of reinforcing social inequalities such as gender, class, or race. Prevailing cultural beliefs, religion, the state, media, legal and medical institutions, gender, racial, and class differences implicitly or explicitly control what is acceptable, or normal, or frowned upon, or unacceptable, or where sexual desire has no meaning.

Seeing matters this way, we recognize that our sexualities, our seemingly most private and personal experiences, are socially regulated. Additionally, sexuality is also itself a conduit to broader social regulation and control in our lives. Social control that affects our personal pleasures and desires shapes more than the sexual realm; it shapes our identities, patterns of leisure and consumerism, national political beliefs and institutions, and so on. This is not to say that people do not resist sexual regulation by engaging in premarital sexual activity, same-sex sexual fantasies, or adultery in cultures where this might be strongly prohibited or at least frowned upon. But whether one plays by the rules or resists them, sexuality has meaning only within the context of culture, its mechanisms for social regulation, and creating and sustaining social inequalities.

Typically, we see sexual repression as the primary form of sexual control in our lives. Some national cultures, such as those of Iran and Afghanistan, are frequently cited as examples of sexual repression. But Euro-American cultures are not thought to be fully sexually liberated either. Calls to educate schoolchildren about sex, to end the sexual double standards that continue to exist between women and men, and to encourage frank and open discussions of sexuality in the United States come from those who believe in greater freedom, since repressing sexuality is one kind of social control too far. With predictable consistency and mind-numbing detail, any number of popular women's magazines, such as *Cosmopolitan*, *Glamour*, and *Elle*, routinely advise their readers how to lead sexually free and liberated lives.

There is a paradox here. In the United States, for example, it is hard to get away from discussions about sexuality, whether educational, popular, or titillating. Between the media, school, family, medical, and legal institutions the problem does not seem to be a lack of discussion on sexuality but an overload of it! This situation is not characteristic only of the United States but can be extrapolated to most cultural contexts. The problems in most places are not so much the repressions and silences in the area of sexuality, but the nature of the discussions and where they occur. This is precisely the starting point for Foucault's work on sexuality. Foucault argues that contrary to prevailing ideas, sexuality is not regulated through repression, but through incessant discussion and revelation.[4]

Through our day-to-day lives, through the legal and medical institutions, Foucault suggests, sexuality is controlled through expression of what's pleasurable, and what's normal. In this way, regulation defines, shapes, and limits sexual pleasure and sexual normality.

If sexuality is socially shaped and regulated so that certain forms of sexuality are permitted while others are deemed deviant, and people may resist and challenge these sexual norms, then it stands to reason that there are multiple forms of sexuality in any culture. Furthermore, there are tremendous variations in the area of sexuality that exist across and within cultures and the differences along lines of gender, class, race, ethnicity, religion, and sexual orientations. This is not to simply say that sexuality is a foundational concept with various inter- and intra-cultural differences. Instead, the position taken here is that there may not be consensus, either within or across cultures, about the meaning of sexuality or what counts as sexual; the concept of sexuality may itself be the subject of discussion and difference. For these reasons, it makes sense, whenever possible, to refer to this concept in its plural form, namely, as sexualities.

What does this approach to sexualities mean for a discussion on nationalisms? This approach acknowledges that sexualities may seem a personal issue but are, in fact, cultural practices that shape our personal lives and our social environment, including institutions such as the state and nationalism. This approach sees sexuality as a matter of personal identity, whether lesbian, gay, or heterosexual. Yet it acknowledges that matters and politics of sexuality are so deep-seated and pervasive that they shape how we imagine, express, and experience nationalism. Nationalisms may be expressed through idioms of sexuality and some forms of sexuality may be promoted as part of national cultural identity. Perhaps this is why poets and soldiers have celebrated their passionate love for their country sometimes in the most effusive, eroticized language; the nation is depicted like the beloved, the object of one's love and desire. At the same time, nations and states are key sources of the regulation of sexuality. Along with the family and the media, the nation and state help enforce social regulation by defining what is normal, rather than by repressing sexuality.

Nationalisms, National States, and the Regulation of Sexualities

In 1982, in the state of Georgia, USA, Michael Hardwick was summoned to appear in court and to pay a fine for drinking in public. When he did not do so, a warrant for his arrest was issued. This warrant was not recalled even though Hardwick subsequently did pay the fine. An officer, seeking to arrest Harwick, was inadvertently let into his house by a friend. What catapulted this event into the national limelight was that the officer saw Hardwick in his bedroom engaged in an act of oral sex with another man, behavior that is considered a felony in Georgia. The Georgia statute prohibited anyone, whether heterosexual or homosexual, from anal and oral sexual contact. Hardwick was thereafter charged with violating the law against sodomy. But this charge was initially ruled, by the state court, to have violated Hardwick's rights because his behavior was private and intimate. The case was then taken to the Supreme Court, which in 1996, in a landmark and far-reaching decision, reversed the Georgia state judgment out of concerns about "gay sex."

At one level, one might assume that the United States Supreme Court has little business adjudicating harmless sexual acts between two consenting adults in the privacy of a home. But taking the view that the majority of people in Georgia see homosexual sodomy as immoral, the Supreme Court refused to protect "homosexual sodomy" from being prosecuted as a criminal act and declared that there was no "fundamental right to engage in homosexual sodomy."[5] That this Supreme Court decision discriminated against certain sexual behaviors is inarguable but it did so by criminalizing "homosexual sodomy" and leaving unaddressed the question of "heterosexual sodomy" even though the Georgia statute did encompass it. The ramifications of this explicit focus on homosexuals and tacit silence on heterosexuals will be more fully explored below.

Sedgwick and others note that not only did this decision open a season of gay bashing while implicitly protecting heterosexuals, but it also had the backing of national tradition. Justice White, who wrote the majority opinion had this to say: "to claim that a right to engage in sodomy is 'deeply rooted in this nation's history and tradition' or 'implicit in the concept of ordered liberty' is, at best, facetious."[6] This case shows us how the most private, personal sexual acts can be matters of regulation by the institutions of the national state. What this legal decision also indicates is how representatives of the state can disavow homosexuality and, no less, sexualize national cultural tradition from a heterosexual perspective.

Regulating marginal groups

One striking pattern in this regulation of sexuality by national states is that marginal groups including gay women and men, and men more broadly seen as sexually deviant, are mostly targeted. With the exception of a few nations, gay, lesbian, and bisexual women and men are the objects of repressive state regulation. In the US, the denial of the right to marry or openly serve in the military is not merely a matter of limiting the personal choices of non-heterosexual people, but of withholding some of the benefits of citizenship that married couples or soldiers enjoy. In numerous nation states, lesbian and gay activists are attempting to undo legal prohibitions against homosexual behavior that were made under colonial law. In her study of homosexuality in Zimbabwe, Margrete Aarmo notes that homosexuality is regulated by common law, which was the outcome of colonial Roman-Dutch law.[7] Even though there is no specific law preventing people from being homosexual, homosexual acts are illegal and punishable. Sexual practices that are considered lawful when they take place between women and men become criminalized when they occur between two people of the same sex. Zimbabwe is hardly unusual in this direct regulation of homosexuality by the state.

Men who are seen as especially prone to deviant sexual behavior are often carefully monitored by the state and its affiliates. Estelle Freedman analyzes the attention to sexual crimes and the notion of the "sexual psychopath" that was prevalent between 1935 and 1965 in the US.[8] At the time, the state, psychiatry, and the media all turned their attention to violent sex crimes committed by male sexual psychopaths even though there was no real rise in sex crimes that necessitated this approach or additional laws. The director of the Federal Bureau of Investigation, J. Edgar Hoover, fueled the national hysteria and called for greater law enforcement, Freedman says. Hoover declared a "war on the sex criminal" and claimed that the sex fiend had become a threat to the safety of American children and women.[9] Freedman makes the point that this was less a concern for the safety of children and women than it was a way to distinguish between perverse and normal behavior, and between normal sexuality and homosexuality. Public outrage over rare and shocking kinds of sexual deviance confirmed the normality of procreative, conventional sexual behavior. Even though these concerns brought sexuality into the public arena, as Freedman points out, what was ignored in this focus on the pathology of sex crime perpetrators were the more routine and heterosexual forms of sexual violence that are directed at women and children. The more unusually sexually deviant men are disproportionately under attack while usual sexual violence disappears into the social background.

Depending on their social class and cultural context, women can also be subject to surveillance by the state, especially when they are outside the purview of respectable womanhood, for being sex workers, lesbians, unmarried, or widows, for example. The state is often the vehicle for subjecting the perceived threat of female sexuality to existing social order through legislative or social control. One of the most prominent concerns in the US in the 1990s was welfare or the Aid to Families with Dependent Children. The AFDC was initially formulated to aid single, indigent women with children, and was thoroughly reformed in 1996. It was primarily motivated by the specter of sexual degeneracy of poor women of color, who were thought to be getting a "free ride" by having children and becoming permanently dependent on the state.

In the preamble of the Act aimed at welfare reform, known as the Personal Responsibility and Work Opportunity Reconciliation Act, it is stated: "1: marriage is the foundation of a successful society; 2: marriage is an essential institution of a successful society which promotes the interests of children."[10] While middle-class and professional women can be encouraged to regulate their sexuality and childbearing within marriage, poor women are more vulnerable to enforcement by state laws. Notwithstanding indications to the contrary, i.e. that women do not have "irresponsible sex" and bear children as economic incentives, and that women are dependent on state aid not from choice but from lack of alternatives, the specter of sexual irresponsibility among poor women of color garnered widespread support for this Act. The point here is not simply the regulation and surveillance of women's sexuality that has long existed in most cultural contexts and pre-modern states. Rather, it is that this regulation and surveillance carries the weight of the modern state acting on behalf of national interests, and with the force of national culture and values.

Sex tourism, national development, and the state

The commerce and politics of sex tourism in particular provide a useful glimpse into how the role of the nation state in regulating sexuality and protecting national interests is rarely simple. As a strategy of development for Third World and poorer countries, tourism has been systematically encouraged by international financial agencies and frequently wholeheartedly adopted by these nation states. Enloe points to a fundamental contradiction of tourism, namely, that tourism can make the poverty of poor countries into a magnet that attracts foreign tourists and foreign currency.[11] Rather than an anomaly, sex tourism can be a systematic part of national development in some Third World countries. Bangkok particularly has been described as the global brothel.[12] Perhaps no other place has been more thoroughly scrutinized by journalists, feminist scholars, or student activists for its sex tourism than this city. I refer to this case to show how it exposes the role of the state in actively supporting this form of commerce. Thailand is unusual in its scope, but is joined in this trade by a wide range of national states, such as Korea, India, Indonesia, and Holland. If we consider Thailand an indicator of patterns and trends that are widely pervasive, not only in the countries just mentioned, but also in Malaysia, Bangladesh, Cambodia, the Philippines, and countries in Eastern Europe, it might offer useful insights into the regulation of sexuality through acts of omission and commission by the state to protect national interests.

In 1967, the United States government contracted with the Thai government to provide "rest and recreation" for American GIs at the time of the Vietnam War.[13] A 1992 survey by the Thai Health Ministry estimated that there were 76,863 prostitutes nationwide and 20,366 in Bangkok, estimates that were later known to be absurdly low.[14] In the 1980s, there were 400,000 more women than men living in Bangkok, but male tourists outnumbered female tourists by more than three to one, giving us a sense of who purchased and who provided sexual services.[15] Businessmen and tourists from Japan, United States, Korea, and India and other countries continue to flock toward the promise of sex tourism. Sex workers are typically recruited from poor rural families with lump sum payments that help the family subsist. Directly or indirectly coerced into prostitution by pimps, business owners, acquaintances, and family members, women and young children are the most vulnerable and the exploited in this sex trade. Groups such as EMPOWER (Education Means Protection of Women Engaged in Recreation) have attempted to help sex workers by preventing their exploitation and providing alternative employment, but with limited success.

The reason, however, that sex work remains an enduring problem in Thailand and other countries is that sex tourism and tourism in general are entrenched in the economy. In a particularly influential book on the Thai sex industry, *Night Market*, Ryan Bishop and Lillian Robinson note that a United Nations conference in Rome in 1963 marked the official support by the World Bank and the United States of tourism in developing nations. Tourism was seen as an effective strategy of national development. The United States Department of Commerce published a document (1961) that actively encouraged tourism in developing nations and lent it its support. Like Jamaica, among other nations, Thailand relies not only on tourism for its economic development, but also on sex tourism.

Tourist brochures extol the beauty of Thailand and its women, but sex tourism is only obliquely mentioned. Bishop and Robinson note that while sex tourism is implicitly acknowledged as a state strategy of national development it is directly addressed only in the context of the threat posed by HIV and AIDS.[16] Paradoxically, sex work is still illegal, but there is little attempt to enforce the law. In Bangkok and elsewhere in the Third World, the law is ignored by pimps, business owners, the police, and tourism officials. This heightens the exploitation of women and makes them more vulnerable to their customers, the pimps, the businesses, and the state. Indeed, other legal provisions have enough loopholes to permit prostitution. Along with Bangkok, some of the major cities in the world also rely on income from this industry. But what makes this all of this reprenhensible is the complicity of the state and various groups in promoting the exploitation of women, implicitly, on the basis of national economic interests.

Endorsing Respectable Sexuality and Nationalism

In the above discussion of national and state regulation of sexualities, an implicit point about influencing sexual norms has probably gradually become obvious. To put it explicitly: a central aspect of regulating sexualities is to determine what counts as normal and what is abnormal. This was one reason why I dwelled on Foucault's argument that this regulation may be less about repression and more about shaping the differences between normal and abnormal. One way to approach the issue of normalization of sexuality and its connection to nationalism and the state is to look at how "respectable sexuality" is defined. At heart, the fundamental link between respectable sexuality and nationalism is that what may be ideals or customs of dominant groups are endorsed as national ideals, and socially and legally, albeit unevenly, enforced. The other side of this respectable sexuality is the supposed abnormal or deviant. These definitions of normality and deviance frequently correspond to heterosexuality and homosexuality.

The key point is that these distinctions of normal and abnormal sexualities, i.e. respectable and deviant sexualities, or the heterosexual and the homosexual, are mutually dependent. Examining these distinctions more carefully will shed light on the ways in which nationalisms and nation states privilege certain kinds of sexualities as they devalue others.

Defining respectable sexualities

Morality has become a euphemism for sex. To be moral is to be asexual, (hetero)sexual or sexual in ways that presumably carry the weight of the "natural."[17]

With his book, *Nationalism and Sexuality: Respectability and Abnormal Sexuality in Modern Europe*, George Mosse broke new ground by looking at the interdependence of nationalism and sexuality across modern Germany and England. In this unprecedented scholarship, Mosse persuasively argued that nationalisms are connected to notions of respectability, meaning "decent and correct" manners, which refer to decorum as well as modesty, purity, and the practice of virtue, morals, and proper attitudes toward sexuality.[18] Although conventional standards of behavior have always been present, in the nineteenth century the concept of respectability became the primary way of understanding the human body and sexuality. Especially in the middle classes, respectability allowed people to maintain a façade of high standing and self-respect, while distinguishing them from both the working classes and the aristocracy. Frugality, devotion to duty, and restraint of passion were seen as the hallmarks of this respectability and as the superior qualities that differentiated the middle classes from others.

But by the beginning of the twentieth century, Mosse notes, respectability was no longer limited to the middle classes and firmly entrenched across various social levels in Germany. Nationalism was the vehicle for the spread of sexual respectability. What were middle-class status markers were re-invented as national cultural tradition and ideals to be absorbed by all classes in Germany. Mosse suggests that German nationalism promoted respectability, helped disseminate it, and keep its essence intact while enlarging its parameters. The German "life-reform" movement and its surprising preoccupation with nudism illustrated how these intertwined beliefs of nationalism and sexual respectability were put into practice.[19] For the life-reform movement, nude bodies that were set against natural settings of meadows, gardens, or the sea in life-reform magazines were venerated as national symbols of strength, beauty, and sexual innocence. The conservative, right wing of the life-reform movement took a more intense position on these issues of the body, respectability, and nationalism. Although the left wing of the reform movement saw nudism as part of the overall emancipation of the human body from the harsh demands of labor, the conservative nationalist wing took the stance that nudism furthered nationalist concerns by promoting the regeneration of the race, reconciling social differences, ranking "the people" according to character and physique. Rather than connoting lust, nudism under the right circumstances implied sexual innocence and national sexual respectability.

As part of this effort to maintain national sexual respectability, nationalists also felt compelled to draw the line between normal and abnormal sexuality.[20] In its simplest manifestation, normal sexuality meant reproduction, elimination of non-reproductive sexual practices, and promotion of moral and physical health. Therefore, specific forms of heterosexuality, aimed at supporting the national struggle for survival by reproducing a morally and physically fit people, were the essence of sexual normality. Sexual abnormality was consequently defined as non-procreative sexual practices, vices that were seen as sapping a man's strength or virility, or practices that led to his physical or moral weakness. Homosexuality and masturbation were seen as the crux of sexual deviance and against the interests of the nation, Mosse shows. Moral purity, preventing vices such as homosexuality and masturbation, was advocated in the nation's struggle to survive. But the repugnance was not limited to homosexual acts; rather, the homosexual came to embody sexual abnormality. As a result of the medical scholarship of the nineteenth century, homosexual abnormality was not about sexual acts but about the entire person, his personality and his psychology. So, if national sexual respectability was signified by reproductive heterosexuality then homosexuality came to represent sexual abnormality in modern Germany.

In contemporary life, ideas of sexual respectability, heterosexuality, and sexual normality are often targeted at young people, especially young women. The threat of HIV/AIDS infections has intensified attempts to regulate the behavior of sexual deviants but also promoted sexual respectability. Perusing sex-education materials published by the Family Planning Association of India (FPAI), I was struck by how a seemingly straightforward question of sex before marriage was cast as a matter of national tradition and identity. Although FPAI is a nongovernmental organization, it works closely with the state and reflects prevailing attitudes toward sexuality and nationalism. First published in October 1975, and updated in December 1990, *Teenagers Ask, The Doctor Answers* has this to say on the matter of premarital sexual intercourse:

> *Question*: Am I old fashioned because I think differently from my friends who think it is all right to have sexual intercourse before marriage?
> *Answer*: Generally every person has a right to his own opinions in personal matters. Believing in sexual intercourse after marriage does not make you

old-fashioned at all. In fact, in the context of Indian morality (which does not approve of the "free sex" attitude of the West), you are perfectly right.

Every girl indulging in free sex runs the risk of having an unwanted baby and becoming an unmarried mother. Every year in this country such avoidable tragedies are increasing. Premarital sex being furtive and snatched in dark corners causes tension due to the fear of being found out. Also both the boy and girl can develop venereal disease and AIDS, which can have serious effects on their lives.

Finally, except in rare instances, sex outside marriage often means the loss of love, warmth, kindness and understanding, that are so essential in sustaining a meaningful relationship between the two people involved.[21]

Clearly, the family and the relevant customs of ethnic or religious communities may all bear on personal decisions such as whether to have sex before marriage. The above quotation also points to matters of national culture and morality, a position made possible by posing Indian national traditions against the "free sex" attitudes of the West; sexual activity belongs within marriage according to national customs and traditions. Agencies affiliated with the state take on the task of promoting respectable sexuality. What's important here is that sexuality is to be regulated not by simply denying or repressing. Another way to put this is that sex is normalized within marriage and given the backing of national cultural tradition. The unspoken part of this social mandate, of course, are implicit references to deviant behavior: premarital sex, extramarital sex, sex between people of the same gender, sex workers and their customers, among others.

In line with the above were the opinions of middle- and upper-class women in Mumbai and New Delhi about matters of gender and sexuality. Thirty-four of the 53 women asked about premarital sexual activity also endorsed the links between heterosexuality, sexual respectability, and the national cultural tradition.[22] These women implicitly or explicitly confirmed the importance of chastity for women before and outside of marriage as traditional. Oddly enough, a number of these women had themselves subverted the principle of premarital chastity. On the other hand, one young woman crystallized the connections between respectable sexuality and nationalism in her response to my question about premarital sexual practices. She said that she and her fiancé did not have sexual relations prior to their wedding because, "We are not of that mental outlook, being Indians."[23] Complicating the responses of these middle- and upper-class women in urban India is that which counts as chastity or sexual respectability is by no means unambiguous. Yet sexual practices seem to be spontaneously linked with national cultural identity and tradition.

Not infrequently, respectable sexuality, especially for women, is limited to procreative sexuality. In Chapter Three, we considered the regulation of women's reproduction in the interests of the nation as an example of the interconnections between gender and nationalisms. Geraldine Heng and Janadas Devan's exploration of Singapore tells us more about the links between nationalisms and respectable sexualities.[24] Singapore's Prime Minister, Lee Kuan Yew, charged the nation's women with endangering the nation's future through misdirected sexual practices. The problem, as Lee saw it, was that professional and working-class, Malay, Indian, and Chinese women's reproductive rates were falling, owing to failure to marry or lack of desire to bear children. Instead, married women were enjoined to bear at least three children as their patriotic duty. Underlying this gendered notion of citizenship and national duty was the need to favor women's sexuality within marriage in so far as it was procreative. In contrast, what was unacceptable was women's sexuality that was pleasure-driven and unproductive of babies, or even productive of babies for their own sake, according to Heng and Devan.

Nationalisms' Recourse to the Dualities of Homosexual/Heterosexual

An influential book, *Nationalisms and Sexualities*, starts with the questions, "How is it that the world has come to see itself divided along the seemingly natural lines of national affiliation and sexual attachment? How do these categories interact with, constitute, or otherwise illuminate each other?"[25] With these questions, the editors, Parker and others, highlight two crucial aspects of our selves and identities and ask us to consider how it seems normal that each of us would have a national identity and a sexual identity. Taking its cue from the work of Foucault and Mosse, this collection asks readers to consider how nationalisms and sexualities, national and sexual identities are deeply interconnected and mutually formative. These identities influence how we think of ourselves, the kinds of rights and resources that are available to us, and also to which communities we belong – let us suppose, African-American lesbian.

This is not to say that national or sexual identities are clear or unambiguous. This position will be more carefully elaborated below, but a couple of examples might be useful here. In the Philippines, the *Bakla* are people who are born male but are seen as a third gender, somewhere between women and men. When a *Bakla* has sexual relations with a normative man, the uncertainty whether that counts as homosexuality or a form of

heterosexuality (given the gender differences between *Baklas* and men),
illustrates that distinctions between heterosexuality and homosexuality
may not be easily drawn.[26] In the same vein, David Eng and others have
pointed out that seen from the perspective of Asian Americans, a generic
American national identity is neither inclusive nor adequate. Instead, un-
failingly constructed as immigrants, they remain suspended between arrival
and departure, between Asia and America.[27] Perhaps what best illustrates
the ambivalences of identities – sexual and national – in the United States are
the debates over the hyphens used in adjectives such as "Asian-American."
For Kamala Visweswaran, the hyphen marks the complicated choices of
immigration and the desire to be both "here" and "there."[28] The hyphen,
when used in "Asian-American," represents a kind of shuttling between
two or more worlds and a doubtful attempt to assimilate within the national
community as citizens, Visweswaran believes.

If the dualities of sexuality or national identity appear inadequate given
the complexities of our lives, then the editors of *Nationalisms and Sexualities*
show further concerns about how these categories help preserve underlying inequalities. Here is the rub of sexual identities: in most societies,
heterosexuality and homosexuality are not equally treated. Nationalisms
are expressed through idioms of heterosexuality and the state helps make
heterosexuality seem normal and self-evident in our lives. In contrast, as
reflected in above examples, forms of homosexuality tend to be more
carefully scrutinized and often punished. One hopeful response to this
inequality has been the emergence of various gay movements in countries
– too many to numerate – including Euro-American nations but also
Third World countries. The heightened surveillance of homosexuality
coupled with the emergence of lesbian and gay movements has helped
shape notions of "homosexual communities," and kept the focus on
homosexuality.

The heterosexual community, on the other hand? The awkwardness of
determining "the heterosexual community" is partly due to the fact that
heterosexuality is established as the norm and, therefore, cannot be easily
restricted to the notion of community. This is the basis for the criticisms
that Janet Halley makes of the Supreme Court's approach to the Bowers
v. Hardwick case mentioned above.[29] Her point is that by targeting
"homosexuals" the Supreme Court helped define homosexuals as a class
on the basis of sexual behavior, curtailed the possibility for equal rights for
homosexuals, and, equally disturbingly, protected heterosexual behaviors
simply by not acknowledging them.

To re-state the point, then, heterosexuality is implicitly and explicitly
promoted in national cultural and political contexts. Most readers may be

well aware that gay, lesbian, bisexual, and transgendered people are often denied the same privileges as heterosexuals. But we do not always stop to think about the ways in which heterosexuals are openly or subtly accorded a broad range of benefits within the nation state. There is no clearer indicator of the power of heterosexuality than the fact that it appears to be "natural" and unremarkable. Nonetheless, social, political, and cultural institutions of the national state tend to promote some forms of heterosexuality while disparaging or marginalizing others. Benefits of citizenship are accrued by people who count as heterosexual whereas non-heterosexuals are wrongfully denied such privileges. This has implications not only for people's personal lives but also for nationalisms and social, economic, and political policies of various institutions of the nation state.

In Euro-American contexts in particular, gay and lesbian studies has invigorated the study of sexuality and made valuable contributions. Perhaps counterintuitively, one of this field's most important insights has been critically to explore heterosexuality. The stress on heterosexuality is partly motivated by the argument that homosexuality and heterosexuality exist only in relation to one another. Jonathan Katz finds that Euro-American medical researchers in the last third of the nineteenth century invented the concept of heterosexuality while elaborating new ideas of perversion and deviance, which came to be reflected in the concept of homosexuality.[30] Katz and others have persuasively pointed to the mutual interdependence of the two concepts of homosexuality and heterosexuality; they give meaning to each other so as to make heterosexuality seem normal and homosexuality seem abnormal or deviant; but neither concept would exist without the other. Therefore, if one is to understand homosexuality more fully, one also needs to consider heterosexuality seriously. But focusing entirely on how homosexuality is socially marginalized would be inadvertently to reinforce heterosexuality as normal. Analyzing how certain sexual practices are made to seem normal is equally important to research into how other practices are made to seem abnormal. In other words, both the normal and the abnormal, heterosexuality and homosexuality are socially constructed; if homosexuality is not "natural," then neither is heterosexuality.

The heterosexual nation?

One outcome of the linking of sexuality with national identity and tradition is that the national state and nationalisms are presented through a heterosexual lens. This is what Jacqui Alexander says about the Bahamas and its striving toward national development.[31] She charges that no nationalism could survive without heterosexuality, however violent and coercive it may be; heterosexuality still remains conducive to nation-building. The strategy of national development in the case of the Bahamas hinged on tourism, and promised an idyllic resort, free of western influence and – implicitly – of gay people. Alexander says that the state specifically relied on imperial and heterosexualized symbols of un-spoiled, virgin territory that was waiting to be discovered and a land steeped in pathos and mystery. This was coupled with colorful and sexu-alized images of black women and men, who promised a warm, congenial and service-oriented welcome to primarily (north) American tourists. Less than respectable sexualities, on the other hand, in the form of lesbian or gay sex or prostitution were deliberately hidden by the state. This, despite the fact that state authorities were not only well aware of prostitution but in fact relied on it as part of the unadvertised tourist attraction.

The role of the national state in regulating national identity, hetero-sexuality, and homosexuality typically carries the force of law. Examining the Sexual Offences Bill that was signed into law in Trinidad and Tobago in 1986, Alexander says that in this case the struggle to link sexuality and morality ended up regulating what was seen as sexual deviance, limiting women's sexual rights in marriage, and regulating women and men's sexual relationships within marriage.[32] What was new about this bill is that it attempted to criminalize new areas of sexual activity while decrim-inalizing other areas. It was aimed at changing the moral fabric of society. While the bill prohibited employers from taking advantage of their "minor" employees at the workplace and criminalized rape within mar-riage, it decriminalized "buggery" committed in private between consent-ing adults, be they two men or a husband and a wife. The ensuing public furor over the criminalization of sexual assault within marriage and decriminalization of gay sex led to a redraft, a significantly different account of what counted as public morality. Not only were the provisions against sexual assault completely watered down and homosexual sex recriminalized, but also lesbian sex involving a person 16 or older became punishable under a new category of "serious indecency." Alexander directs our attention to the way the state arbitrated on sexual relations between women and men, promoting the interests of men within marriage, and limiting women's rights as wives. In so doing, the state actively restricted permissible sexual activities and notions of morality.

Heterosexuality, homosexuality, and HIV/AIDS

Looking at the internal politics of national states and nationalisms with respect to HIV/AIDS is further revealing of distinctions between normal and abnormal sexualities, and also their troubling ramifications. In her discussion on homosexuality in Zimbabwe, Aarmo details the unashamed public expression of homophobia by President Mugabe in 1995.[33] Mugabe expressed a common perception that homosexuality does not exist in African cultures, that it is deeply offensive to the moral cultural fiber, that it is something imposed by foreign cultures, that it is about the inversion of sex roles, and that no rights could be accorded to people avowing such identities. A similar attitude led Dr. K. Abhayambika, a professor of medicine and state AIDS program officer in Kerala, India, to say,

> Even at the end of the twentieth century, the Eastern culture is untinged in its tradition of high morality, monogamous marriage system and safe sex behavior. Our younger generation and youth still practice virginity till their nuptial day. The religious customs and God-fearing living habits are a shield of protection against social evils. It will be difficult for the HIV to penetrate this shield except in certain metropolitan populations.[34]

The tragic irony of these statements is that it is estimated that one out of nine people who are currently HIV-positive is Indian.[35]

The privileging of heterosexuality and the marginalization of what are deemed deviant or abnormal sexualities can have complicated consequences for policies of nation states. HIV/AIDS and strategies of how to prevent new infections and the death of people currently infected, and how to manage and alleviate currently infected people's health and social problems, foreground how these policies are riven with the unequal dualities of sexuality and national identities. Cindy Patton has addressed these issues in her work on HIV/AIDS.[36] Patton notes that AIDS-control efforts invented a category of "African AIDS" that was associated with heterosexuality and the "African family." Despite wide cultural differences and differences in patterns of HIV/AIDS incidence in the continent of Africa, Patton suggests that in the 1980s Euro-American media and scientists saw African AIDS as Pattern Two. (Pattern One was identified as being the result of homosexual behavior and drug infections in the West, and Pattern Three marked those other than people in Africa or the West where HIV/AIDS was seen as the result of sex tourism and international bloodbanking.) African AIDS was seen as a heterosexual phenomenon, as if homosexuality and drug-use does not exist there, and attributed to practices such as polygamy. The South African President, Thabo Mbeki, who to his credit highlighted the importance of correlating incidence of poverty with rates of HIV/AIDS, nonetheless also disavowed the part played by homosexuality in HIV/AIDS prevalence in the country; he endorsed the approach that African AIDS was a heterosexual phenomenon.

Not only does this approach obscure the complexities of HIV/AIDS across the continent of Africa, but also, Patton persuasively notes, these characterizations bolstered notions that in the West HIV/AIDS was limited to homosexual males.[37] Implicitly, heterosexual males in the West were absolved of the need to practice safe sex. In effect, the dualities of homosexuality and African and Euro-American AIDS protected the heterosexual men in the US from sexual surveillance or restrictions on their sexual practices. In contrast to the outright privileging of heterosexuality, homosexual HIV/AIDS was targeted in the US. This is an example of how Africa becomes homogenized and characterized by "traditional" heterosexuality to the detriment of AIDS-control there.

The example illustrates more than the complexities and inequalities of heterosexuality and homosexuality that are attached to nationalisms, especially since "Africa" and the "West" cannot be strictly defined as nationalisms; it points us toward the inequalities between national states in the global arena of sexuality and, more specifically, in the fight to control HIV/AIDS. Writers Salih Booker and William Miner use the term "global apartheid" to gesture toward the fundamental global inequalities that constrain efforts effectively to control HIV/AIDS.[38] They describe the signs of global apartheid as differential access to basic human rights, differences in wealth and power that are consonant with race and place, racism embedded in global economic processes and institutions, and the practice of international double standards that do not uphold the same rights for others. Perhaps this is what leads Ramòn Castellblanch to note that each day 5,500 people die of AIDS in sub-Saharan Africa. Even though Saturday is traditionally the day for funerals, a Kenyan minister said that so many people are dying there that "we bury each day of the week."[39] Perhaps the most telling example of the constraints on some national states with high incidences of HIV/AIDS are the efforts by the South African government to make available drugs to HIV-infected people at cheaper prices or free of cost. Pharmaceutical companies such as Bristol-Myers Squibb and Merck sought help from the United States government to pressure the South Africa state by threatening to withdraw

United States aid if South Africa did not stop importing cheaper, generic versions of the drugs. HIV/AIDS incidence may not be entirely attributable to sexual behaviors, but this phenomenon certainly reveals inequalities between national states in the efforts toward AIDS-control.

Looking at Nationalisms from a Queer Perspective[40]

In light of the marginalization of homosexualities by nationalisms and less than equal rights granted to gay, lesbian, and bisexual citizens, what possibilities are there for the unequivocal inclusion of lesbian, gay, bisexual, and transgendered peoples into the community of nations or the reimagination of nationalisms from alternative perspectives? In his article on the exclusion of gays and lesbians from participation in the affairs of the nation and the possibility of their inclusion, Richard K. Herrell says that three areas of social life are crucial to the meaning of "good citizens" in the United States.[41] He identifies religious association, family life, and local politics as the crucial spaces where homosexuality is marginalized. In reaction to this, he argues, the banding together in lesbian and gay politics since the 1960s, in order to bring change in the public policy on HIV/AIDS, has been useful in claiming to be citizens of the nation.

But this strategy, which may be possible in the United States, may not be applicable elsewhere. The promotion of individual rights of lesbian, gay, transgendered, and bisexual people may be only partly effective especially when these individual rights come into conflict with collective or communal rights. In her discussion on homosexuality in Zimbabwe and President Mugabe's unashamed public expression of homophobia that was mentioned above, Aarmo shows how the more individual rights-based language of lesbian and gay identities can go only so far. She suggests that organizations such as Gays and Lesbians in Zimbabwe (GALZ) and social practices and activities, such as drag shows, help them to find alternatives to their exclusions from national life, church, and family.[42] However, she finds, demanding rights as gays or lesbians often elicits counter-accusations of being westernized or culturally inauthentic, thereby creating the backlash against them.

Echoing the complexities of including homosexualities in non-Euro-American nations, Tan beng hui notes that there is greater surveillance of female sexuality and, in particular, deviant female sexuality as part of the larger project of nation-building in contemporary Malaysia.[43] In a highly publicized case, a 21-year-old Malay woman impersonated a man in order to marry another woman. While impersonating a man may not seem effective in the long-term search for equality as citizens for lesbians, transgendered, bisexual, and gay people, beng hui says that gender impersonation is one available strategic means to challenge the exclusion of deviant female sexuality in Malaysia. Clearly, then, there is not a single strategy for the inclusion of citizens of various sexual orientations into the national community.

If elsewhere I made the argument that mere inclusion, without substantially reimagining the national community, is insufficient, then a relevant question is whether nationalisms can be imagined from a non-heterosexual or queer perspective. Although the term "queer" can be variously defined, here I refer to it as an approach that does not take heterosexuality as its normal and natural starting point and includes people who are gay, lesbian, bisexual, transgendered, two-spirited, transvestites, or third-gendered. Furthermore, a queer approach, including the work of Sedgwick mentioned early on in this chapter, remains skeptical of the mere divisions between homosexuality and heterosexuality. Therefore, whether there can be an "imagined community" of citizens that does not privilege heterosexuality or reproduce the problems of dual categories of sexual difference is the question.

Queer Nation, founded at an ACT UP meeting in New York in 1990, is perhaps the clearest example of a national community imagined from a non-heterosexual perspective. In their definitive article on the nature and politics of Queer Nation, Lauren Berlant and Elizabeth Freeman describe its premise and the limitations.[44] Queer Nation changed putative meanings of nationalism to reimagine lesbian, gay, bisexual, and transgendered sexualities at its core. This approach used an "in-your-face" politics to appropriate national icons from day-to-day life to make them safe for all persons, every day. Queer Nation appropriated the most corporate of spaces, including the shopping mall and the print and advertising media, to position homosexuality as a "product" that consumers find both pleasurable and unsettling in order to transform public culture; it wanted to manipulate the commodification of sex to imagine an alternate nation, one that does not draw distinctions between normal and abnormal sexualities. Indeed, a wide range of sexualities was foregrounded in representations of the nation. But, if Queer Nation can undermine separations between straight and gay politics only through notions of queer identity, then it has not been able to avoid the assimilationist pitfalls of American nationalism, say Berlant and Freedman.

Undoubtedly, Queer Nation poses an intriguing alternative by raising the possibility of a national community that is pleasure- and consumer-centered and that does not reproduce the distinctions between homosexuality and heterosexuality. Nonetheless, like other forms of official nationalisms, Queer Nation privileges a particular citizen-perspective. In this case, a queer, white, male subject is at the center of Queer Nation's insurgent politics. In so far as ethnic, racial, economic, and immigrant differences are ignored, Berlant and Freeman find that Queer Nation also mimics misplaced notions of a homogenous and inclusive nation that are true of official American nationalism. Therefore, the idea of Queer Nation is hardly free from the politics of inclusion and exclusion that is the questionable basis of hegemonic nationalisms to begin with.

Why this persistent search for national communities? Eng questions what he calls an enduring yearning for contained boundaries where the national state and home are neatly aligned as the privileged location for the benefits of citizenship.[45] Gayatri Gopinath suggests that this nostalgia shapes Berlant and Freeman's analysis of Queer Nation.[46] Although they point out the exclusionary potential of Queer Nation by showing that it privileges the white, male queer subject, they nonetheless see Queer Nation as strategic in redefining notions of citizenship and nationality. Nevertheless, Gopinath argues that by side-stepping the vexed relation of many queers of color to the disciplinary and regulatory mechanisms of the state and the nation, Berlant and Freeman do in fact support an exclusive and exclusionary vision of nation. Perhaps more than anything else, exploring the example of Queer Nation tells us much about the persistent effects of nationalisms, even or especially for groups that are typically relegated outside official nationalisms. Queer Nation also suggests that perhaps the search for inclusive nations is inherently fraught. The problem may not be a matter of "good nationalisms" or "bad nationalisms," but that enduring inequalities related to race, gender, sexuality, ethnicity, class, and religion make inclusionary nationalism virtually impossible.

Conclusion

Comparatively little attention has been given to issues of sexuality by scholars writing on nationalism, and vice versa. To be sure, some researchers have shown how nationalisms are colored by the idiom of sexuality and how nations and states have systematically promoted certain kinds of sexualities and sexual behaviors in the interests of nationalisms. The relatively little attention to this area despite its relevance is therefore more striking. In an effort to bridge the gap in this area, this chapter drew upon a limited but rich body of literature in order to consider the juncture between nationalism and sexuality.

This chapter was built around the ways in which national states both promote and regulate sexualities. Contrary to the view that sexuality is essentially a private matter under little institutional control, we took the approach that sexuality is a particularly important site for state regulation on behalf of national interests. Taking our cue from the work of Foucault, we understood regulation not simply as restriction or denial but also through promotion of respectable sexuality. Therefore, while "deviant sexualities" are closely monitored and regulated through laws and law enforcement, respectable sexualities are simultaneously encouraged by the state through prescriptions of normality.

Furthermore, nationalisms are themselves cast within a sexualized framework. Most typically, the idiom of heterosexuality and the nation as made up of heterosexuals is embraced. If nationalisms and states seem to avow "normal" sexualities while disavowing "abnormal" sexualities, it is hardly coincidental. The underlying question explored was how do national and sexual identities become so effectively entwined and to what effect. While normal sexualities are embraced and abnormal sexualities are frequently displaced on to other nationalities, as was especially evident in the discussion of so-called patterns of HIV/AIDS, the links between respectable sexualities and nationalisms are not uncomplicated. But it would be no overstatement to say that the links between nationalisms and normal sexualities make for unequal citizens of the national community.

A final aspect that was explored in this chapter had to do with looking at alternative possibilities of nationalisms. Turning the concept of nationalism to examine it through the lens of sexuality, we raised the possibility of nationalisms from the perspective of the marginalized. What was intriguing about Queer Nation is that it remained critical of the dualities of heterosexuality and homosexuality. Queer activists have argued that maintaining the boundaries between these sexual dichotomies does not make for an effective politics in the long term. To this purpose, Queer Nation took a more pleasure-driven, consumer-oriented approach to the concept of nation. Yet, as critics point out, Queer Nation was unable to avoid the pitfalls of official nationalisms. Like its more dominant versions, Queer Nation implicitly promoted a national community from the perspectives of gay, white males. Perhaps the more important lesson here was the limitations of nations as imagined communities. It is either a poverty of our imagination or a poverty of the mold of nations and nationalisms that they are beleaguered with the problems of exclusion.

NOTES

1   Eve Kosofsky Sedgwick, *Epistemology of the Closet* (Berkeley and Los Angeles: University of California Press, 1990), esp. pp. 27–35.
2   Ibid., p. 2.
3   Ruth Vanita, "Introduction," in Ruth Vanita (ed.) *Queering India: Same-sex Love and Eroticism in Indian Culture and Society* (New York and London: Routledge, 2002), pp. 1–11.
4   Michel Foucault, *History of Sexuality, Vol. 1* (New York and London: Vintage Books, 1990).
5   Jonathan Goldberg, "Bradford's 'Ancient members' and 'A case of buggery . . . amongst them'," in Andrew Parker, Mary Russo, Doris Sommer, and Patricia Yaeger (eds.) *Nationalisms and Sexualities* (New York and London: Routledge, 1992), p. 61.
6   Sedgwick, *Epistemology of the Closet*, p. 6.
7   Margrete Aarmo, "How homosexuality became 'un-African': the case of Zimbabwe," in Evelyn Blackwood and Saskia E. Wieringa (eds.) *Female Desires: Same-sex Relations and Transgender Practices across Cultures* (New York: Columbia University Press, 1999), pp. 255–80, esp. p. 261.
8   Estelle Freedman, " 'Uncontrolled desires': the response to the sexual psychopath, 1920–1960," in Kathy Peiss and Christina Simmons, with Robert A. Padgug (eds.) *Passion and Power: Sexuality in History* (Philadelphia: Temple University Press, 1989), pp. 199–225.
9   Ibid., p. 206.
10 Cited in Denis Altman, *Global Sex* (Chicago and London: University of Chicago Press, 2001), p. 144.
11 Cynthia Enloe, *Bananas, Beaches and Bases: Making Feminist Sense of International Politics* (Berkeley and Los Angeles: University of California Press, 1989), p. 31.
12 Altman, *Global Sex*, p. 10.
13 Ryan Bishop and Lillian S. Robinson, *Night Market: Sexual Cultures and the Thai Economic Miracle* (New York and London: Routledge, 1998), p. 8.
14 Ibid.
15 Enloe, *Bananas, Beaches and Bases*, p. 31.
16 Bishop and Robinson, *Night Market*, esp. ch. 4.
17 M. Jacqui Alexander, "Redrafting morality: the postcolonial state and the Sexual Offences Bill of Trinidad and Tobago," in *Third World Women and the Politics of Feminism* (Bloomington and Indianapolis: Indiana University Press, 1991), p. 133.
18 George L. Mosse, *Nationalism and Sexuality: Respectability and Abnormal Sexuality in Modern Europe* (New York: Howard Fertig, 1985), esp. ch. 1.
19 Ibid., esp. ch. 3.
20 Ibid., esp. ch. 2.
21 Quoted in Jyoti Puri, *Woman, Body, Desire in Post-colonial India: Narratives of Gender and Sexuality* (London: Routledge, 1999), pp. 35–6.

22	Ibid., p. 111.
23	Ibid.
24	Geraldine Heng and Janadas Devan, "State fatherhood: the politics of nationalism, sexuality and race in Singapore," in Parker et al., *Nationalisms and Sexualities*, pp. 343–64.
25	Andrew Parker, Mary Russo, Doris Sommer, and Patricia Yaeger, "Introduction," in Parker et al., *Nationalisms and Sexualities*, p. 2.
26	Martin F. Manalansan IV, "Searching for community: Filipino gay men in New York City," in Russell Leong (ed.) *Asian-American Sexualities: Dimensions of the Gay and Lesbian Experience* (New York and London: Routledge, 1996), pp. 51–64, esp. p. 63.
27	David L. Eng, "Out here and over there: queerness and diaspora in Asian-American studies," *Social Text* 52/53, 15, 3/4 (1997), pp. 31–52.
28	Kamala Visweswaran, "Predicaments of the hyphen," in The Women of South Asian Descent Collective (eds.) *Our Feet Walk the Sky: Women of the South Asian Diaspora* (San Francisco: Aunt Lute Books, 1993), pp. 301–12.
29	Janet Halley, "The construction of heterosexuality," in Michael Warner (ed.) *Fear of a Queer Planet* (Minneapolis and London: University of Minnesota Press, 1993), pp. 82–102.
30	Jonathan Katz, "The invention of heterosexuality," *Socialist Review* 20/1 (1990), pp. 7–34.
31	M. Jacqui Alexander, "Erotic autonomy as a politics of decolonization: an anatomy of feminist and state practice in the Bahamas tourist economy," in M. Jacqui Alexander and Chandra Talpade Mohanty (eds.) *Feminist Genealogies, Colonial Legacies, Democratic Futures* (New York and London: Routledge, 1997), pp. 63–100.
32	Alexander, "Redrafting morality," pp. 133–52.
33	Aarmo, "How homosexuality became 'un-African'," pp. 259–60.
34	Quoted in *Less Than Gay: A Citizen's Report on the Status of Homosexuality in India* (New Delhi: AIDS Bhedbhav Virodhi Andolan, 1991), p. 48.
35	Eileen Stillwaggon, "AIDS and poverty in Africa," *The Nation*, May 21, 2001, pp. 22ff.
36	Cindy Patton, "From nation to family: containing 'African AIDS'," in Parker et al., *Nationalisms and Sexualities*, pp. 218–34.
37	Ibid., pp. 218–19.
38	Salih Booker and William Miner, "Global apartheid," *The Nation*, July 9, 2001, pp. 11ff.
39	Ramòn Castellblanch, "AIDS in Africa, drug makers need more scruples," *Toronto Star*, July 26, 2000.
40	A version of this section appears in Steven Seidman and Diane Richardson (eds.) "Nationalism has a lot to do with it! Unraveling questions of nationalism and transnationalism in lesbian/gay studies," *Handbook for Lesbian and Gay Studies* (London: Sage Publications, 2002), pp. 427–42.
41	Richard K. Herrell, "Sin, sickness, crime: queer desire and the American state," *Identities* 2/3 (1996), pp. 273–300.
42	Aarmo, "How homosexuality became 'un-African'," p. 271.

43 Tan beng hui, "Women's sexuality and the discourse on Asian values: cross-dressing in Malaysia," in Blackwood and Wieringa, *Female Desires*, pp. 281–307.

44 Lauren Berlant and Elizabeth Freeman, "Queer nationality," in Warner, *Fear of a Queer Planet*, pp. 193–229.

45 Eng, "Out here and over there," p. 36.

46 Gayatri Gopinath, "Funny boys and girls: notes on a queer South Asian planet," in Leong, *Asian-American Sexualities*, pp. 119–27.

CHAPTER FIVE

In the Name of God, Community, and Country: Nationalisms, Ethnicity, and Religion

In her novel, *Cracking India*, Bapsi Sidhwa tells a poignant story set in the last few years of the colonial era, when India was fracturing into the independent nations of India and East and West Pakistan.[1] The story is told through the eyes of a young Parsi girl, Lenny, who is afflicted with polio. Parsis are an ethnic group who traveled from Persia several hundred years ago and settled in the Indian subcontinent. Through the eyes of Lenny, we see how the lives and identities of the people around her gradually change over a four-year period, with the rising tide of religious divisions within colonial India. At the time, political leaders on various sides of religious divide, including those from the minority Muslim community, argued that religious differences were more important than ethnic and cultural similarities, and powerful enough to warrant a separate nation of Pakistan made up primarily of Muslims.

In Sidhwa's story, an ethnic Punjabi identity – based on a common language, shared folk culture, similar dress and food – was by 1947 eroded by the religious divisions along Hindu, Muslim, and Sikh lines. The interplay between broader political tides that led to the creation of the two independent nations and the changing ethnic and religious identities of ordinary people in what was then the region of Punjab accentuates how ethnicity, religion, and nationalism can feed off one another to have wide-ranging consequences. Within a relatively short period, religious differences superseded ethnic commonalities (and other divisions of social class and caste), becoming deliberately politicized, leading to cultural nationalisms and a tussle over territory. But we can see this another way: ethnicity was re-imagined as religious affiliation and made the basis for political sovereignty. As young Lenny takes account of the bewildering changes that are taking place among those closest to her, we learn how the confrontations lead to bloodshed, terror, and rape, unprecedented in their scale and intensity. The unaffected viewpoint of the 8-year-old makes the violence all the more distressing.

Since the 1940s we have witnessed the rise of numerous newly independent national states, and the proliferation of movements consistently expressed in the idiom of nationalisms and nations. In this regard, the partition of colonial India into India and East and West Pakistan, and the subsequent redivision of Pakistan into Bangladesh and Pakistan, are part of a broad trend toward cultural and, more importantly, political sovereignty. Following the principle of self-determination, the realignment of the world into separate national territories not surprisingly triggered further demands for political autonomy. A leading scholar of ethnicity and nationalism, Walker Connor, makes the important point that once the doctrine of self-determination had been expressed through the French and American revolutions, it became a catalyst and justification for independence movements throughout the world and ultimately led to the decolonization that took place after World War II.[2] The right to exist as a distinct nation within the boundaries of a sovereign state and the right to be recognized as such by other national states emerged as the overriding requirement of the time. Movements for cultural autonomy by ethnic groups preceded the model of nations and modern states; but what was distinctive about the post-World War II period was the expectation that each people is entitled to a state.

Ethnic separatist movements, ethnic violence and conflict are the other side of the principle of self-determination and the rise of national states. In recent years, the rise of frequently violent, ethnic nationalist conflicts is seen as the greatest challenge to the stability and viability of the model of nation states. As noted in Chapter One, most states are multinational and multi-ethnic; this is particularly obvious in state-centered, political nations. Yet, even in cases where cultural nationalisms arise first and then seek sovereign states, we cannot assume ethnic or cultural uniformity. Ethnic nationalist movements therefore expose the fundamental tensions in the model of the nation state: the inconsistency between the promise of political sameness regardless of social and cultural differences and the reality of inequality; and the near impossibility of equating a people, a nation, and a state. To put it a different way, ethnic nationalist movements arise out of the crisis of state legitimacy. The more they push the principle of cultural and political sovereignty to demand that territorial boundaries and notions of citizenship and belonging be re-drawn, the more they seem to raise the specter of innumerable, unviable nation states.

Armed conflicts in the recent past that can be described as ethnic conflicts against national states are all too frequent. And there are also several relatively nonviolent ethnic separatist movements, such as the Québecois movement in Canada. Ethnic nationalist movements have arisen especially in Asia and Africa in the post-World War II period; such political groups have attempted to secede from an existing national state. They include the failed Igbo attempt to separate from Nigeria and the struggle between the Tamils and Sinhalese in Sri Lanka. The settlement in the latter case grants increased autonomy to the Tamils but within the political boundaries of Sri Lanka. Connor argues that ex-colonies in Asia and Africa are especially vulnerable to the rise of political ethnic movements because postcolonial states were based on arbitrary colonial administrative boundaries and not on the basis of ethnicities, some of which are now attempting to gain political sovereignty.[3]

Yet Europe, Latin and North America are hardly unaffected by ethnic conflict and separatism; to name a few countries: Mexico, Spain, Canada, Belgium, ex-Yugoslavia, and Russia. Thomas H. Eriksen notes that indigenous populations in Europe and North America, the Saami and the Inuit, have organized themselves to get state recognition for their ethnic identities and to be granted territorial autonomy within existing boundaries.[4] In May 1992 voters in Canada approved an Inuit self-governing homeland, and by 1999 the map of Canada was redrawn to create the Nunavut Territory in the northwest. Similarly, the Saami, who are spread across Norway, Sweden, Finland, and Russia, have parliaments in the three Scandinavian countries. But not all political movements will settle for greater cultural and political autonomy. The Basques, Bretons, Scots, and the Welsh demand the right to self-rule and sovereignty. This is not to say anything of the intensifying ethnic and national identities in Europe and North America following the influx of migrant labor and refugees, which have resulted in the creation of new, permanent ethnic minorities. The political and economic integration of Europe, in turn, has also intensified ethnic and cultural nationalisms.

These concerns about the intensity and violence of ethnic nationalisms in the latter half of the twentieth century are outstripped only by the threat of religious nationalisms; religion has come to be regarded as one of the most dangerous forms of ethnicity. Religious nationalisms invoke particularly troubling images of strife, hatred, and violence, often for good reason. The recourse to religion as a means to redefine national community can and has led to violence of staggering proportions. At the same time, as suggested by the formation of Pakistan, religious nationalism can lead to a new, independent nation. Nonetheless, unlike other aspects of ethnicity, religious nationalisms are seen as a threat not only to the political integrity of national states, but also to the secular principles of civic nations.

The previous chapters have alerted us to the influence and complicated effects of colonialism and modernity on how we understand and experience nationalisms. These chapters also attested to how idioms of nationalism are realized through notions of race, gender, and sexuality. Building on that approach, this chapter is devoted to understanding nationalism through the lens of ethnicity. Here, I want to explore ethnicity as a fundamental aspect of the form and content of nationalism. Indeed, some scholars do not differentiate between nationalisms and ethnic nationalisms. Yet, maintaining a difference between nationalisms and ethnicities, this chapter focuses on the politicization of ethnicity as nationalism. The argument pursued here is that ethnicities do not inevitably lead to nationalisms; they have to be politicized and re-imagined within the framework of nationalism. The first section considers the ethnic bases of nationalisms and elaborates on how ethnicities are refashioned within the framework of nationalisms. This section also looks at the influential role of the state in mediating between nationalisms and ethnicities.

A second line of inquiry relates to the perceived threat of ethnic nationalisms to national states. Thus attention is given to the conditions under which ethnicities become nationalist movements and their revolutionary as well as reactionary implications. The second section of this chapter focuses on religion and its links to nationalisms. The rise in numerous parts of the world of religious nationalist movements that are aimed at redefining the dominant nation and gaining control of the state has caused some concern, necessitating a careful look at the often violent manifestations of religious nationalisms. The chapter ends with reflections on the danger posed by fundamentalist nationalist movements.

Nationalisms and Ethnicities

> We still have a great deal of work to do to decouple ethnicity, as it functions in the dominant discourse, from its equivalence with nationalism, imperialism, racism and the state, which are the points of attachment around which a distinctive British or, more accurately, English ethnicity have been constructed.[5]

In these words, Stuart Hall, a well-known scholar and activist on race and culture in Britain, clearly does not show optimism about the "ethnicization" of British national identity, i.e. that Britishness is being reconfigured in favor of plural ethnic identities. Since the end of the colonial era, Welsh, Scottish, and English nationalisms are reasserting themselves as a result of the loss of a broader British national identity.[6] In relation to her point that British national identity was forged in reaction to its Other (Chapter Two), Linda Colley suggests that this break-up of Britain is not the outcome of cultural differences between the four nations, but because the Other – in the shape of Catholicism, France, Germany, or the colonies – no longer exists. The result, suggests Hall, are projections that the English are just another ethnic group with their own language, peculiar customs, rituals, and myths. So, what is wrong with this ethnicization of English identity or with the inward focus on England rather than Britishness? What does this shift from Britain to England and from notions of a superior, imperial race to "just-another-ethnicity" indicate?

Defining ethnicity

Ethnicity is typically defined as a form of collective identity based on shared cultural beliefs and practices, such as language, history, descent, and religion. Even though ethnicities often allude to enduring kin-based and blood ties, it is widely recognized that they are cultural, not biological, ties. Italian Americans, Yoruba, and Quebeçois are examples of ethnic identities. The shared similarities may be real, such as a common language, or perceived, as in stories about a common past. Yet such factors do not inherently constitute an ethnic group; rather, ethnicity varies by historical and cultural context. For example, Jewish Americans living in the US may be defined and identify as an ethnic group because of their religious affiliation and perceived cultural commonalities. Within Israel, a predominantly Jewish state, religious affiliation may not be the decisive criterion for ethnic differentiation – unless one is non-Jewish. Ethiopian Jews are ethnically distinguished by their perceived cultural, racial, and socio-economic differences from other Jewish groups living within Israel; for non-Jewish Arabs, on the other hand, their religious difference defines them as an ethnic minority. In effect, what defines a group ethnically is that it is held together by a shared cultural identity; however defined, it recognizes itself, and is recognized by non-members as such.

Ethnicity may refer to shared cultural characteristics such as language, customs, the group within which people are expected to intermarry, but in modern societies it also refers to political aspects, including access to state and civil resources. Hall suggests that ethnic identities become important whenever multiple groups exist in a common territory and when internally similar and distinct peoples are pulled into relationships with each other or, notably, with the state. This is the reason why ethnic groups in multi-ethnic postcolonial societies routinely lobby for special considerations, job and education quotas. These competitive conditions bear on an ethnic group's upward mobility, right to exist and maintain cultural integrity, and, in some cases, lead to ethnic conflict between competing groups or between a group and state institutions.

Nigeria is a country made up of more than two hundred ethnic groups, which were gradually brought under a single decentralized colonial state in the early twentieth century. Since Nigeria's independence from Britain in 1960, three ethnic groups have dominated: the Hausa-Fulani in the north, the Yoruba in the west, and the Igbo in the east. In their overview of ethnicity and conflict in Nigeria, Rian Leith and Hussein Solomon note that ethno-regional divisions are further overlaid with religious and socio-economic differences, since the northern states are predominantly Muslim, more heavily populated, agriculture-dependent, and impoverished and the southern states are mostly Christian, better-educated, and more resource-rich.[7] In 2000, after the defeat of Nigeria's military dictatorship, a resurgent Islamic movement backed and won the right to re-implement *Sharia* penal law across twelve northern states, causing clashes between the Muslims and the Christians in these areas. Although religious tensions are an important dimension of this conflict, the struggle over resources and the need to increase political influence along ethnic lines are no less relevant. Indeed, Leith and Solomon argue that even though ethnic conflicts are often about material issues that can be resolved through conventional methods, they are infused with intractable cultural symbolisms.[8] Surely, then, the concept of ethnicity is not simply about a group's "culture," benignly defined, but spans the material and symbolic, the cultural and political realms.

Ethnicity encodes important questions about identity, belonging, tradition, boundaries, race, and a group's past and future, questions that are especially relevant from the perspective of nationalism. Contrary to some views that associate ethnicity with minority groups, ethnic identity relates to majority or dominant groups in a society as well. According to Hall, ethnic identities are always imagined "through the eye of the needle of the other"; they are always in relation to other groups and their perceived characteristics.[9] In his discussion of what constitutes ethnicity, Eriksen raises the complicated question of whether an ethnic group necessarily has a distinct culture or whether two groups can be culturally identical but constitute two different ethnic groups.[10] He suggests the key issue is whether the groups have a minimum amount of contact and whether each does see itself as distinct from the other group. Looked at from a different angle, ethnicity is a social identity and way of relating between people who consider themselves culturally distinct from other groups against whom they define themselves. This is important to note about ethnic identity: while it is shaped out of a group's relations with outsiders, members of the group set store by it.

An influential scholar of nationalism, Paul Brass, argues that ethnic identity formation involves three sets of struggles: the group's attempts to define itself symbolically and materially, its rules for inclusion and its boundaries; ethnic groups compete for rights, privileges, and social resources; the state struggles with its dominant groups and the populations within the territory.[11] For example, census-taking, measuring, and cataloging a population has been especially instrumental in creating and altering ethnic identities. Brass argues that colonial states expended much effort to count and classify people within their territories and fit what were in many cases overlapping, multiple identities into discrete categories. For this, colonial authorities created new categories some of which endured as ethnic identities while others did not. These categories, Brass says, also served as the basis on which some groups were favored over others.

For most of us, our ethnicities give us a sense of belonging to a group or community of people. Whether we live physically within this group or in touch with it culturally, ethnic identification unites us with a larger community of people, gives us a sense of our past, and sometimes seems to explain quirks in our behavior and attitudes. For an ethnic group, who belongs within the group and how to determine ways of including new members, whether through birth or other criteria, are important questions. These criteria can be clearly or more ambiguously defined. Of course, the flip side of inclusion is exclusion; ethnic groups identify what distinguishes themselves from outsiders, and have to set the boundaries of their identities. Feminist scholars are especially interested in the importance of women's bodies and roles to a group's ethnic identity and its boundaries. For example, similarly to expressions of nationality, ethnic identity may be articulated through ideals of womanhood and respectable sexuality; "our women are not like theirs." Further, only children born to mothers who belong within the group may be included; those of women who marry into the group may be excluded.

If the point that ethnic groups, despite their claims, are products of their circumstances and are partly shaped out of their shifting relations with other groups and state institutions is clear, then what also needs to be emphasized is that markers of ethnic identity – tradition, history, etc. – have to be constantly reiterated. The notion of tradition is especially tricky. Tradition connotes enduring, relatively unchanging practices, but there is nothing self-perpetuating about it. As noted in Chapter One, Hobsbawm showed that seemingly long-standing national traditions were, in fact, invented and depended on repetition for their power. Counterintuitively, traditions have to be self-consciously reinforced and continually reiterated in order to have meaning. They are not unchanging, and are the products of the relations among members of the group and between members and outside groups and state practices and institutions. Further, Craig Calhoun notes that when traditions go from being closely tied to the lives of people in small groups and told through word of mouth to being written down, televised, or made into films to accommodate the needs of people in large groups, their meanings do not remain the same.[12] Looking at ethnic traditions with this realization does not make them less real or lessen their power in any way; rather, it helps us understand how ethnicities constitute themselves, their distinctive traditions, and under what circumstances.

As a concept, ethnicity is often confused with race. In routine conversations and sometimes in scholarly work, ethnicity is to gender what race is to sex. Just as gender is understood as the outcome of cultural attributes that make us into men or women and sex is seen as biology, ethnicity and race lie either side of a culture/biology divide. Ethnicity is identified with the cultural realm and race is often thought to be biologically based. According to this framework, ethnicity is about self-identity and, therefore, is subjective and politically neutral. However, race is seen as a more objective category, hierarchical, and marred by power differences. By this token, it seems much easier to envision peaceful and pluralistic multiethnic societies than it is to imagine multi-racial societies.

But just as the distinctions between sex and gender are hardly clear-cut, the difference between ethnicity and race is not easily captured. Indeed, there is a complex and volatile interaction between ethnicity and race. As critical scholars of race have long pointed out, race is hardly a simple biological distinction. Even though by definition the concept of race refers to different biological characteristics of groups, it is culturally prescribed and varies from one time period to another and from one culture to another. In its turn, like race, ethnicity is not a neutral concept. On the contrary, ethnicities are shaped and expressed in unequal relation to one another.

Hall reminds us that to be English is shaped by history, by economic and political relations, and by cultural influences. When one visualizes an English person, a back woman is not what comes to mind. Hall suggests that a free-born English person is a race- and class-based, and a gendered concept: it is of a English *man*, and is associated with a stiff upper lip form of masculinity.[13] The problem, and this is his concern with endorsing the ethnicization of Britain mentioned above, is that despite the fact that Englishness connotes a specific and peculiar form of ethnic identity, it is presented as being more widely applicable. Instead of representing common characteristics that are relevant to some and not others, English-ness is presented as normal, homogenous, and unitary. Hardly a neutral concept, then, ethnicity is like race in being riven with differences and inequalities. These inequalities exist between ethnic groups as well as among members of an ethnic group, by virtue of social class, gender, age, sexuality, or other significant social factors. Put differently, as an ethnic identity, Englishness is not equally available to all groups within England, and social inequalities complicate the ethnic homogeneity of those who seem quintessentially English.

Speaking to the political possibilities that lie in this interplay between ethnicity, race, gender, and class, an insightful scholar of race and ethni-city, Kobena Mercer, describes how black identity was "redefined" in Britain in the early 1980s.[14] Where "black" was a racialized category that loosely referred to non-whites, various people of Asian, African, and Caribbean descent collectively took on the mantle of black identity on the basis of political similarities. Redefining a racial category into a subjective cultural and political self-identity, these groups transformed "black" into a kind of ethnic category. This self-identity allowed disparate cultural groups brought together by common experiences of racism to express their alliances and solidarity. What this example also compellingly dem-onstrates, as Mercer reminds us, is that ethnic identities, such as "black," are not just there or immutable, but can be constructed out of political and cultural struggle. In sum, recognizing the contextual, constructed nature of ethnicity, recognizing its reach across cultural and political issues, and seeing it as an arena of inequality and contestation better positions us to see its relevance to and interconnections with nationalism.

Framing the interplay between ethnicity and nationalism

If readers are anticipating the potential overlap between ethnicity and nationalism by now, then it will be clear to them why some scholars of nationalism look carefully at its links with ethnicity. Like ethnicity, nationalism is about questions and concerns of identity, belonging, his-tory, homeland, boundaries, strategies of inclusion and exclusion and, no less, is an arena of power and contestation. Both nationalisms and ethnicities are understood as forms of solidarity, shared culture, and shared descent. Nationalisms systematically draw upon long-standing ethnic identities and long-established links to territories, thereby also giving each nation its distinctive character and history. Nationalisms can significantly affect which ethnic groups are seen at the heart of the nation, how these groups are identified, how ethnicity is defined, and which of its aspects are foregrounded. National states can play an especially crucial role in creating categories of ethnic affiliation, documenting their origins, and determining access to critical social resources. The point is that there is no simple causal link between ethnicity and nationalism but they become inextricably linked under some circumstances.

Two kinds of ethnic nationalist movements are discernible: those that seek sovereign independent territory by breaking away from an existing national state on the basis of ethnic/national differences; or those that seek to redefine the existing national community and redraw territorial boundaries, most typically by purging targeted ethnic groups. If the separatist movement of Basques in Spain, of Chechans struggling against under Russian authority, and of Palestinian aspirations of political sovereignty are examples of attempts to found new independent nation states, then Hutu attempts to purge Rwanda of Tutsis or Serb-led attempts to do away with Muslims in Bosnia through sustained violence were about re-shaping existing national and territorial boundaries through a process of elimination.

But there is one difference between ethnicity and nationalism, namely the relationship to the state. In modern societies, ethnic identities are related to the state, as argued above, but not in the same way as nationalism. An essential aspect of nationalism is its relationship with territorial boundaries, whereas many ethnic groups do not demand territorial control. For that matter, ethnic groups do not regulate the economy in a planned way or have a centralized legal structure. They may express attachment to a territory as their homeland, but not all ethnic groups seek sovereignty over political boundaries. Indeed, an ethnic group becomes nationalist when it makes such demands; this is also called political ethnicity. To put it simply, not all ethnic groups are nationalist but most nationalist movements use the language of ethnicity to make claims about their legitimacy, their history, and their distinctive features. Eriksen qualifies this by saying that there are some nationalist movements that are either pluralistic or depicted as supra-ethnic; for example, despite some underlying tensions and conflict between national and ethnic identities, Mauritian nationalism alternately tries to present itself as a "mosaic of cultures" and a supra-ethnic community that transcends ethnicity.[15]

In his overview of what he calls ethnonationalism, Connor identifies key links between ethnicities and nationalism.[16] At its most basic, there are questions about whether two or more ethnic groups can co-exist within the political unit of the state. A related question is about which model, the homogenous nation state or the multinational state, is more conducive to democracy. On the one hand, if the answer is the nation state, then, given their rarity, the question is whether to encourage ethnic separatist movements and the proliferation of innumerable but unviable states. Yet multination states seem plagued by fundamental tensions between unity and diversity. While most modern states incorporate more than one nation within their boundaries, the pervasiveness of ethnic unrest makes this arrangement hard to sustain. Marked by a duality between state-based unity and the centrifugal impact of ethnonationalisms, the model of the national state and its political efficacy is in doubt. The pervasiveness of ethnonationalist movements not only in Africa and Asia but also in Latin America, Europe, and North America testifies to the enduring and influential nature of the principle of self-determination and, in effect, the limitations of multination states.

Processes of modernization and the rise of intergovernmental institutions raise further questions about the proliferation of ethnonationalisms. Connor claims that the fact that many scholars of nationalism have not paid adequate attention to ethnonationalisms is partly due to the idea that modernization will herald the decline of ethnicity and ethnic identities.[17] It was believed that modernization would help shift identification with ethnic groups to the state. Instead, not only do we observe counter-trends, but also these trends raise the possibility that modernization has itself caused ethnic separatist movements. As we shall see below, the insight of scholars of ethnicity and nationalism, including Brass, is that the unevenness and unequal nature of modernity may help trigger ethnic nationalisms in recent times. Yet, Connor finds, socioeconomic aspects of modernity are not the sole causal factor in ethnonationalisms; this is born out by the relatively recent rise of ethnic consciousness at various levels of modernity: the movement among the Basques and Catalans in Spain; the demands of the French-speaking from the German-speaking peoples in Berne; the resurgence of Scottish and Welsh nationalisms, among others. Similarly, the rise of intergovernmental and multi-state institutions raises the question whether nationalisms are too parochial to meet contemporary political, economic, and social needs. Connor argues that ethnonationalisms are not inherently incompatible with these organizations; this is an issue to be further explored in the following chapter.

Approaches to ethnic nationalisms

At its most influential, ethnicity can serve as a seedbed of nationalism. It can contribute to the development and strengthening of nationalism, a national identity, and solidarity. This link between ethnicity and nationalism leads influential scholars of nationalism, Anthony Smith, Walker Connor, Thomas H. Eriksen, Paul Brass, and John Armstrong to rethink the origins and meaning of nationalism. It is useful to consider how at least three of them have theorized the interaction of ethnicity and nationalism.

In his work on nationalism, Smith focuses on the importance of ethnicity through the concept of "ethnies," the French term for ethnic communities. He defines ethnies as named human populations with the shared ancestry myths, histories and cultures, having an association with a specific territory, and a sense of solidarity.[18] To recap the discussion in Chapter One, Smith believes that the framework of nations – the sentiments and symbolism of nationalism – are to be found in pre-modern ethnies. According to him, there are two main routes to nation-formation that depend on the kind of ethnic community from which it is drawn: in one, loosely formed, aristocratic ethnies mobilize the middle classes into a territorialized nationalism with the help of the state; in the other, native intellectuals appropriate and remake a selective ethnic identity and past out of popular cultural practices in order to mobilize a nationalist movement. He suggests that there is also a third route, evident in the United States, Canada, and Australia where nations were forged out of the fragments of immigrant ethnic communities.

With this approach to nationalism, Smith is not only able to show the pre-modern roots of nationalisms, but also to bridge the gap between perennialist and modernist perspectives on nationalism. As explored in Chapter One, perennialists argue that nations are not merely modern phenomena, but have their roots in these long-standing collective cultural identities, namely, ethnicities. Modernists, on the other hand, see nationalism and nations as modern phenomena that are qualitatively distinct from pre-existing forms of collective identities. Through his emphasis on ethnies, Smith rejects the idea that nations are a primordial part of our evolution in favor of a thesis emphasizing the cultural rather the biological ties of a group, and their shared myths, memories, symbols, and values that are retained over a period of time. But, Smith is not convinced that nationalisms and nations are a modern phenomenon either. The role of ethnicity is therefore key to his theory of nationalism and his approach that nations and nationalisms are neither simply modern expressions nor endemic to human history.

This approach may well suggest that ethnicities and nationalisms are inherently and closely linked in so far as pre-existing ethnicities are the source of modern nationalisms and nations, but it is flawed. Smith is right to draw our attention to how nationalisms may tap into ethnic identities, traditions, and myths, thereby forging points of continuity between pre-existing ethnic communities and modern nationalisms. After all, nationalisms are not forged out of thin air. But this approach does not adequately acknowledge how nationalisms appropriate ethnicity by fundamentally refashioning its meaning and significance. While there is little doubt that a fundamental aspect of nationalism is its claim to a long-standing community, ethnic identities and communities are not simply available as its raw material. On the contrary, nationalisms reinvent ethnic communities by highlighting some traditions, cultural markers, and versions of history over others. Two claims are implicit here: that ethnicities are contextual, constructed, and constantly shifting identities; and that ethnicities can be transformed into nationalities only through political interventions. In that sense, the transformation of ethnicity into nationalism represents less a point of continuity and more a point of departure.

As hinted earlier, Connor's scholarship on ethnonationalism has helped in understanding the interplay between ethnicity and nationalism. Like Smith, Connor does not essentially distinguish between ethnicity and nationalism; for Connor ethnonationalism and nationalism are interchangeable terms. Not surprisingly, then, he defines a nation as a self-differentiating ethnic group and sees nationalism as loyalty to the ethnic group.[19] Connor's approach to ethnonationalism is driven by five concerns: the need to avoid imprecise and confusing terminology, such as confusing nationalism with patriotism or loyalty to state; greater attention to the psychological and emotional aspects of nationalism; the importance of comparative approaches to nationalism; the recognition that ethnonational demands are essentially political rather than economic demands; and avoiding overemphasis on elites in ethnonationalist movements.[20]

While Connor's work usefully directs attention to the rise of ethnic nationalisms, he conflates the two concepts. The problem is that Connor does not see an essential difference between ethnicity and nationalism. He challenges the more general use of ethnicity to connote cultural similarities of language, religion, etc. in favor of restricting the term to its links with nations. For Connor, a group's self-awareness is what makes it a nation rather than just an ethnic group. In effect, all nationalist movements are seen as political extensions of ethnicities and, as noted above, this approach ignores how nationalist movements may selectively fashion an ethnic identity and invent ethnic traditions. Another limitation is Connor's emphasis on the political and cultural aspects of ethnicity over the importance of mobilizing for socioeconomic resources. Although Connor is right to not reduce ethnic mobilization to socioeconomic concerns, his approach runs the risk of granting culture an independent status. As mentioned in the case of the Hausa-Fulani, political, symbolic, and socioeconomic aspects of ethnic mobilizations are often tightly interconnected. Lastly, while Connor is right to caution us against conceding too much ground to social elites, there is a danger in ignoring the key role that they can play in some ethnonationalist movements, and erroneously seeing ethnicities as fundamentally homogenous and egalitarian.

Brass's approach to ethnicity and nationalism is different on at least two accounts. First, he distinguishes between ethnic groups and nations. According to him, ethnicity or ethnic identity "also involves, in addition to subjective self-consciousness, a claim to status and recognition, either as a superior group or as a group at least equal to other groups."[21] Members may claim ethnicity to demand greater resources for individuals within the group or demand rights for the group as a whole. A nation, according to him, can be seen as a particular type of ethnic community or as an ethnic community politicized.[22] Nations may be created out of the politicization of an ethnic community or through the amalgamation of diverse groups and the creation of a composite national culture through the state; in other words they may be ethnic or state-centered. One outcome for Brass of not conflating ethnicity and nationalism is that he has to explain how ethnicities are transformed into nationalities. According to him, an ethnic group first makes the transition to a self-conscious community on the basis of language, religion, or other salient factors.[23] For example, language is transformed from a means of communication to a heritage of the community. At the second stage, social, political, and economic rights are articulated for members or for the group as a whole. In cases where the community demands recognition as a political body, it establishes itself as a nationality, Brass believes. The corollary is that many ethnic groups do not seek to or are unable to make the transition to nationality.

A second point of distinction is that Brass emphasizes the role of elites in politicizing ethnicities; he is an avowed instrumentalist. He argues that particular social groups, elites, or leaders are crucial in the creating of communities out of ethnic groups, including in the selection of historical symbols, cultural practices, dialects, or religious customs. Indeed, Brass argues that ethnic self-consciousness, ethnically-based demands, and ensuing ethnic conflict only occur when there is conflict either between indigenous and external elites and authorities, or among indigenous elites. Undoubtedly, Brass's approach may be faulted for overemphasizing the role of social elites and for underestimating the participation of a wider cross-section of ethnic members – the point developed in Chapter One and implicitly echoed by Connor. Yet Brass's approach to ethnicity and nationalism helps us to recognize them as interrelated but not synonymous. In fact, it becomes important in explaining the conditions under which ethnicities may become nationalist and when nationalisms take on the mantle of ethnicities.

The point that I am leading up to is that in many cases there are continuities between pre-existing ethnicities and the nationalisms that emerge in these settings. Ethnicity can and does bind people together and, in some cases, may be the basis for something that Hobsbawm calls proto-nations.[24] But what is equally important to note is that there is no direct correspondence between pre-existing ethnicities and nationalisms. Rather than providing an inevitable basis for nationalism, ethnic identities and solidarities might be selectively deployed to drum up support for nationalist claims and claims for a sovereign national state. This leads Hobsbawn to point out that very few modern national movements are based on a strong ethnic consciousness; in fact, this consciousness is often invented to bolster claims to nationhood. Therefore, what kinds of ethnic identities are projected, what elements of pre-existing ethnicities are reinvoked as the markers of the ethnic-national groups, and which customs followed by small subsections, are resurrected as traditions for the entire ethnic-national group are issues that complicate assertions that ethnicities are the well-spring for nationalisms and national states.

On the contrary, nationalisms privilege certain ethnicities over others. Hall's discussion of the ethnicization of English identity makes clear how particular ethnicities might be represented over others in order to constitute a national identity, and why he calls for the "decoupling" of ethnicity and nationalism in the passage quoted at the start of this section. In his words, "It was only by dint of excluding or absorbing all of the differences that constituted Englishness, the multitude of different regions, peoples, classes, genders that composed the people gathered together in the Act of Union, that Englishness could stand for everybody in the British Isles."[25] Nationalism is expressed through the idiom of a particular ethnic identity to the exclusion of others and the nation is seen as the authentic place of belonging of that group. In the case of England, this viewpoint may lead to overt forms of racism towards non-whites or to calls for assimilation into some vaguely conceptualized notions of an authentic English identity. This explains why Home Secretary David Blunkett called upon immigrants to "feel British," such as by speaking English, amidst a report on race riots that occurred earlier in the year. This stance was backed by calls to make immigrants take citizenship classes, and give up incompatible customs, including forced marriages.

The role of language in ethnic nationalisms

In terms of the active creation and recreation of ethnicities to bolster nationalisms, two aspects are especially noteworthy: the role of history and the role of language. The importance of language in our lives, its potential to unify certain groups, and its role in demarcating boundaries between two groups has lead to widespread interest in the significance of language to nationalisms and national states. But, from the perspective of the interplay between ethnicity and nationalism, the issue of greater importance is when language serves to create national consciousness and becomes the flash-point in ethnic political conflict.

With regard to the way language may facilitate the formation of a national consciousness, Anderson says that the turning point was mechanical printing and the dissemination of languages.[26] He identifies three factors in the formation of a national consciousness. First, these languages made it possible for wider ranges of people to communicate with one another. Prior to mechanical printing, classical languages, such as Latin, were limited to small sections, and the languages and dialects spoken by ordinary people were often incomprehensible in other regions. Print-languages, according to Anderson, made it easier for people to understand one another and know that there was a much wider community that shared the same language. Particularly if nationalism is held to be a popular sentiment or of "the people," then classical, elite languages are ill-suited to its purpose. Second, the printing of languages reinforced notions of an ancient past and continuity with that past, traits that are characteristic of nationalisms and nations despite evidence otherwise. It made these languages and the groups within which they prevailed seem more eternal. Through print, the words and thoughts of past generations could be accessed. Third, printed languages created a hierarchy of languages based on how closely they resembled the print-language. Educational institutions were especially important in normalizing some languages. Anderson cites the examples of High German, the King's English, and Central Thai being elevated to new politico-cultural influence. In these ways, print-languages gave shape to emergent ideas of national community. This is well reflected in that almost all national states today have a national language that facilitates the functioning of state institutions even in cases where they continue to be spoken by relatively few people.

The more important point about language as a major indicator of ethnicity is that the rise of print-languages may have facilitated the emergence of a national consciousness; but as a central marker of nationalism, language has to be actively politicized and often at the cost of sidelining the language of other groups. In France, French is not only the national language but also stirs great national pride despite variations in how it is spoken. The irony, though, is that when the France was constituted 12–13 percent were deemed to speak it "correctly," and the rest spoke it either very little or not at all.[27] Hobsbawm argues, therefore, that contrary to nationalist mythologies that national languages reflect the primordial nature of the national community and its psyche, national languages are almost always semi-artificially created and sometimes even outrightly invented. To acknowledge that national languages are products of nationalisms rather than the product of a shared national culture hardly lessens their significance, especially when it is used to administer the national territory, is taught in schools, and is necessary for career advancement.

History in the making of ethno-nationalisms: the case of Serbian nationalism in the 1990s

If language is important in consolidating ethnic identities and in lending validity to nationalist projects, then projections of history are equally strategic in the forging of a national cultural and political consciousness. Even though the past seems made up of indisputable facts, historians remind us that history is less about the past than it is about the present. In other words, history or the past is always recounted through the lens of the present. In Chapter Two, we considered how projections of history were central to emerging anti-colonial nationalisms in order for them to resolve a fundamental contradiction, namely, the nationalisms were new but nations were claimed to have existed since time immemorial. Projections of history make this claim legitimate. But the malleability of history was not important just in nineteenth-century anti-colonial nationalisms. How the past continues to play a central role in ethnicized claims of nationalisms is nowhere better illustrated than by the promotion by Serbian political leaders of a nationalist agenda in Bosnia-Herzegovina.

In the ethnic conflict that gripped Bosnia in 1992–3, the rekindling and revising of Serbian nationalism is most notable; the process was well underway in the 1980s under the leadership of Serbian President Slobodan Milosevic. Bosnia was part of the Yugoslav Federation organized by Marshall Tito and started to come apart in the decade after his death in 1980. The boundaries of the republics in the federation were drawn in a way to ensure ethnic intermixing in each case. Calhoun contends that it was the post-1992 attempt to make national boundaries coincide with ethnic identities that produced the human devastation and misery.[28] Not withstanding the horrifying outcomes of ethnic cleansing that was triggered by Serbian nationalists in Bosnia, the project was in keeping with the thrust of nationalisms elsewhere, i.e. to control a territory within which people shared an ethnic origin, spoke a single language, and shared a religion. If Calhoun is correct in his analysis, the question is how did this form of ethnic nationalism become powerful enough to lead to the murder of 7,500 Bosnians by the Serbian army in Srebrenica in just one week between July 13 and July 19, 1995?

The "cleansing" of Bosnia of Croats and Muslims was justified through the combination of old history and the exigencies of the present. Although Serbs and Croats had a common language and ethnicity, they did not share a religion. In the nineteenth century Serbs became Orthodox, under the influence of Russia; Croats were Catholics and maintained stronger ties to the West. It was only then that the two groups laid stress on differences between languages, styles of pronunciation, and literary styles, thereby laying the basis for the legacies of ethnic differences.[29] However, the economic woes of Serbia, linked to the weakening of the Soviet economy and the parallel strengthening of Croatia and Slovenia, fueled the rhetoric of Serbian nationalism put out by leaders such as Milosevic. As a means to mobilize the economically impoverished and demoralized Serbs, Milosevic and Bosnian Serb nationalists, such as Radovan Karodzic, tried to create a Greater Serbia that would include Bosnia, but without its Muslims and Croats.

Numerous writers have noted that Serbs accused Bosnian Muslims of being "Turkish progeny" and aiding the Ottoman empire in the victimization of Serbs. These historical events were invoked to justify the cruelty to Bosnian Muslims. But it would be a mistake to say that simple memory kept these events alive for memory has to be actively nurtured. Julie Mostov points out that especially in the late 1980s and early 1990s, images of heroic figures from the distant past, stories of suffering and sacrifice, and visions of glory for a defiant nation were spun by Serb nationalist literary elites.[30] These tales were supported by historical "facts" about atrocities toward "their" nation and visions of an ethnic nationalist identity as the path out of foreign oppression. These messages, revisions of history, and promises for the future were widely disseminated over Serbian state television, radio, newspapers, and public meetings. Perhaps nothing less would have been necessary to carry out the ensuing ethnic cleansing in Bosnia and elsewhere.

Conditions of the politicization of ethnicities

The argument developed thus far, that nationalism entails the politicization of ethnicity, raises the obvious question about the conditions under which this can happen. Brass sets out four factors that decide whether an ethnic group is mobilized into a nationalist movement: the unequal distribution of resources, the building of organizational resources necessary for a political movement; the responses of the state; and the general political context.[31] Recognizing that by itself inequality is insufficient to trigger a nationalist movement, Brass suggests what is important is the competition for resources by two or more groups in an ethnically and socioeconomically stratified society.[32] He notes that while this is more likely in societies that are industrializing and have a centralized state, ethnic mobilization is also evident in industrialized societies with significant socioeconomic and political disparities.

The formation of political organizations are an important stage in the gathering momentum of nationalist movements; they are necessary both to make political demands on behalf of the ethnic group and to fulfill political and incipient nationalist goals. Setting up these political units, acquiring skilled leaders, and marshalling resources are some of the ways in which we can measure the transition from an ethnic to a nationalist group, according to Brass.[33] Political organizations that can command community resources and identify themselves with the community are likely to be most effective. The challenge for these organizations is to be the sole political representative of the community and to shape the political identity of the community that they represent.

A third, and arguably the most important, factor has to do with the role of the state.[34] The structural arrangement of the state may facilitate the transition from an ethnic community to a nationalist movement. For example, the administrative demarcations of the state may conform to the concentrations of ethnic groups. While this is not a sufficient criterion for the mobilization of an ethnic political movement, it does foster ethnic communal consciousness that can be politically mobilized. In cases where states adopt one or two official languages over others and where these languages are seen as key to educational and job opportunities, ethnic groups may be mobilized into political action. Brass finds that the state's distribution of economic resources and the jobs it commands can be another important source of conflict. Whether such ethnic grievances develop into full-fledged nationalist movements will depend on the state's responses. On the one hand, states can accommodate such demands and, where necessary, grant more political and cultural autonomy; for example through federalism. On the other, Brass says, states may attempt – in response to conflict – to quell the political aspirations of ethnic nationalisms by co-opting such movements, violently repressing them, or through deporting key political figures.

Finally, the broader political context can influence the rise of ethnic nationalist movements.[35] In Brass's view, the possibilities for realignment of political and social forces and organizations, the willingness of dominant ethnic elites to share power, and the potential availability of alternate political arenas are among the key factors. To this, we might add two additional, related factors. First, external and international influences may either support or hinder the surge of ethnic nationalisms within a particular state. Second, as many scholars of ethnicity and nationalisms argue, the gradual erosion of national states under the onslaught of globalization is leading to an intensification of ethnic nationalist movements. These movements are triggered by a weakening of the state's ability to enforce nationalist unification or by the capacity of the state to protect various ethnic groups from neo-liberal policies.

The case of Rwanda

The background to the 1994 genocide in Rwanda is an example of the complex conditions under which ethnic nationalisms can be mobilized and, worse, turn violent. It shows how socioeconomic factors, political organizations, the response of the state, and external influences both past and current can lead to the brutalities of ethnic nationalisms. The population is composed of a Hutu majority, a Tutsi minority, and a small population of Twa, who are held to be the original inhabitants. The Hutus are thought to be a Bantu people who migrated from the south and west, and the Tutsis a Nilotic people who migrated from the north and the east. By April 1994 an estimated 500,000 to 800,000 Tutsis had been killed over a hundred days, giving this genocide the dubious distinction of having the fastest rate so far recorded. One reason that the estimates of killed Tutsis vary is the difficulty of telling the difference between Tutsi and Hutu corpses, pointing to the tragic irony of this ethnic genocide.

A seemingly ancient ethnic hostility wreaked havoc on the Tutsis despite the fact that the division became influential relatively recently as a result of pre-colonial, colonial, and postcolonial state policies. Historically, Hutus and Tutsis shared a language and a religion; they intermarried and lived intermingled with one another, making it difficult to categorize them as distinct ethnic groups.

What did distinguish the two groups was that Hutus tended to be cultivators and Tutsis herdsmen, and by the 1860s the latter were firmly entrenched as the political and economic elite. Despite the fact that Tutsis enjoyed greater access to the state and its resources and greater financial power, the lines between Hutus and Tutsis remained porous. In fact, Philip Gourevitch, a reporter and author of the book, *We Wish to Inform You that Tomorrow We Will be Killed with Our Families*, says that in the nineteenth century the categories of Hutus and Tutsis had little local significance and made sense only in relation to state power and, significantly, it was possible for Hutus to become Tutsis.[36] But out of these differences, the two groups developed ideas about themselves and each other, and in the absence of clear-cut differences details of diet and physical traits took on larger significance.

Exacerbated by European racial typologies and the Belgian colonial presence, ethnic and class differences were subsequently heightened. The Hamitic myth – that alongside the Africans who were dark-skinned, short, with thick lips were other Africans who more closely resembled Europeans – helped not only perpetuate the idea of two distinct racial/ ethnic groups in Rwanda but also the beliefs that the Tutsis were superior owing to their more European appearance. Despite the countless exceptions, the physical archetypes – the coarse, shorter, stocky, round-faced, dark-skinned, flat-nosed Hutu and the "nobler," "aristocratic," lanky and long-faced, lighter-skinned, narrow-nosed, and thin-lipped Tutsis – came to endure. Belgian colonial policy after World War I systematically exploited these differences and re-engineered Rwanda along these ethnic lines.[37] Ethnic identity cards labeled people as either Hutu or Tutsi, making it impossible for Hutus to become Tutsis and thereby institutionalized apartheid. For example, Hutus were forced to toil on plantations, as construction and forestry crew, and Tutsis were placed as their taskmasters. Although Hutus and Tutsis continued to intermarry, the irreconcilable ethnic/racialized differences dominated the political landscape.

The tide turned in the transition to independence, starting in 1959, when Hutus seized state control in a violent struggle and about half of the estimated 17 percent of the population who were Tutsis migrated to neighboring countries. Tutsi efforts to return to power in the 1960s led to the massacre of domestic Tutsis by the Hutus in 1963, causing a further exodus of Tutsis. A coup in 1973 by an authoritarian Hutu officer, Juvenal Habyarimana, imposed a fifteen-year period of stability. The more recent devastation, however, was triggered in 1990, when an expatriate rebel force made up mostly of Tutsis, the Rwandan Patriotic Army, invaded northern Rwanda. Habyarimana's government survived because forces from France and Zaire supported its troops. Pressure from the international community forced Habyarimana to share power with this group but also incited the ire of Hutu extremists over what was perceived as his concession to the Tutsis. In an effort to retain power, Habyarimana allied with extremist Hutus to train militias, broadcast anti-Tutsi rhetoric, and plotted to kill Tutsis and moderate Hutu leaders. The shooting down of a plane carrying Habyarimana, probably by members of his presidential guard, prompted the massacre of Tutsi civilians and moderate Hutu leaders. Indeed, the first felled in the city of Kigali were these moderates. They and thousands of Tutsis were the victims of what was called Hutu Power.

Sadly, what sets this genocide apart is not simply the scale of the killings. Rather, it is the efficiency with which vast numbers of Tutsis and tens of thousands of moderate Hutus were killed over a short period of time. Along with Hutu extremists, the army and the national police conspired to kill Tutsis who had sought refuge in gathering places: churches, schools, and hospitals, among others. Estimates are that perhaps 250,000 Tutsis were killed within a two-week period. On this occasion, Hutus were enjoined not to spare Tutsi women and children. This scale of genocide, which Gourevitch calls the most efficient mass killings since the atomic bombings of Hiroshima and Nagasaki, was impossible without the participation and complicity of local political leaders such as mayors, religious leaders such as pastors, and civilian authority figures such as teachers and doctors. In the early 1990s foreign aid had continued to pour into Rwanda despite reports of the killings of Tutsis even at the time. International intervention was slow in coming and has been the subject of much criticism later. The United Nations Security Council authorized France to lead an intervention only on June 22, 1994. The killings temporarily abated when the Tutsi rebel Rwanda Patriotic Front advanced into and captured Kigali in mid-July.

It is not difficult to peg Rwanda's case of ethnic genocide to the pervasive pattern of ethnic rivalry in poor and Third World countries. Besides being simplistic and pejorative in its implications, this explanation makes ethnic strife seem inevitable. Instead, the unimaginable ethnic massacre tells us more about the ways in which ethnicity is actively created and deployed to "cleanse" a nation of its other. Rather than automatically reflecting natural, enduring differences, ethnic differences and, more importantly, ethnic inequalities have to be created and constantly invoked for them to have significance. The role of the state in exacerbating and channeling ethnic tensions is especially relevant. Upon the assassination of Habyarimana, members of Hutu Power used the government radio and newspapers to call Hutus to their machetes in order to rid Rwanda of Tutsis. The causes of the genocide included: an economy devastated by the crash in the price of coffee and tea, Rwanda's chief exports; relatively little arable land; a renewed reliance on international aid; and the building of solidarity among the Hutus by inciting them against the Tutsis. As Calhoun reminds us, genocide does not automatically follow from the racist rhetoric of nationalism and is usually a more complicated result of ethnic differences and state-centered political projects.[38]

Religion and Nationalism

In this section, I focus on the interplay between religion and nationalisms. Since I am treating religion as one possible aspect of ethnicity, much of the discussion about the links between ethnicity and nationalisms in the preceding section has relevance here. But examining nationalism by focusing on religion is helpful in assessing the particular threat of religious nationalisms, in unraveling putative links between religion, fundamentalism, and nationalism, and in considering the rise and limitations of religious nationalisms.

As noted in the introduction to this chapter, religious nationalisms can seem an especially potent threat to the viability of national states and secular principles of civic nationalism. Needless to say, the secular nature of nationalism can be the very source of the problem for religious nationalists. Depending upon our political and religious affiliations, we may also see religious nationalisms as inherently fundamentalist. Since the late twentieth century, and especially since September 11, 2001 in the United States, religious fundamentalism is posed as arguably the greatest threat to political stability and order. While there are various forms of fundamentalism, it is most typically associated with religion. The specters of wild-eyed zealots, violent nationalist movements, conservative rhetoric, and closed-minded beliefs come to mind all too quickly when there is a reference to fundamentalism.

In contrast, the argument made here is that religious nationalisms are not inevitable or inherently dangerous. The reason is that religion is not always politicized, and may in fact be inimical to nationalism. The more interesting questions are therefore about how and under what circumstances religion is forged with nationalism, and when it does become ominous. Studying the links between nationalism, religion, and fundamentalism also helps us to see that religious nationalisms and fundamentalisms are not the same. No less, we can question how religious fundamentalism is associated with some religions – Islam in particular – and not others. An insightful observer of how religion, fundamentalism, and Islam are being interchangeably used, Minoo Moallem, argues that representations of Islamic fundamentalism in the West are driven by racism; these representations reduce all Muslims to fundamentalists, and are founded upon the duality of irrational, morally inferior, and barbaric men and passive, victimized, and subservient women.[39] This link between Islam and fundamentalism reinforces questionable distinctions not only between "our faith" and "their fundamentalism," but also between "our patriotism" and "their nationalism," as mentioned in the Introduction to this book.

Religion and fundamentalism

In his book, *Nations and Nationalism since 1780*, Hobsbawm asks, "Why and how could a concept so remote from the real experience of most human beings as 'national patriotism' become such a powerful political force so quickly?"[40] The general answer for Hobsbawm is to be found in the pre-existing feelings of collective belonging. Religion may be the context for some of those feelings. Religion serves many functions in our lives, and creating forms of solidarity between people of the same faith is surely one of them. What else would explain why Christian evangelists from the United States travel to predominantly Islamic countries that have only small groups of Christian believers but the desire to show solidarity with these minorities and, of course, to spread the word of God as they understand it? From the point of view of the sociologist Emile Durkheim, religion is a system of beliefs and practices related to sacred things that unifies believers into a community or institution. In this sense, religion can be seen as one possible aspect of ethnicity. Further, it is not easily distinguishable from definitions of cultural nationalism. However, unlike nationalists who aspire to territorial sovereignty, religious communities do not necessarily imagine themselves in such political terms.

For our purposes here, I limit my discussions to non-fundamentalist and fundamentalist variations of dominant religions, such as Buddhism, Christianity, Confucianism, Hinduism, Islam, and Judaism. When we consider the role of these "world religions" in relation to nationalisms and national states, a complex, ethno-cultural understanding is necessary. For example, Christianity does not look uniform across cultural contexts; it is shaped by existing local and regional cultural, ethnic, class-based beliefs and practices. So other aspects of ethnicity, such as language, folk culture, or myths of a common past, interact with the specific local or regional expressions of religions such as Christianity to create multiple varieties, of which some are fundamentalist.

In their five-volume series, *Fundamentalisms Comprehended*, the editors, Martin E. Marty and R. Scott Appleby, use a working definition of the concept of fundamentalism. It is: "a tendency of some members of religious communities to separate from fellow believers and to redefine the sacred community in terms of its disciplined opposition to nonbelievers and 'lukewarm' believers alike."[41] This definition is somewhat limited because it defines fundamentalism in terms of religion, but, given our focus, that is not a major concern here. Contrary to widely prevailing stereotypes that link fundamentalism and Islam, the term "fundamentalism" was first associated with Christian groups in early twentieth-century United States. Faced with the perceived threat from Catholic immigrants into the United States, Protestants took on the name Fundamentalist (c.1910) in order to profess their faith and register their differences not only from Catholics but also from the more liberal, modernist Protestants.[42]

Non-fundamentalist and fundamentalist religious groups are hierarchically organized. While some of them do aspire to a more egalitarian system, they still have a minimal authority structure that guarantees influence to the leadership. In fact, most groups are shaped by the teachings and presence of a charismatic leader. One aspect of the organizational and ideological structures of most religious groups is that women tend to take a secondary place. It is not to suggest that women do not participate or even occupy positions of authority. Rather, a typical characteristic of fundamentalist and non-fundamentalist religious groups is the, albeit varying, emphasis on the patriarchal, heterosexual family unit and on clearly prescribed different gender roles for women and men, in which women are primarily recognized as mothers and wives. Even when religious groups do not actively advocate inequality between men and women, confining women to the roles of biological reproducers and as companions to their husbands has the effect of reinforcing social inequalities.

What is notable is that differences between fundamentalist and non-fundamentalist groups are neither unambiguous nor are they stable. Yet religious fundamentalist groups tend to display in exaggerated form some of the characteristics of the non-fundamentalists. If religious communities observe some distinctions between believers and nonbelievers, fundamentalists groups tend to have more sharply defined boundaries. Gabriel Almond, Emmanuel Sivan, and R. Scott Appleby note that these distinctions might be metaphorical or spatial.[43] Members of fundamentalist groups might be required to live within a certain area or organize their lives around specific institutions. Their behaviors, rituals, and clothes might be regulated in order to distinguish between believers and non-believers. These distinctions are compounded by a dualistic worldview where divisions between believers and nonbelievers coincide with good and evil, with virtue and sin, with redemption and damnation. The category "outsiders" would include not only members of other faiths and agnostics, but also the more moderate and mainstream members within the same faith. This attempt to create sharply defined boundaries to the religious community is one of the most striking aspects of fundamentalist groups.

Another defining aspect of fundamentalist groups is claims of "true" or "pure" interpretations of religious teachings from the ancient past. This is what makes them fundamentalist in the proper sense: the refusal to acknowledge the possibility of other interpretations of the same religious tradition. Further, fundamentalist claims that their interpretations are continuous with ancient or pre-modern traditional and orthodox religious practices cannot be backed up. On the contrary, fundamentalism is a hybrid of new elements and resurrected traditions from the past. Moallem describes its paradoxical nature: fundamentalisms are both an offshoot of and response to modernity, but also seek to counter modernity.[44] Syncretic rather than either new or traditional, religious fundamentalisms selectively borrow from the contemporary while resurrecting notions of the past. They tend not to simply defend tradition, but to re-create selectively certain aspects of tradition.[45] Even though fundamentalisms would strongly root themselves in scripture and emphasize their continuities with the past, they are rarely eager to return to those golden antique times. In fact they may deliberately take up some products of modernity, asserting that to be conservative or traditionalist in contemporary life is inadequate or even counterproductive. Fundamentalists adopt new technologies, such as cellular phones, faxes, and web pages, resort to new ideologies, and new methods to disseminate their teachings. In some cases, fundamentalist movements might creatively borrow from the ideas of groups they oppose as well as the traditions that they claim as their own. For example, in the United States, Christian fundamentalists indict feminism as a source of social ills but, ironically, do not fail to use one of feminism's central tenets – that women and men are equal – to expand their own following. At the same time, fundamentalist movements typically indict what they consider the deplorable aspects of modernity and so-called westernization, in order to justify the expanded role of religion; they may mobilize against the option to choose abortion in the United States, deny the presence of gay and lesbian people in India, or attempt to ensure tight control of women's sexuality in Iran.

The politicization of religion and religious fundamentalisms

Undoubtedly, there is close interaction between institutionalized religions and nationalism. Religious identification can be the basis for national solidarity. Indeed, there is notable similarity between the "imagined communities" of religion and those of the nation. Like nationalism, religion fosters a ways of establishing unity and brotherhood among people who otherwise have little direct contact or little in common. Examples such as Ireland, Israel, and Iran clearly indicate the connection between religious and national communities.

But the point is not that there is any easy or inherent coincidence between religious and national communities. In fact Anderson argues that for nationalism to predominate as a way of imagining community, it had to supersede the factors that made world religions and their communities possible.[46] Perhaps the most important of these was a sacred language. Sacred languages made possible communion between members belonging to different ethnic and cultural groups but sharing the same faith. Yet they were regarded as sacred because they represented the word of God and the truth of the religion. That a relatively small elite knew these languages only reinforced the idea of hierarchy and authority as natural. The community of religion, Anderson believes, was founded on the sanctity of a language and its relation to truth, and was hierarchical rather than horizontal and boundary-oriented. Nationalism could arise as an alternative form of community only with the demotion of sacred languages, the decline of the belief that truth was encoded in them, and the burgeoning possibility that communities could be horizontal and egalitarian. Indeed, Anderson's approach seems to explain better why in recent times some groups aspire to religious communities extending beyond national boundaries.

On the basis of Anderson's thesis, then, it seems harder to account for national communities that are imagined through the idiom of religion and the cases where religiously based groups seek sovereignty over a territory. Keeping in mind both the coincidences and the tensions between religion and nationalisms, it seems that religion is neither a sufficient nor necessary criterion for nationalism, but it can be tremendously important. The link between religion and nationalism can be summarized in two ways: religion is instrumental in rising nationalisms; and religion is inspirational in nationalist movements.

Instrumental role of religion: In some cases, nationalisms are not inspired by religion as much as they seek religious justification, religious symbolism, and religious interpretations to garner support for their cause. Put simply, religion is an instrument for some nationalist movements, and sometimes it is religion of a fundamentalist kind that is used to garner political support. Almond, Sivan, and Appleby call these "fundamentalist-like" movements because they are inspired by political rather than religious considerations.[47] In contrast to fundamentalist movements that are drawn into politics only as a result of their religious beliefs, fundamentalistlike movements merely invoke religion to justify their political purposes.

Ulster Protestants in Northern Ireland can be seen as an example of fundamentalistlike movements. In the case of Northern Ireland, the religious conflict between Protestants and Catholics is typically described as a conflict between unionism and nationalism. In this framework, Catholics who aspire to a united Ireland are characterized as nationalists and the Protestants who seek to be part of Britain, as unionists. Recasting it as a clash between two nationalisms, Elizabeth Porter argues that, after all, the Protestant desire for union with Britain is also a form of nationalism.[48] Other scholars go so far as to say that Ulster Protestantism is an ethnic nationalist movement that resorts to religious symbolism in order to overcome its opponent.[49]

Religious iconography can be especially important to legitimize nationalisms. Hobsbawm suggests that religious icons and practices, such as prayers in school or the Virgin of Guadalupe in Mexico, give a palpable reality to the otherwise imaginary community of the nation.[50] Those icons and practices that have the backing of the state can be especially powerful symbols. Perhaps therefore, in the United States, the issue of whether the state can mandate prayers in school is highly charged on both sides. For conservative religious leaders like Jerry Falwell, the US Supreme Court decision against prayer in public school signifies the dangers of secularism in the United States. For others in favor of the

Court's decision, maintaining a line between the state and the religion is a foundational principal of the (north) American nation. More recently, the rise of religion among the nation's political leaders in Washington DC in the aftermath of the September 11 terrorist attacks has been noticeable. For those who strongly believe in the principles of a secular American state, prayer meetings, and a more general expression of religiosity by political leaders, has been a cause for concern.

The organizational structures of religious groups may also be instrumental in launching and supporting nationalist movements. Palestinian nationalism is closely allied with the organization Hamas. Initially, Hamas emerged as an Islamic movement resisting Israeli occupation. The Intifada, or the religious uprising that was declared in 1987, brought Hamas into prominence, and, after the 1993 Oslo Accord, it emerged as the best-organized and most influential force in the Palestinian territories.[51] As a political movement, Hamas combines nationalist resistance against Israeli occupation, the movement for a sovereign Palestinian Islamic state, and the strengthening of Islam's role in civil institutions. But the key to its success was its organizational capacity; for example, Hamas ran schools, health clinics, and food aid programs. Not only did this gain widespread grassroots support, but it also enabled Hamas to emerge as one of the leading religious-nationalist movements in the occupied territories.

Inspirational role of religion: Following the broader line of argument developed in the preceding section on ethnicity and nationalism, religion can be a central aspect of nationalist movements, but not without active political intervention. In contrast to the instrumental role of religion in some nationalist movements, religion can help shape the aims of nationalist movements. Despite the threat posed by religious nationalisms to the principle of secular nationalism, religion can and does inspire nationalist movements. No doubt, nationalisms so inspired have significant limitations, but not inherently more so than secular nationalisms.

In the case of Iran, in 1979, Ayatollah Khomeini brought to fruition a religious nationalist movement that had been gathering momentum since the 1960s. This revolutionary movement was the outcome of several factors.[52] Rapid but unequal economic development had created a situation in which there was a wide gap between the profiteering elites and the old merchant and lower classes. Despite the expansion of education, university students were often left without suitable employment or opportunities for political expression, producing a discrepancy between aspirations and reality. The basis for the movement, the traditional merchant classes, students, and professionals, were inspired by Ali Shari'ati, who advocated a revival of Shi'ite Islam to combat the tyranny of ruling elites and the onslaught of western ideas and culture.[53] The modernization policies under the Shah of Iran, such as the unprecedented presence of women in the public sphere in the cities, and the problems of rapid urbanization, such as delinquency and alcoholism, were seen as symptoms of moral laxity. Khomeini repeated Shari'ati's call to make Shi'ism the activist political solution to all forms of oppression, exploitation, and social injustice.

Under Khomeini's leadership, the nationalist revolution was marshaled against the legitimacy of the existing state. At this point, religion was neither an inevitable nor simply a functional aspect of the nationalist movement. The nationalist revolution sought the legitimacy of religion in its challenge to the Shah's regime and the existing secular state but it also recast the role of religion in political life. Religion was used to reimagine the national community; to imagine a different sort of modern state; and to reframe the relationship between religion and state. The mix of reformist Shi'ism and revolutionary beliefs resulted in the formation of the Islamic Republic of Iran.

The case of Ireland is similarly illustrative of the interplay between religion, nationalism, and the state. Angela Martin finds that the roots of Irish nationalism can be located in the Devotional Revolution of the mid-nineteenth century.[54] This revolution gave the Irish Church greater control over religious practices, education, gender and sexual practices and the Irish nationalist clubs modeled their approach on the Devotional Revolution. The Irish Free State, founded in 1922, enshrined Irish Catholic morality in the juridical structures of the state and the constitution by underscoring the patriarchal nuclear family and limiting the access of married women to work outside the home. However, especially since 1973, when Ireland joined the European Community, geopolitical, economic, and juridical boundaries of the Irish state have seemed to be in question. Martin argues that widespread perceptions that the Irish nation is itself dissolving are precipitating a crisis of Irish nationalism and a sense that Irish Catholic morality is under threat.

Not surprisingly, highly emotive, religiously linked issues, such as contraception, abortion, and divorce are the grounds upon which questions of religion and nationalism are being sorted out. These questions came to a head with "The X Case" in 1992, involving the rape of a 14-year-old girl by the father of a schoolmate. What catapulted this case into national prominence was the girl's plan to travel to England for an abortion, since the Irish constitution prevents women from obtaining an abortion. In effect, the courts played the decisive role in this case. Martin reports that this case was tied up in the courts for a while until, shortly before it would be too late in the pregnancy to obtain an abortion in England, the Irish High Court permitted her to travel; the deciding factor seems to have been that the court was convinced that the 14-year-old girl would commit suicide if denied this right.

Fundamentalism and nationalism

If nationalisms and religions are intertwined and not inherently dangerous, the question is under what circumstances do they become ominous. Part of the answer lies in the difference between religious and religious fundamentalist nationalisms. As noted earlier, even though these differences are not always clear or stable, the inherent tendency of religious fundamentalisms to draw sharp differences between those who belong to the community and those who do not is what makes them of concern. Further, when fundamentalist movements seek the political idiom of nationalism in order to rethink the relationship between the state and members of the faith and to place non-members outside of the religious and national community, they become dangerous. While not all fundamentalist groups seek direct control of the state or aspire to make the religious and national communities synonymous, their concerns with matters of modernity and secularism prompt them to vie over political issues affecting the nation.

One pattern underlying the diversity of fundamentalisms in the twentieth century is that they seem to emerge against the perceived threat of a secular world and what are seen as the ills of modernity. For fundamentalists, not only does the secularization of local and national communities and the world at large imply a pluralistic, unreligious setting in which there are fewer followers, but also that the religious community might itself be dissolved. Almond, Sivan, and Appleby argue that a chief perceived enemy of fundamentalist movements is the secularizing state that has a rationalized bureaucracy, propagates secular education, prohibits or restricts religion and religious practices in schools, and encourages what are seen as sinful practices, such as divorce, extramarital sex, homosexuality, greater rights for women.[55] The crux of the problem of the secularizing state for fundamentalists is that the state fails to provide support for religion. As a result, a fundamentalist movement may seek to gain control of the state to restore the sanctity of religion in the workings of the state and to oppose any attempts to draw lines between the state and religion. Indeed, the separation of state and religion is anathema to fundamentalist movements with aspirations for expansion outside their own community.

Another side of the state's inadequacy, from the perspective of fundamentalist groups, is its intrusion into the religious sphere. State legislation that curbs the financial operations of these movements, schools run by them, and their move toward militancy in the form of hate speech or arms build-up are examples of state intrusion into the religious sphere that might be considered intolerable by fundamentalist groups. More significantly, efforts to suppress and eradicate these movements for fear that they will take over political institutions can instead increase their aspirations. Egypt and Algeria are countries where political leaders who endorse the importance of keeping apart religion and the state have also struggled to suppress the rising influence of more extreme and fundamentalist religious groups. Egypt and Algeria exemplify how the repressing of religious fundamentalisms detract from efforts to forge democratic regimes. Mark Juergensmeyer notes that, in Algeria, Islamic movements have been a source of discomfort for Algerian nationalists since independence in 1962.[56] Even though the front Islamic de Salut (FIS) won 55 percent of the vote in the 1990 local elections and 40 percent of the vote at the first stage of the national elections in 1991, it was routed by the military. In lieu of continuing with the national elections, the army established a secular military junta in 1992, thereby prompting a civil war that continued until 1993. The threat of an Islamic state, on the one hand, and a military, repressive regime, on the other hand complicated Euro-American responses to Algeria. Alternating between tacit and later more open support for the Algerian dictatorship that aimed to contain the threat of fundamentalisms, the Euro-American response was inadequate and confused, and showed how Islam and democracy, or democracy and repression, are not as exclusive as widely believed.

The RSS and Hindu nationalism

I would like to conclude this chapter by focusing on the escalation of Hindu nationalism in the 1990s and its links to the Indian national state. This is not only an example of the links between nationalism and fundamentalism but also turns our attention to their underlying danger. At stake, I argue, are revised, exclusionary notions of citizenship.

Hindu nationalism is based on a coalition of three fundamentalist organizations, namely Rashtriya Swayamsevak Sangh (RSS, or National Organization of Self-helpers), the Vishwa Hindu Parishad (VHP, or World Hindu Society), and the Bharatiya Janata Party (BJP, or Indian People's Party). The RSS emerged out of the strife between Hindus and

Muslims in colonial, pre-partition India, and in reaction to the formation of Muslim organizations. The VHP was founded in 1964 at the initiative of RSS to spread the philosophy of *Hindutva*. *Hindutva* specifies a realm that is based in the racial, cultural, and religious superiority of Hindus. Almond, Sivan, and Appleby describe that its basic tenets reject a secular, pluralistic state, and aim at the creation of a Hindu state that observes traditional sacred boundaries and includes only practicing Hindus.[57] This equivalence of Hindu fundamentalism and a Hindu state leads these researchers to note that "Hindu fundamentalism appears to be as much a militant nation- and state-building (or rebuilding) movement, as a traditional religion-affirming movement."[58] As Paola Bacchetta persuasively demonstrates, the RSS sought to "unify" Hindus and "build" their "character" to resurrect a Hindu state, thereby making the religious and political domains the same.[59]

In a more nuanced discussion of the relationship between the Hindu nation and state than that by Almond, Sivan, and Appleby, Bacchetta notes that the state as a political apparatus is subordinated to the higher ideal of the Hindu nation. Yet the effort to make state and civil society sacred led to the founding of the BJP in 1980 as the political instrument of the RSS. The BJP successfully contested national elections in the 1990s and by the turn of the twenty-first century emerged as the leading party in the Indian parliament, realizing an important step toward the creation of this Hindu, rather than secular and pluralistic, state.

The membership of these three groups sheds light on the continuing appeal of this Hindu fundamentalism. Elite members of the three groups are drawn primarily from the upwardly mobile middle class, from lower middle-class professionals, merchants, and cash-crop farmers. They tend to be upper-caste, and either school or college graduates, but not from elite universities. The rank and file recruits, however, are either school-educated or illiterate. What Valerie Hoffman has said about the economic causes of Muslim fundamentalists is also true here. Post-independence development and modernization may have led to some improvement in the lives of the middle and lower middle classes, but the limited nature of these benefits aggravate disappointment and frustration; there are significant discrepancies between their increased access to education and their disappointed hopes of higher social status and economic gain. Increasing landlessness among peasants and large-scale migration to urban areas has created vast numbers of urban and semi-urban poor. In sum, the widening socioeconomic disparity between the upper classes and the lower middle classes, and the continued impoverishment of large numbers of people provide fuel to fundamentalist rhetoric. No less, these disparities indicate important social and economic differences among those who respond to the call of fundamentalism.

This fundamentalism is male-centered and often virulently masculinist. Until the 1980s, Hindu women were not mentioned in the writings of the RSS.[60] Thereafter, Bacchetta notes, Hindu women were invoked as mothers who would impart Hindu culture to their sons, nurture their virile qualities, and raise them to be nationalists willing to defend the nation against its enemies. Notably, there is little discussion on women as wives and references to women are to them as mothers and "little sisters." But, since then, Hindu women have been mobilized within this masculinist framework in a different way: as promulgators of this fundamentalist discourse. Each of the three organizations discussed now has a distinct women's component that allows women to participate in Hindu nationalism. What complicates the albeit limited role of women, according to Amrita Basu, is that a number of women attained greater prominence in the Hindu nationalist movement than women in the more secular nationalist movements.[61] The women who emerged as powerful proponents of Hindu nationalism openly incited violence against the perceived enemy, especially by magnifying the threats to their sexual honor from Muslim men. By invoking patriarchal norms of a woman's honor as sacred and placing the responsibility on men to seek revenge when it is violated, these women rouse both Hindu masculinity and Hindu nationalism.

However, it is difficult to claim that these women are simply instruments of male-centered Hindu nationalism. Basu believes that the BJP's representations of the rape of Hindu women as symbolic of the victimization of the entire Hindu community are effective because it invokes the violence that women routinely suffer.[62] Further, Bacchetta notes that what women's groups say often differs from male fundamentalist accounts. Where the men focus on Muslim men as the enemy, women also indict Hindu men for contributing to the problems faced by them. Yet they surely help consolide the boundaries of the religious and national community, albeit in somewhat different ways from men.

If the loosely defined community of Hindu fundamentalism and nationalism is fraught by internal differences of social class, and caste, and gender, then these differences are obscured in representations by non-Hindus, especially Muslims. Among the various non-Hindu groups in India, Muslim communities are by far the most targeted, by Hindu fundamentalists. It was not coincidental that one of VHP's massive undertakings in 1990 was to launch a *rath yatra* (a pilgrimage on a chariot, actually a well-equipped Toyota van) to demolish a mosque that was supposedly built on the birthplace of the Hindu god, Ram.[63] After a couple of unsuccessful attempts, on December 6, 1992, 200,000 Hindu "self-helpers" tore down the over-four-hundred-year-old mosque.[64] Significant revisions of history and historical mythology were necessary to this task. The Hindu fundamentalists claimed that originally there was a temple to commemorate the exact spot of Ram's birth, but that it later fell into disuse. According to them, a Hindu ruler from the fifth century CE ordered a reconstruction of the temple, among others, after a divine revelation. In 1528, Babur, the founder of the Mughal dynasty, ordered the temple destroyed and a mosque erected in its place, in this historical account. Both claims are open to question. Yet, so-called reputed historians and the alleged self-revelation by Ram to a Muslim guard in charge of the mosque were called on to justify the demolition of the mosque. The ensuing riots in far-flung cities such as Mumbai (formerly Bombay) bear testimony to the terrible passions aroused by the dark side of Hindu nationalism.

Harjot Oberoi maintains that the crux of the problem is that for these Hindu fundamentalist groups there are no distinctions between religious members and citizens.[65] In the case of Hindu nationalism, as in others, members do not see themselves as fundamentalist. Since fundamentalism is tantamount to the claim that there is only one truth, it is unable to recognize itself as such. Oberoi argues that Hindu fundamentalism claims to represent the true forces of nationalism, and speaks of themes that have long been the preserve of nationalism, namely, injustice, exploitation, territory, and inherent rights of people, among others. Like fundamentalism, nationalism seeks to transcend parochial identities, such as religion, region, sect, clan, etc., in exchange for the rewards of citizenship. That the social and cultural entitlements of citizenship will accrue only to Hindus, Oberoi says, is the expected outcome of a nationalism that is defined on the basis of religious affiliation. However, the differences of gender, social class, and caste intrinsic to the Hindu fundamentalist/nationalist community further ensure that the benefits of citizenship will not be equally distributed.

What compounds this threat of Hindu fundamentalism is BJP's rise to political power. Religious cultural nationalisms thereby gain political clout and influence. No doubt, the rhetoric of who belongs to the Hindu nation is more complicated than might initially appear. Partly in order to stay in power, the BJP actively solicits political votes from religious minorities, including Muslims, Sikhs, and Christians, by relying on *Hindutva* rhetoric. This rhetoric sees the ethnic-religious national community of Hinduism as including all manners of Hindus, but also reinterprets minority religions, such as Jains, Buddhists, and Sikhs, as off-shoots of the font of Hinduism. In some cases, there are even attempts to recast Christians and

Muslims as "Hindu by blood," on the basis of the idea that prior to conversion they were Hindu; not surprisingly, Muslim and Christian leaders resist this appropriation of their faith and erasure of their religious beliefs.

But momentous political events can test how belonging and citizenship is imagined, how boundaries of the national community are drawn, and when religious fundamentalisms have the clout of state actors and agencies. According to leading accounts, in February 2002, a Muslim mob in Godhra, Gujarat, deliberately set fire to a train containing Hindu religious volunteers, killing 59 of them. Under the leadership of well-respected Supreme Court justices, the report of this event is being contested by citizen rights groups. If it did occur, it was a reprehensible act of violence that belongs in the larger, historical, and regional context of ongoing tensions between Hindus and Muslims.

However, there is little doubt about what followed. It is estimated that more than 1,000 Muslim adults and children were killed by a murderous mob in an unimaginable rampage. Residential areas, mosques and other places of worship, and businesses were targeted to maximize physical, sexual, and psychological trauma and economic devastation to Muslim communities in surrounding areas. The carnage committed through rape, murder of the young and the unborn, slaughter of hundreds of Muslims, setting women and men on fire was not only brutal but also systematic. There is no question about the dehumanization of Muslims that is necessary to enable this kind of bloodshed; there is no question about the idea that women's bodies were metonyms of their communities, which encouraged their defilement by Hindu aggressors. But what needs to be underscored is that this scale of violence could hardly occur without the involvement of the state.

The issue here is as much the brutality of Hindu sectarianism as it is the complicity of the state. In some cases, state agencies actively participated in the atrocities and, in other cases, stood mute and refused assistance to traumatized Muslims. There is now every indication that this was a systematically orchestrated attack under the leadership of the head of the state of Gujarat, Chief Minister Narendra Modi. In fact, well-founded allegations suggest that the possibility of an attack was already in place prior to the spark allegedly lit by the Muslim mob. What further compounds the collusion of the state is that Modi is a member of the BJP and despite repeated calls for his resignation no formal charges have been brought against him. What is more difficult to fathom is that in the elections held in the fall of 2002, Narendra Modi and the BJP party won a landslide victory in the state of Gujarat. But perhaps this is an indication of how the fear of the other, especially in the aftermath of such brutality, has taken a firmer hold among Gujarati Hindus, both fundamentalist and non-fundamentalist.

The Hindu fundamentalism in question here is by no means unified or homogenous; it is masculinist, class- and caste-based. These internal differences are partly obscured even as they are magnified manifold and violently enacted on external groups, in this case Muslim communities in the surrounding areas. But this discourse of Hindu fundamentalism can thrive in so far as it draws political support from the state, in this case the BJP. Ethnic and religious tensions can inspire passion and violence, but with the force of fundamentalism and the political clout of state actors and agencies, the results are terrible indeed. Ultimately, what this kind of collusion between fundamentalism and nationalism does is not only to ensure that the meaning of citizenship and belonging is revised. With support from the state, denial of belonging and citizenship takes on deadly meanings. And, without concerted effort against such revisions, citizenship's scope may get narrower and narrower.

Conclusion

In a world that appears riven by sectarian violence and religious fundamentalisms, it is interesting that nationalisms still seem to be significant. This chapter therefore explored the possibility of ethnic communities as the bases for nationalisms as well as the potent effects of ethnically defined nationalisms. The argument developed in this chapter was that despite compelling reasons to map the links between nations and pre-modern ethnic formations, there is no natural congruence. If anything, nationalisms have continually to give shape to the ethnic community and its past. More importantly, ethnicity and notions of ethnic identity are politicized through the framework of nationalism. Ethnicity is an important aspect of social identity and not inherently given to violence. In its link to nationalism, it can also inspire a movement for cultural and political sovereignty. But clearly, the kind of inclusion and exclusion the ethnic nationalist community practices can lead to terrible sectarian hatred and violence.

The second part of this chapter dwelled on the links between religion and nationalism, with a particular focus on the role of religious fundamentalisms. Religious movements can take on the guise of nationalism in striving for more control, and nationalisms can take on the mantle of religious fundamentalisms in their search for greater legitimacy. But when religion serves as the basis for sharp divisions between citizens and aliens, as do religious fundamentalisms, there is every reason to be concerned about nationalism. There seem to be few positive or reassuring trends in these interconnections between fundamentalisms and nationalisms. Both are essentially imagined as egalitarian forms of community with ideas of who belongs or does not belong to the community. When they take strength from each other, the exclusions are heightened with violent and direct consequences. Seen in this light, fundamentalisms do not have to be religious in order to be dangerous.

NOTES

1 Bapsi Sidhwa, *Cracking India: A Novel* (Minneapolis: Milkweed Editions, 1991).
2 Walker Connor, *Ethnonationalism: The Quest for Understanding* (Princeton, NJ: Princeton University Press, 1994), esp. p. 5.
3 Ibid., esp. pp. 8–12.
4 Thomas H. Eriksen, *Ethnicity and Nationalism*, 2nd edn. (London and Sterling, Vt.: Pluto Press, 2002), esp. p. 2.
5 Stuart Hall, "New ethnicities," in Bill Ashcroft, Gareth Griffiths, Helen Tiffin (eds.) *The Post-colonial Studies Reader* (London and New York: Routledge, 1995), pp. 223–7, esp. p. 227.
6 Linda Colley, "Britishness and otherness: an argument," *Journal of British Studies* 31 (October 1992), p. 328.
7 Rian Leith and Hussein Solomon, "On ethnicity and ethnic conflict management in Nigeria," *Africa Journal in Conflict Resolution* 1 (2001), http://www.accord.org.za/web.nsf.
8 Ibid., p. 2.
9 Stuart Hall, "The local and the global: globalization and ethnicity," in Anthony D. King (ed.) *Culture, Globalization and the World System: Contemporary Conditions for the Representation of Identity* (Minneapolis: University of Minnesota Press, 1997), p. 21.
10 Eriksen, *Ethnicity and Nationalism*, esp. p. 12.
11 Paul R. Brass, *Ethnicity and Nationalism: Theory and Comparison* (New Delhi, Newbury Park, and London: Sage Publications, 1991), p. 247.
12 Craig J. Calhoun, *Nationalism* (Minneapolis: University of Minnesota Press, 1997), p. 50.
13 Hall, "The local and the global," esp. p. 21.
14 Kobena Mercer, *Welcome to the Jingle: New Positions in Black Cultural Studies* (New York and London: Routledge, 1994), pp. 270–3.
15 Eriksen, *Ethnicity and Nationalism*, esp. ch. 6.
16 Connor, *Ethnonationalism*, esp. ch. 1.
17 Ibid., pp. 35–8.
18 Anthony D. Smith, *Nationalism and Modernism: A Critical Survey of Recent Theories of Nations and Nationalism* (London and New York: Routledge, 1998), p. 191.

19   Connor, *Ethnonationalism*, p. 42.
20   Ibid., esp. chs. 2 and 3.
21   Brass, *Ethnicity and Nationalism*, p. 19.
22   Ibid., p. 20.
23   Ibid., esp. pp. 23–5.
24   Eric J. Hobsbawm, *Nations and Nationalism since 1780: Programme, Myth, and Reality* (Cambridge: Cambridge University Press, 1990), esp. ch. 2.
25   Hall, "The local and the global," p. 22.
26   Benedict Anderson, *Imagined Communities: Reflections on the Origin and Spread of Nationalism*, revised edn. (London and New York: Verso, 1991), esp. ch. 3.
27   Hobsbawm, *Nations and Nationalism*, p. 60.
28   Calhoun, *Nationalism*, pp. 58–65.
29   Ibid., p. 62.
30   Julie Mostov, "Sexing the nation/desexing the body: politics of national identity in the former Yugoslavia," in Tamar Mayer (ed.) *Gender Ironies of Nationalism: Sexing the Nation* (London and New York: Routledge, 2000), esp. pp. 90–2.
31   Brass, *Ethnicity and Nationalism*, esp. ch. 2.
32   Ibid., pp. 41–8.
33   Ibid., pp. 48–50.
34   Ibid., pp. 50–5.
35   Ibid., pp. 55–62.
36   Philip Gourevitch, *We Wish to Inform You that Tomorrow We Will be Killed with Our Families: Stories from Rwanda* (New York: Farrar Straus and Giroux, 1998), esp. p. 50.
37   Ibid., pp. 55–8.
38   Calhoun, *Nationalism*, p. 35.
39   Minoo Moallem, "Transnationalism, feminism, and fundamentalism," in Caren Kaplan, Norma Alarcón, and Minoo Moallem (eds.) *Between Woman and Nation* (Durham, NC and London: Duke University Press, 1999), pp. 320–48, esp. pp. 322–4.
40   Hobsbawm, *Nations and Nationalism*, p. 46.
41   Martin E. Marty and R. Scott Appleby, "Introduction," in Martin E. Marty and R. Scott Appleby (eds.) *The Fundamentalist Project*, vol. 5, *Fundamentalisms Comprehended* (Chicago and London: University of Chicago Press, 1995), p. 1.
42   Ibid., p. 13.
43   Gabriel Almond, Emmanuel Sivan, and R. Scott Appleby, "Fundamentalism: genus and species," in Marty and Appleby, *Fundamentalisms Comprehended*, pp. 399–424, esp. pp. 405–8.
44   Moallem, "Transnationalism, feminism, and fundamentalism," p. 323.
45   Almond et al., "Fundamentalism," p. 406.
46   Anderson, *Imagined Communities*, esp. ch. 2.
47   Almond et al., "Fundamentalism," pp. 419–21.
48   Elizabeth Porter, "Identity, location, plurality: women, nationalism and Northern Ireland," in Rick Wilford and Robert L. Miller (eds.) *Women, Ethni-*

city and Nationalism (London and New York: Routledge, 1998), pp. 36–61, esp. p. 37.

49 Almond et al., "Fundamentalism," p. 420.

50 Hobsbawm, *Nations and Nationalism*, esp. p. 72.

51 Gabriel A. Almond, Emmanuel Sivan, and R. Scott Appleby, "Examining the cases," in Marty and Appleby, *Fundamentalisms Comprehended*, pp. 445–82, esp. p. 450.

52 Nayereh Tohidi, "Modernization, Islamization, and women in Iran," in Valentine M. Moghadam (ed.) *Gender and National Identity: Women and Politics in Muslim Societies* (London and Atlantic Highlands, NJ: Zed Press and Karachi: Oxford University Press, 1994), pp. 110–47.

53 Ibid., esp. pp. 120–3.

54 Angela K. Martin, "Death of a nation: transnationalism, bodies and abortion in late twentieth-century Ireland," in Mayer, *Gender Ironies of Nationalism*, pp. 65–86, esp. p. 66.

55 Almond et al., "Fundamentalism," esp. pp. 405–6.

56 Mark Juergensmeyer, "Antifundamentalism," in Marty and Appleby, *Fundamentalisms Comprehended*, pp. 353–66, esp. pp. 355–6.

57 Almond et al., "Examining the cases," esp. pp. 464–9.

58 Ibid., p. 467.

59 Paola Bacchetta, "Hindu nationalist women as ideologues: the Sangh, the Samiti and differential concepts of the Hindu nation," in Kumari Jayawardena and Malathi de Alwis (eds.) *Embodied Violence: Communalising Women's Sexuality in South Asia* (New Delhi: Kali for Women, 1996), pp. 126–67, esp. p. 129.

60 Ibid., esp. pp. 148–51.

61 Amrita Basu, "Feminism inverted: the gendered imagery and real women of Hindu fundamentalism," in Tanika Sarkar and Urvashi Butalia (eds.) *Women and the Hindu Right: A Collection of Essays* (New Delhi: Kali for Women, 1995), pp. 158–80, esp. p. 159.

62 Ibid., pp. 170–4.

63 Harjot Oberoi, "Mapping Indic fundamentalisms through nationalism and modernity," in Marty and Appleby, *Fundamentalisms Comprehended*, pp. 96–114, esp. p. 110.

64 Ibid., p. 100.

65 Ibid., esp. pp. 97–101.

Speculations on the Future of Nationalisms

By way of concluding this book, I want to recapitulate the multiple accounts of nationalism that crisscross through the preceding chapters. At one level, the chapters describe nationalism, its rise, its different manifestations, and its important facets. Clearly, as the chapters reflect, there are disagreements about what various scholars have to say about nationalism and its patterns. At another level, then, are the questions of how to approach nationalism and what broader themes are encoded within its idiom, such as race, gender, sexuality, and ethnicity.

A culturalist approach to nationalism is shaped by, but also critical of, what are loosely described as modernist theories of nationalism. Partly shaped by Anderson and Hobsbawm's insights, the culturalist approach sees nationalisms as modern phenomena that are conceived, but are not unreal. I also want to emphasize that this is not to simply acknowledge that nationalisms are culturally constructed but to push the argument further: that nationalisms need to be continually imagined, reproduced, and reiterated in order for them to appear normal and natural. Therefore, a second point is that both the banal as well as the spectacular moments of nationalisms can provide important insights. The persisting influence of nations and nationalisms is not merely a factor in moments of crisis or spectacles such as independence-day celebrations in former colonies and the USA, for that matter. If anything, nations and nationalisms are woven through the fabric of everyday life. Third, a culturalist approach departs from modernist theories in two related ways: it argues against a single theory of nationalism and its origins; and it challenges Euro-American-centered perspectives on nationalism that either disregard non-western settings or, worse, create disreputable stereotypes of non-western nationalisms. A fourth aspect is to see nationalisms as inherently ambivalent: reactionary and revolutionary, inclusionary and exclusionary, patriotic and dangerous, unifying and divisive, homogenizing and discriminating, usually at the same time. Another related approach is to explore the potential role of social elites and intelligentsia in nationalist movements as well as its more popular expressions without mechanically disparaging one and romanticizing the other. The sixth aspect of the culturalist approach is to recognize the racialized, gendered, sexualized, and ethnicized roots and implications of nationalisms. Finally, it is to see nationalism as an idiom that is politically linked to the state but is expressed in cultural terms.

From this vantage point, one would say that the concepts of nationalism and nation took shape in Western Europe and North America, especially under the influence of the French Revolution (1789–92) and the American Revolution (1776). This is different from claiming that nations and nationalisms originated with these revolutions. Making such a claim is difficult because it simplifies a complex set of processes. Rather than seeing these revolutions as crystallizing factors, the claim reduces the origins of nations and nationalisms to two or more historical and culturally specific moments. We need to take a complicated rather than a reductive approach to nationalism. For example, as Benedict Anderson notes, nationalism may have been imagined by creole populations in the American colonies and then exported elsewhere. The gradual crystallization of an ethnic, cultural nation in Germany through the early nineteenth century, further undermines the position that nations and nationalisms everywhere have the same trajectory. And Chatterjee's persuasive argument about the fundamental differences between anti-colonial and metropolitan nationalisms moves us further away from treating nationalism monolithically.

Nations and nationalisms are part of the broader social conditions that characterized the late eighteenth century and the turn of the nineteenth century. The possibilities of nationalism existed before this period but it was the interactions between nationalisms and other aspects of modernity – the rise of the modern state, industrial capitalism, and colonialism – that gave it a recognizable form. Colonial expansion, industrialization, increasing capitalist accumulation, and capitalist markets, the centralizing and bureaucratizing state and its militarization were the conditions for the rise of nationalisms.

What was distinctive about its rise under these conditions was nationalism's revolutionary potential. Nationalism became a means to demand

accountability of state governance and rule. Rather than divine or mon-
archial authority, nationalism elevated the subjects of the state as its
supreme authority. It emerged as the principle through which to define
a political community of citizens with a specific and individual relationship to the state. It defined not only the political rights and obligations of
citizens to the state but also the cultural basis of this community: one
where loyalty to the nation ideally superseded all other loyalties of ethnic
group, family, or religious community. Nationalism was about the cultural unification of a group of people dissimilar in social class, race,
ethnicity, religion, and other significant variables into a nation through
state-influenced nationalisms. In effect, it was the French Revolution that
helped people reimagine political and cultural relations between citizens
and the state through the principle of nationalism.

Scholars have argued that there is at least one other broadly defined
route to the formation of nations: one where nations are constructed on
the basis of common origin of a people, or of shared culture, whether of
language, customs, or religion. But the important point is that there is no
natural continuity between pre-existing communities and nations. In that
sense, nationalism marks a point of transformation rather than a point of
continuity with the past. Ethnic communities do not naturally evolve into
nations but have to be actively transformed within its cultural and political idioms. Nations and their distinctive aspects have beginnings in pre-
existing groups but always emerge through the filters of belonging, territory, patriotism, and a horizontal community of citizens. Whether the
nation was forged as a civic community or whether it was conceived as
an ethnic, cultural community, nationalisms were innovative in how they
reconstituted the cultural basis of communities and their relationship to
the state as sovereign political territory.

Nations or national communities were therefore the inventions of nationalism, and required the forging of a national consciousness, ideas of a
national culture, a national past and common destiny. Not surprisingly,
nationalisms imagined a pre-existing community that naturally evolved
into a nation, with a distinctive history and culture. Ethnic commonality
on the basis of language, origins, a shared culture, or territory were
crucial to giving shape to the form and content of nationalism. Amidst
changes wrought by industrial capitalism, especially to the family and the
home, nationalisms also relied heavily on metaphors of kinship and
belonging. These metaphors are not inevitable; rather, this is the means
for nationalism to normalize itself. Nothing less would meet the challenges
of national consciousness and national unity, given the differences and
tensions that divide ethnically or politically unified people.

If nationalism was a means to legitimize the modern state, then the state was crucial to fostering a nation. The centralizing state, the building of communications and transportation infrastructure across the territory, the gradual standardization of language and education, creating and planning a state-wide market economy, identification of a common external enemy, making war, a standing police force and army, and colonial expansion put into place conditions that would help foster a sense of national identity. At the same time, national unity and national consciousness were more self-consciously promoted through the fundamental tasks of the modern state: defining and managing the boundaries of the state, determining the criteria for citizenship, protecting its people, representing their interests, educating, monitoring, and regulating them. State governance through the careful counting, measuring, and classification of its population simultaneously splintered people into individuals and helped recreate them into ethnic, regional, religious groups, and, at the highest level, into a nation. The point is that even though nationalism emerged as a revolutionary cultural and political principle, its spread was not inevitable or organic. It required the structures and intervention of the modern state, thereby blunting its radical possibilities.

Through the eighteenth and nineteenth centuries nationalisms took root in places such as Britain and France through making war and through empire building. Rather than a culturally and historically innovative set of ideas associated with politically radical intellectuals, nationalism became the whip of political conservatives. Notions such as the "political will of the people" and "national interests" are easily appropriated to serve diverse political ends. There is no doubt about the role of radical intellectuals and educated social elites in catalyzing nationalism as a revolutionary movement. They were able to tap into broad-based discontentment among other social groups even as they reworked these frustrations into a nationalist framework. But as nationalisms took root and became institutionalized, they could also be used to garner support for wars, for imperial expansion, and for militarization of nations. Capitalists, bureaucrats, and conservative political leaders, often successfully, sought control of facets of nationalism to further a variety of causes.

If British and French nationalisms were sparked through their mutual conflicts and rivalries then they were also forged out of their encounters with colonial societies. In that sense, nationalisms in Europe, and elsewhere, were complex, multilayered, and relational; for example, there was more than one version of British nationalism, whether in relation to its foremost colonies or its competition and rivalry with France. This does not suggest that there weren't themes consistent across these relationships, such as Britain as a master, Protestant, imperial race, but simply underscores the point that nationalism is neither monolithic nor does it develop outside of perceived relations with other national communities.

In the colonies, nationalism was the means through which subjugated groups imagined their independence from colonial rule. No doubt, it could have been imagined differently; for example, as demands for greater cultural and political autonomy short of independence and the right to self-determination. Nonetheless, nationalism was the principle upon which anti-colonial movements questioned the legitimacy of colonial states and made demands for sovereign statehood and self-rule. If political independence was the primary aim of nationalisms in the colonies, then claims of cultural distinctiveness helped shape the nation. Fostering national consciousness through political movements, literature, and writing histories, defining the national community, and promoting national unity were crucial to anti-colonial nationalisms. However, political movements of subaltern groups, equally aimed against the colonial state and native elites, belied notions of national unity and homogeneity. A significant aspect of the challenge faced by anti-colonial nationalisms was that in order to justify self-rule they had to define how they were culturally unique as a nation but otherwise comparable to metropolitan nationalisms. Points of difference and comparability gave anti-colonial nationalisms their liberating potential and vigor.

If a nationalism is formed in relation to some other group, then the part played by race and racism is easy to see. The nineteenth century was marked not just by the ascendancy of nationalism but also of changing notions of race and racial terminology. As the twin pillars of modernity, both race and nation misleadingly appear to be natural, self-evident categories. Under the broad political context of colonialism, of the ascendancy of science and scientific inquiry, race was seen as biological matter, demonstrating opposite, unequal characteristics of people. Race, so conceived, played a contradictory role in colonial rule: it justified colonial expansion but rationalized its "rule of difference." Colonial encounters racialized national differences and national differences were seen as expressions of racial differences. What these differences meant, of course, depended upon one's vantage point. Therefore, even though discourses of race and unequal racial categories of self and other shaped metropolitan nationalisms and colonial rule, these differences were recast and the racial hierarchies were unsettled in the framework of anti-colonial nationalisms.

Notions of ideal womanhood, itself class-, race-, and ethnically-based, and respectable sexuality were central to characterizations of nationalisms and their specific contents. Both metropolitan and anti-colonial nationalisms were shaped through representations of women and sexuality, but as mirror opposites, in the heyday of colonial rule. It was not that representations of men and masculinity were unimportant; on the contrary, under colonial rule, issues of maleness, male vigor, and respectability shaped national and racial differences. Regardless of whether indigenous women were viewed as subordinate or relatively free of the constraints of European middle-class white womanhood, the status of indigenous women was key to debates over the legitimacy of colonial rule. Not surprisingly, then, representations of womanhood figured prominently in the question of what made anti-colonial nationalisms distinct from metropolitan ones.

Differences of race, gender, and sexuality did not simply mark external boundaries of the nation; they also marked the *internal* boundaries of inclusion and exclusion, of belonging and foreignness. And perhaps there is no better indication of how these internal differences and boundaries were relevant and how they had to be constantly re-drawn than the presence of groups seen as marginal to the national community but living within the political boundaries of the state. Further, if, as is being argued here, nationalisms are selectively imagined, then notions of ideal womanhood and respectable sexuality filtered which women, of which social and cultural groups, were seen as the essence of the nation and which groups of women were thereby marginalized. Lest it seem that what is at stake here are simply abstract notions of belonging, it is important to underscore that for some groups internal differences restricted full access to the rights and protections of citizenship, whether through racial segregation or through denying women the right to own property.

The ascendancy of nationalisms in the colonies and the metropoles coincided with the rise of race-based movements, such as the Black Nationalist movement in the USA, and women's movements seeking equality. Perhaps never before had liberal notions of citizenship, of equality regardless of class, race, ethnicity, gender, among other factors, seemed so much to contradict the unequal treatment of racially-marked groups and women of various social classes. In the second half of the nineteenth century, and the early twentieth, middle- and upper-class women organized for full rights of citizenship, including the right to vote, in the USA, Britain, Australia, and France. In the USA, middle-class white Protestant women often highlighted their superiority to working-class women, women of color, especially Native American and African-American women, in their struggle to obtain the right to vote. In the colonies, the movement toward equality and women's reform was linked to the rise of nationalism and the colonial state. Women's movements were a significant part of anti-colonial nationalist movements, not just through the very presence of women but also, as noted above, through their symbolic value. In most cases, the demands of women's movements were subordinated to the nationalist goals and were realized to greater or lesser degrees after the formal end of colonialism.

The aftermath of World War I was a defining moment for principles of self-determination and sovereign national states, paving the way for demands for self-rule and sovereignty in the remaining colonies. Just before the end of World War I, President Woodrow Wilson gave a now-famous speech in which he outlined fourteen points that would lay the basis for an international order of nations with political independence and territorial integrity. The creation of the League of Nations crystallized this vision of a new international order made up of sovereign national states. Coupled with the weakened hold of nations such as Britain, France, the Netherlands, and Belgium after World War I was an escalation of anti-colonial movements aimed at securing political independence from foreign domination. In the continuation of a pattern seen earlier in Latin America, formal colonialism began to give way to more informal but influential relations of domination even as colonies became independent national states.

These anti-colonial nationalist movements eventually culminated in a wave of decolonization and the rise of newly independent national states after World War II. Beginning with the Philippines, several other countries became independent states during the 1940s and 1950s: Syria, Lebanon, Burma, Sri Lanka, India, Pakistan, Indonesia, Laos, Cambodia, and Vietnam. The early 1950s witnessed the independence of former colonies in North Africa, including Libya, Morocco, and Tunisia. Between 1958 and 1962, 23 independent postcolonial states were established in Africa and between 1963 and 1968 another ten were added.[1] What is remarkable about this is that, without exception, independence from colonial rule was expressed in the modern idiom of the national state. Each of these emergent nations was shaped by nationalism, and had the trappings of an identifiable national flag, anthem, language, and its own particular history. Built upon the foundations of the colonial state, the postcolonial state was typified by centralized and bureaucratic systems of administration.

The interwar years coincided with scholarly attention to the concept of nationalism. The political events of World War I and the intensification of nationalisms in Europe led western intellectuals to analyze nationalism and to express concerns about its more ominous side. Coming to a head during World War II, fascism at the national level under the Nazi regime in Germany confirmed the worst fears about the dangerous potential of nationalism. Not surprisingly, later scholars, such as Elie Kedourie, understood nationalism as an ideological rather than a revolutionary movement. There is no doubting the horrors of World War II or the distressing results of what happens when fascism is mixed with nationalism. There is no arguing with nationalism as a potentially ominous ideological force. But a view from Europe in the context of two world wars misses the coeval but very different roles and meanings of nationalism elsewhere, such as in the colonies or ex-colonies in Latin America. While anti-colonial nationalisms cannot be romanticized, neither can they be simply reduced to the vested interests of indigenous social elites, nor can they be simply seen as an ideological delusion of the masses. What is more, even though much can be said about the role of European nationalisms and war in the first half of the twentieth century, ironically, nationalism came to be seen as the dark force of the East.

In the realignment following World War II, power shifted from the former colonial powers of Britain and France to the relative latecomers in the imperial race, namely the United States and the Soviet Union, and the end of formal colonial rule did not mean the end of imperialism. In most cases, newly independent states were derived from the administrative boundaries of colonies that extended over contiguous territories including diverse ethnic peoples. Nationalism may have precariously held together multiple, different groups through empire- and war-making or through the struggle toward decolonization, but it faced different challenges in this new era of national states.

As noted in the last chapter, the last fifty years or more have witnessed the rise of numerous ethnic nationalist movements, many of which have been bloody and tragic. Though hatred against the external colonial enemy was enough to mobilize national liberation movements, it was hardly enough to manage an independent state. Fraught with the inequalities of class, religions, genders, and ethnicities in newly independent nations carved out of colonial administrative boundaries, the new states have been the scene of tragic events in numerous instances. Indeed, the violent suppression of the separatist Igbo movement by the Nigerian state (the Biafran War), the long Tamil struggle against the state in Sri Lanka, the protracted violence of the Indonesian state in East Timor in an effort to suppress secession, among other conflicts, indicate the dark side of state-led nationalism and the repressive aspect of the state. European and North American nations may not have witnessed ethnic violence on the same scale but they have not been immune from separatist movements or from state-sponsored violence. More strikingly, the Cold War provided a foil for rival ideologies and nationalisms, leading to numerous wars and occupations, in Vietnam, Afghanistan, Nicaragua, and Korea.

The inconsistencies in the concept of equal citizenship have triggered another set of challenges across postcolonial and Euro-American states. In many postcolonial states there have been demands for decentralization and less state intervention, which are counterbalanced by demands to extend the privileges of citizenship in new ways. Movements for the political, economic, cultural, and civil equality of minority groups, for gender equality, and anti-war protests are some of the phenomena in which the limits of liberal citizenship have been challenged in places such as the USA, France, Britain, and Australia. Critical studies of nationalism, which are attentive to the gender and the racial implications of nationalisms, or to the links and the differences between postcolonial and Euro-American states, lead these critical considerations of nationalism..

Through this critical scholarship, we can identify two challenges to the framework of nationalism: the rise of ethnic nationalist movements and neo-liberal threat to the national state. Much has been written about these two threats to national states, especially from the vantage point of rapidly intensifying globalization. The concern is that national states are on the decline – either because they have outlived their purpose or because they are losing the fight against the relentless force of globalization – and that there is a parallel rise of cultural nationalisms. A dangerous combination, indeed. But a more careful look at the globalization thesis suggests that, externally, the greater concern is about deepening inequalities between national states and, internally, the failed promise of liberal citizenship. I would like to end this book by briefly exploring the globalization thesis with respect to nationalisms, nations, and states. I will suggest that we need to be more vigilant about the internal inequalities of citizenship by race, gender, sexuality, and ethnicity. The worrying concern is that the chasm between the promise and limits of nationally based citizenship for many is inherent to the model itself.

Nationalisms, Nations, States, and their Futures

One overriding opinion about the futures of nationalisms and nations is that the era of nationalisms and national states is in decline. Surely, the state will endure in some altered form, but it not clear that it will be organized through the framework of nationalism. In the ending to his book, *Nations and Nationalism since 1780*, this is what Hobsbawm has to say:

> After all, the very fact that historians are at least beginning to make some
> progress in the study and analysis of nations and nationalism suggests that,

as so often, the phenomenon is past its peak. The owl of Minerva which brings wisdom, said Hegel, flies out at dusk. It is a good sign that it is now circling around nations and nationalism.[2]

In this passage, Hobsbawm raises two points: that nations and nationalisms may be past their heyday; and that scholars are making some headway in understanding what these phenomena mean. While Hobsbawm's suggestion that historians need the benefit of hindsight to analyze social occurrences is an important one, nonetheless it raises an important question: if nations and nationalisms are on the downswing, then why is it still important to understand them as contemporary phenomena? Hobsbawm is surely not suggesting that nations and nationalisms are no longer relevant or important. Indeed, their heyday may have passed precisely because they are so thoroughly entrenched in our contemporary lives. They may be past their peak simply because it can be taken for granted that their influences will endure in significant ways. Hobsbawm's claim that nations and nationalisms are on the decline needs to be discussed rather than conceded.

Nothing supports the position that the future of national states is in question more than the discourse of globalization. National states face an unprecedented challenge from the processes of globalization. While proponents of globalization may view this optimistically, critics of globalization are generally concerned. In a process often described as a "space-time" compression, globalization is the proliferation of neo-liberal policies, the rapid mobility of finance and trade, people, and ideas across national borders.[3] The fostering of international trade and foreign capital investment by reducing regional, national, and sub-national barriers, deregulating domestic markets, and reducing the role of the public sector in favor of the privatization of goods and services are among the chief characteristics of neo-liberalism. In neo-liberal policies and cross-border flows, coupled with the rise of intergovernmental and supra-governmental organizations and the clout of multinational corporations, critics of globalization see a dual threat to national states: that they are losing their sovereignty; and that they are less able to protect the interests of citizens, thereby leaving them exposed to the upheavals of market forces. The net result is the downsizing and decentralizing of states, with non-state institutions taking up the regulation of law, punishment, education, religion, "welfare," and other social tasks.

A related but different concern about globalization has to do with cultural nationalisms. In the previous chapter, we discussed the rise of ethnic and religious nationalisms at length. But from the perspective of globalization, the significance of cultural nationalisms is somewhat different. The argument and concern is that the cross-border flows, which – ironically – favor some nations over others, are aggravating cultural nationalisms. In this view, cultural nationalisms are the outcome of the declining sovereignty of nations, of reduced state capacity, and of the erosion of distinct national and regional cultures. The discourse of globalization therefore refers to two opposing tendencies.

Globalization has become the dominant lens through which scholars, activists, state actors, among others, have analyzed issues such as the cross-border mobility of capital, the proliferation of neo-liberal policies, and the rapid transfer of cultural ideas and entertainment. Such is the strength of the globalization lens that only two positions have seemed possible: globalization as a positive or a negative force. No longer just a way of describing the realities around us, it becomes a way of shaping perceptions of those realities. And, such is the impact of globalization and neo-liberal policies that, whether we support it or condone it, many of us subscribe to the thesis of a globalizing world. There is no denying the presence of processes loosely defined as globalization, but we also have to entertain the idea that globalization may not be as global as believed.

The point that I am leading up to is that there are compelling indicators of cross-border flows and other aspects of globalization. But the counter-indicators are more compelling: the rootedness of people, the heightened roles of states, the national bases of most multinational corporations, among others. Contrary to some fears, the national state is not withering away. I am sympathetic to the claims and fears of the anti-globalization position; as such, I will focus on related concerns and sidestep the pro-globalization position. Yet, if we do not raise questions of globalization, nationalisms, and states in a more nuanced way, we surely run the risk of giving globalization more coherence and power than it deserves. And we may lose sight of the continuing sovereignty and accountability of at least some national states. A second claim I make is that the globalization lens does not adequately account for cultural nationalisms, that cultural nationalisms encode a range of issues – racism, cultural autonomy, citizenship – that cannot be neatly accounted within the globalization framework.

The indicators of globalization: globalizing trade, finance, and the compromised state

In academic and popular writing, the concept of globalization is not always defined and readers are frequently left to intuit its meanings. But there appears to be some consensus on its most important indicators.

One important indicator is the rise of intergovernmental and supragovernmental organizations to manage the growth of so-called free trade and open markets. The foremost example of this is the World Trade Organization (WTO), which was formed on January 1, 1995 with independent jurisdiction on trade in manufactures, agriculture, services, investment, and intellectual property, and its rules are binding on all of its members. Member states are encouraged to lower trade barriers and protections of their national industries, and permit the flow of foreign investment, thereby reducing an individual state's ability to make and execute national economic policies. The International Monetary Fund (IMF) and the World Bank (WB) are two other examples of organizations that can compromise state sovereignty, mostly in the Third World, by insisting on reduced state spending and the increasing privatization of social services, including health care, the communications and transportation infrastructures, and other public services.

At the regional level, free trade agreements (FTAs), such as NAFTA (North American Free Trade Agreement) and the more recent FTAA (Free Trade of Americas Agreement), the Asian Pacific Economic Community (APEC), or bodies such as the European Union (EU) further promote this supranational model of trade and economic liberalization. The power of decision-making or wielding influence shifts away from national states to "denationalized" urban centers, subject to the competing influences of a variety of interest groups. As a result, as Saskia Sassen, a keen observer of the globalization process, notes, major cities around the world, such as New York, London, and Tokyo, emerge as the denationalized centers of power.[4] The implicit penalties of being left out of these regional networks pressure states to liberalize domestic markets and deregulate foreign investment, shifting the control over resources and policy-making to these regional centers. For example, NAFTA regulates the flows of goods, services, and capital between Canada, Mexico, and the United States. NAFTA has forced Mexico to reduce its agricultural subsidies, curtail its infrastructural investments in rural areas, allow foreign ownership of land and financial institutions, and privatize the railways.

Another dominant trend that signals the erosion of individual state autonomy is the sway of multinational and transnational corporations (MNCs and TNCs). Frequently, the terms "transnational" and "multinational" are used interchangeably. However, multinational corporations may be based in one nation while operating in others, and a truly transnational corporation is not tied to any single nation but is adrift and mobile. They are influential in two primary ways: through the production and marketing of commodities and services and through the flows of capital across national boundaries. Governed by the logic of expanding markets and profitability, MNCs and TNCs focus on internationalizing the production and consumption of goods and services and managing the flow of financial transactions across national borders.

Each of these aspects poses a challenge for nation-centered models of economic growth and more conventional expectations about the role of national states. TNCs and MNCs represent a vital concentration of power especially against some national states, primarily because these states are dependent on these corporations for capital investment, for job creation, for foreign currency, and sometimes for technological diffusion. Permitting the unrestricted flow of capital (often of staggering amounts of money) across national borders has led to currency speculation. As a result of the technology and neo-liberal fiscal policies that allow speculators instantaneously to move around massive amounts of money, national currencies and economies are vulnerable to instability. Although nations such as Chile, Malaysia, and China try to avert the threat by mandating a minimal period for foreign investment, proponents of neo-liberalism and globalization challenge these as protectionist policies that undermine the spirit of the market. In contrast, the leverage of multinational and transnational corporations is put in sober light when we consider that in 1998, of the 100 largest economies in the world, 51 were global corporations and only 49 were countries.[5] The combined sales of the 350 largest corporations were almost a third of the combined Gross National Product (GNP) of all industrialized countries and exceeded the individual GNPs of all Third World countries.[6]

On the matter of the transnationalization of production, MNCs exceed the autonomy of many Third World states in some respects, as mentioned in Chapter Three. This is apparent in the practice of sub-contracting or "sweating," a means to farm out various aspects of the production of goods and commodities in order to reduce costs. While this used to be more common in garment manufacturing, it is now widely used in the automobile industry, electronics, toys, and furniture, among other trades. Sweating not only permits the exploitation of labor in various Third World countries and in cities such as New York and Los Angeles, but in many cases it also undermines the ability or willingness of Third World nations to enforce labor protectionist laws. So afraid are some nations of losing foreign investment that they will ignore local regulations against child labor, poor wages, unacceptable working conditions, and against prevention of unions. That this fear is not misplaced is also well evident from the fact that while countries like South Korea and Taiwan were attractive to corporations looking for cheap labor, when they allowed labor protection and unionization these corporations moved to the more externally dependent nations such as Vietnam, Indonesia, and Bangladesh. Nations more heavily indebted to international lending agencies are more likely to promote their labor as cheap, give tax breaks, and even absorb the bill for resources such as electricity and water in production.

Clearly, fears about the pitfalls of globalization are not ill founded. For scholars, activists, and more popular critics of globalization, the concerns about globalization and the declining role of national state are three-fold. First, there is concern that the proliferation of neo-liberal policies and intensifying globalization implies the strengthening influence of some states, especially the USA, within the international economic, political, and social arena. Second, with the influence of intergovernmental organizations and MNCs, there is a crisis of accountability. Ideally, state institutions are responsible for protecting citizens from exploitation by ensuring a minimum living wage, reasonable terms and conditions for employment, the ability to unionize, and provide a safety net in some cases. However, under conditions of globalization and the decreasing leverage of many states and of their ability to ensure the welfare of citizens *vis-à-vis* corporations and international trade organizations and other stronger states, the fear is that corporate influence will expand unchecked.

Third, there is concern about the polarizing effects of globalization across national borders. The promise of globalization is hard to reconcile with profound social inequalities. Recent reports indicate the failure of the promise of globalization for most people in Africa, Latin America, Asia, and the Middle East. The vast majority of the people living in these places have seen no improvement in their lives since 1989, the year when the Berlin wall fell and capital expansion spread.[7] In March 2002 a United Nations conference on how rich nations can help the poor ones with aid and trade was held in Monterrey, Mexico, often touted as a model of the positive outcomes of neo-liberal policies in the Third World. Ironically, Monterrey is not just an example of prosperity and development triggered by NAFTA and measured by the number of millionaires, wealthy suburbs, air-conditioned malls, Pizza Huts, and Kentucky Fried Chicken stores. It is as much an indicator of the darker side of globalization. While globalization did not make the vast majority, who live around Monterrey, poor, it has done nothing to help them.[8] People are dirt poor, sometimes living in shanty towns without sewers or street, in other cases with little running water and no indoor plumbing, and with little hope of a better future for their children.

Weaknesses in the anti-globalization position

In his overview of the global state, Martin Shaw highlights two fallacies of the globalization debate: that globalization is a linear process; and that global and national/international categories are inherently opposed.[9] On the contrary, globalization occurs at various levels, has multiple centers, and takes different forms at different historical moments. Moreover, the set of processes that we refer to as globalization has considerably different impact on different states. This leads us to Martin's second point about how we define the "global," "national," and "international" and how we posit their relationships. Martin argues that both sides of the globalization camp take a dualistic view, in which trade within a national economy is non-global and that which exists across state boundaries is global. He maintains that, in contrast, most trade is measured in national and international terms.

To further unpack some of the misleading assumptions underlying the anti-globalization argument, it is useful to distinguish between state sovereignty and state autonomy. In a helpful contribution, David Held argues that while loss of sovereignty usually refers to the loss of a nation state's power to control the course of its future, to make final decisions, and to enforce law within the territory, loss of autonomy is about the diminution of the capacity to achieve national policies.[10] Autonomy is not about the ability to set goals but to achieve those goals and policies that have been put into place. Held qualifies the globalization thesis with the point that the diminution of state autonomy or the loss of sovereignty are not only two different questions but that these questions do not uniformly apply across states. Two arguments are implicit here. First, it is difficult to talk about globalization in general because different states are more or less involved in the globalization process and are varyingly impacted, making it necessary to take a contextual approach to questions of sovereignty and autonomy. Second, the globalization discourse obscures the profoundly unequal relations between states; the problem may not be globalization per se but the political and economic hegemony of some states over others.

As noted above, although one aspect of the anti-globalization position relates to the reigning supremacy of the USA, in particular, there is good reason not to overemphasize it to the exclusion of the role of other states, especially in regional economies. In an especially useful exploration of national states against the backdrop of the globalization thesis, Linda Weiss shifts attention to the international political and economic arena. Questioning whether globalization exists, Weiss says that what we are witnessing is the heightening of differences among various national states.[11] The ability of some states effectively to transform their capacities in the international arena is what makes the difference between "stronger" and "weaker" states, according to her. In her discussion of state capacity, Weiss argues that there is no such thing as state capacity in general; states may mobilize consent, pursue foreign policy, may follow an import-substitution model, for example, with more or less efficiency. But her point is that some states, such as Japan and Germany, have adjusted to economic change more effectively than others, leading to predominance in their region.

Not only does Weiss's approach help us consider the international political and economic arena in a more nuanced way, but also another aspect of her argument offsets conventional wisdom about the intensification and scale of globalization. She argues that despite evidence that national economies are highly integrated there is insufficient support for globalization or the flattening of national differences.[12] She shows that the bulk of trade is intra-regional and as much as 90 percent of production in industrialized nations is for domestic production. Contrary to beliefs about the growing power of foreign direct investment, it is on the decline and domestic financial institutions have sway internally. On the issue of MNCs, Weiss says that although they operate within an international arena, they have national bases and are better analyzed as "national" corporations.

So the globalization thesis needs to be qualified by shifting its emphasis on to the role and hierarchies of national states. The point is not that the model of nation states is under assault but that some states are experiencing reduced autonomy and perhaps a loss of sovereignty. George Steinmetz rightly distinguishes between a state's lack of political will and its institutional incapacity to respond to the exigencies of globalization.[13] When national states pursue trickle-down policies of prosperity, it is not so much because they are unable to face up to external pressures as because they are unwilling to ensure social parity. Further, economic integration does not mean homogeneity or the loss of political sovereignty. Held gives the example of the formation of the European Community, which helped European national states meet the challenges of the dominance of the USA in the decades after World War II, and of the subsequent ascendancy of the Japanese economy. If anything, Held argues, the European Community strengthened the national states' ability to function effectively at home and abroad.[14]

Equally importantly, functions associated with the modern state are undergoing change; they are being revised and reprioritized. The national state is underscored as the primary arbiter of social justice and protector of its citizens. The state certainly controls crucial functions, including the capacity to define citizenship and its benefits, the use of violence, and the coordination of various institutions involved in governance, both nongovernmental and civil. If anything, there may be greater pressure than before on states to ensure political stability, to regulate labor and labor laws, to provide adequate levels of education in the interests of international trade and money, and to ensure a "hospitable" climate for foreign investment and production units. Some states in particular, such as the USA, increasingly emphasize the control and regulation of immigration. The Keynesian welfare state may have declined but national states retain their political functions, including taxation and legislation; they defend the internal and external territory through the military and police; they also continue to control or indirectly shape administrative and ideological functions such as education, mass communication, and national/patriotic rituals.[15] Indeed, at this historical moment, militarization and making war remains an important function of the national state. Perhaps there is no better evidence of this than the proliferation and strengthening of state agencies in the USA to make "war on terrorism," especially after September 11, 2001.

The flow of people across state boundaries

But what about the flow of large numbers of people across national boundaries? Even though most of the attention to globalization is directed at trade and money, the numbers crossing borders is probably as important as an indicator of globalization.

Among the groups that traverse national boundaries, Leslie Sklair calls attention to transnational elites, as both the product and instrument of globalization.[16] By transnational elites, Sklair means the corporate executives and their local affiliates, state bureaucrats who facilitate globalization, capitalist-inspired politicians and professionals, and consumerist elites from the media and merchant groups. Despite the fact that they are few in sheer number, these elites exert influence in at least three ways. They tend to have global rather than local perspectives, they often have affiliations to more than one country and see themselves as "citizens of the world," and they tend to share similar consumer patterns. Not only do they derive benefit from, and support, the push toward globalization but they also are less likely to be driven by nationalist concerns. Indeed, according to Sklair, their task is to purvey consumer products, entertainment, news, and ideas to a rapidly expanding public and to persuade others that their interests coincide with those of transnational corporations.

In contrast to this select group are much larger numbers of people who traverse national boundaries out of economic and political pressure, quite apart from motives of pleasure and tourism – as many as 100 million migrants. Of these, 20 million refugees change countries each year, more than 35 million people work in other than their own country, and 10 million are displaced by environmental degradation, so the mobility of people across borders is hardly an unusual phenomenon.[17] When one adds the flow of temporary visitors as tourists, the volume of border crossings is larger still and a striking pattern is discernible. Speaking about migrants in their book, *Nations Unbound: Transnational Projects, Postcolonial Predicaments, and Deterritorialized Nation-States*, Linda Basch, Nina Glick Schiller, and Cristina Szanton Blanc note what is distinctive about current patterns.[18] They suggest that it is no longer easy to make clear distinctions between immigrants, who uproot themselves to make a new home elsewhere, and migrants who are temporary and transient groups. Instead, immigrants are more likely to develop and maintain multiple familial, economic, social, religious, and political relationships that span the borders of two or more national states, of places of settlement and of "back home." Basch et al. see these changing and intensifying patterns of transnational migration in relation to global capitalism and the global relations between labor and capital.

But what this focus on transnational and temporary migration leaves out is how most people and communities remain rooted within their national units. There is more intranational and regional mobility of voluntary and involuntary migrants. More importantly, this rootedness is shaping how displacement and diaspora are constructed within a nationalist framework. Indeed, taking on the increasingly widespread forced and voluntary displacement of peoples, Liisa Malkki argues that there is a disjuncture between putative ideas of nation, home, and rootedness and the realities of homelessness, and the deterritorialization of identities.[19] Her point is that nationally based notions of identity and belonging provide the framework for interpreting the mobility of diasporic groups, refugees, and migrant labor. The term "diaspora" is a way to capture the displacement of temporary and long-term migrants, of refugees, and of the exiled, such as Palestinians living in Lebanon, the United States, Australia, and elsewhere; people from the Caribbean in Britain and the United States; Indians in Canada; and Filipinas in the Middle East. Indeed, given the inadequacy of nationally based notions of identity for diasporic groups,

Malkki recommends the development of alternative, deterritorialized, and denationalized conceptions of identity to accommodate the scale of displacement.

The persistance of nationally based notions of belonging and citizenship lead to more stringent measures against immigration. Numerous Euro-American states and Japan have adopted harsher measures on immigration in response to the political clamoring of their citizens. In Europe, (north) America, and Japan, declining opportunities for relatively well-compensated, unionized jobs cause some of the anger toward newer migrants and exacerbate divisions between citizens and foreigners, between territorialized ethnic groups and landless aliens, often regardless of the duration of their presence. Sassen notes that in the USA, since immigration is thought to be the result of unfavorable socioeconomic conditions in other countries and not due to the needs of the USA or broader international changes, immigration policy is erroneously thought to be humanitarian; despite prevailing misconceptions that migrants are admitted by choice and generosity, economic and political need are more important factors.[20] For example, despite close regional, cultural, and economic ties, anti-immigration sentiment is rife in California and has shaped public policy. Calls by the Mexican President, Vincente Fox, to loosen immigration restrictions against Mexican immigrants have prompted no immediate or significant changes in US immigration laws.

Cultural ideas and entertainment

Turning to another facet of the globalization thesis, the concern is about globalizing culture, cultural homogenization, and cultural imperialism. In his introduction to the book, *Global Culture: Nationalism, Globalization, and Modernity*, Mike Featherstone firmly rejects the possibility that we are living in a world with a global culture.[21] One has only to look around high-density urban areas or travel across the national border to another place to note that, indeed, there is little evidence of a global culture. On the contrary, one is faced with differences in language, religion, customs, and practices. Yet, as Featherstone notes, there is ample evidence that culture is globalizing. Writing on the globalization of cultural ideas and practices, Benjamin Barber identifies this new cultural economy as the welding together of telecommunications technologies with information and entertainment software.[22] The result? The export and consumption of the Internet and the World Wide Web (WWW), Michael Jackson, Hollywood and Disney movies, Pepsi, blue jeans, Nike sneakers, and Star Trek. From the globalization of resources and then of manufacture of goods, in the past few decades the emphasis has gradually moved from services (banking, etc.) to information, telecommunication, and entertainment, as Barber shows. More recently, the emphasis is on images and sound bites put together by advertising agencies and movie studios. Hardly innocuous or superficial, these forms of information, entertainment, and images are about our deep-seated pleasures and desires. Or, as Barber puts it, "infotainment" is aimed at nothing less than the human soul.[23]

The ongoing concern about globalizing culture is that this is really the Americanization of cultural forms and practices, which is a threat to the multitude of diverse national cultures. The examples of globalization cited above are all, without exception, American. This is not to deny the export of Japanese animation or of Hindi films from Mumbai (Bombay) or of Franco-Maghrebi rai music; instead, the concern is about the hegemony of American popular culture and corporate interests that rely on an American template. Barber observes that what are being marketed are not just American images and products but also the idea of America itself; parochial American forms get exported as the essence of a common world taste. Malls and theme parks are new centers of public life and congregation, and American logos, advertising slogans, brand names, celebrities, and jingles are widely recognizable in numerous locations. These cultural forms can succeed only by suppressing other cultural forms. Hollywood films, for example, have undermined film production in France, Sweden, Spain and Italy. In 2001, Paris was inundated with posters of the film *Lara Croft: Tomb Raider*. Film industry that has survived elsewhere, for example in Mumbai, has been through a similar pattern of exporting blockbuster films to Africa and the Middle East, partly imitating Hollywood styles, and at the cost of wiping out other independent film production. For the volume of Hollywood films that are exported a comparatively small number flows into the US, indicating that cultural globalization typically flows one way, its wellspring is in the West, and especially in the USA.

However, arguing against a simplified view of cultural globalization as the homogenizing influence of American consumer culture, Hall makes the case for a more complicated stance.[24] Taking issue with the tale of unchecked replication of American or western cultures told elsewhere, Hall suggests that cultural globalization does not aim to do away completely with existing and evolving forms of non-western culture. Indeed, globalization and cultural homogenization are aimed at absorbing and recasting cultural differences within a western idiom that can be re-marketed to audiences everywhere. American and western capital seek sources of cultural difference and innovation in order to sustain consumer interest and profit-making, while "Americanizing" or "westernizing" these forms. The success of novelists using "Third World" subject matter – Salman Rushdie, Naguib Mahfouz, and Arundhati Roy – may be as much about the need to find, absorb, and market cultural difference not only to the West but also to the Third World as it is a reflection of their talent. Indeed, what seems to underpin much of the work on globalization is that both cultural homogenization and cultural differences are at play and, in fact, interdependent. Making this point with respect to the furor over Rushdie's *Satanic Verses*, Janet Abu-Lughod notes that if the blockbuster success of this book indicates how globalized culture is becoming, the disparate mobilizations against this book in Muslim and non-Muslim countries also shows how "unglobalized" and locally specific cultural practices can be.[25] What seems true is that Americanized or westernized cultural forms do not exist quite in the same way everywhere; they are incorporated into the daily settings and the local landscape.

Another crucial reason to complicate the globalizing culture position is that it does not distinguish between fears of cultural standardization and unequal access to consumption. Alongside the problem of cultural standardization is also the problem of inequality of access to resources and consumption. A variety of political groups may decry how American-centered cultural globalization corrupts the integrity of national culture. But the power of corporate-driven models of consumption also highlights the social and economic differences among groups within and across states.

Globalization and cultural nationalism

The rise and intensity of cultural nationalisms is the other side of the perceived threat of globalization to the integrity of national states. As noted earlier, although we considered the rise of ethnic nationalisms in the previous chapter, these cultural responses are specifically tied to the disruptive effects of globalization. Hall takes the position that the erosion of national states, national economies, and national cultural identities are complicated by the fact that powerful entities are at their most dangerous when they are ascending or descending.[26] Nationalism, ferocious warfare, racism, and jingoism are among the responses to the threats posed by economic and cultural globalizations. As he tellingly puts it, "All I want to say about this is, that when the era of nation-states in globalization begins to decline, one can see a regression to a very defensive and highly dangerous form of national identity which is driven by a very aggressive form of racism."[27]

These cultural identities can be described in two ways: as cultural autonomy and as reactionary culturalism. Especially in response to what is perceived as (north) American cultural imperialism, groups in any number of nations seem to be engaged in a struggle for national cultural autonomy. From this perspective, if national culture is seen as essentially unique and reasonably pure, Americanized cultural globalization must be nothing less than a threat to its sanctity and continuation. The differences are especially heightened in nations that do not see themselves as western or European, although American popular culture is considered a threat in parts of Europe as well. Conservative and radical political groups in a variety of places in Africa, Asia, and the Middle East express concern about the threat posed by the infiltration of Americanized or westernized images and practices, such as beauty pageants, consumer-based cultures, romance novels, Hollywood films, and American television programs, which have little relevance for the majority of their citizens. Their fear may be compounded by what is seen as the hedonistic and West-oriented turn of many middle- and upper-middle class young people in these countries to discos, rap music, denim, and McDonalds. Precisely because American and Americanized global cultural forms have the power to influence leisure, entertainment, pleasures, and desires, they seem to compromise national cultural integrity. In response, cultural resistance to the perceived American cultural imperialism can take a variety of forms, such as elaborating national culture, its distinctive cultural traditions and history, and its importance in people's lives.

Taking a somewhat different approach to globalization and its cultural implications, Barber emphasizes how intensifying globalization is matched by the intensification of ethnic, religious, and racial hatreds that threaten to "tribalize" or fragment the world.[28] He describes the rise of reactionary culturalisms amidst a rapidly globalizing world. Extrapolating the term from its prevailing meanings of a religious struggle on behalf of a faith or a holy war against enemies of the faith, Barber refers to *jihad* to include all kinds of dogmatic and violent expressions that seek to forge communities rooted in exclusion and hatred, and are intolerant of democratic values and institutions. Barber's argument is that these tribalized forms of Jihad are the other side of globalization, what he succinctly calls, McWorld. McWorld and *jihad* are interdependent responses though tending in opposite directions. If McWorld is driven by making national borders porous and universalizing markets, then the other is driven by anger, hatred, and the re-creation of exclusionary communities. For Barber, however, the crucial point of similarity underlying the difference between Jihad and McWorld is that both undermine the sovereign national state and its democratic institutions. One emphasizes particular ethnic or racial characteristics to fragment the national community and the other seeks to make national borders irrelevant. The net result, Barber says, is a weakening of democratic civil society and institutions to protect the political and economic rights of a nation's citizens. He concedes that the national state does not guarantee democracy, democratic institutions, and the welfare of its citizens. Nonetheless, for Barber, democratic and civil institutions are important attributes of national states. Therefore, he believes, the twin assaults by Jihad and McWorld are a powerful threat to democracy and civil society, and the overall model of national states.

The problem with Barber's approach is not the counter point that the struggle for cultural autonomy and reactionary culturalisms are benign; on the contrary. Despite his attempt to use the term *jihad* in a broader way, he continues to associate these culturally reactionary responses primarily with Islamic groups. A second problem is that he does not address how reactionary culturalisms are also frequently tied to the unevenness of state policies, economic capabilities, and distribution of economic, political, and cultural resources. The problem is that insufficient attention is given to the national unit and to state-based policies.

In contrast, I suggest that we shift the critical focus back on to the national unit. In the previous chapter, we explored at length the rise of ethnic and religiously defined conflicts. My thesis in that chapter was that in some cases they pose a significant threat to the stability of existing national states, either through demands for sovereignty or through control of the state. To underscore an implicit aspect of the argument in the chapter, examples such as Serbian and Hutu cultural nationalisms are better situated in a national/international framework. These reactionary cultural nationalisms have much to do with intra-national policies: the impact of state policies, the roles of state actors, and attempts to narrow the scope of citizenship through the annihilation of others within the same territory. Taking a globalization approach would obscure how frequently the source and site of conflict is around the proverbial corner. The discourse of globalization gives insight into the threat and virulence of narrowly defined cultural identities, but it does not tell us much about why control over the state, struggle for political autonomy, and, in some cases, aspirations for sovereign territories continue to figure prominently in ethnic and cultural nationalisms.

Observing the relocation of long-term migrants, Smadar Lavie and Ted Swedenburg agree that the First World is being "Third-Worlded,"[29] that is, is being irrevocably and significantly changed in its make-up. Numerous scholars have commented on the emergence of hybrid groups, especially in Euro-American nations as well as in Japan. These hybrid groups and their hybrid practices are most noticeable in what Sassen has called global cities, including New York, London, Tokyo, and Los Angeles. While many have celebrated this "multiculturalism," marked by the presence of visibly different-looking people, Chinese, Thai, and Indian restaurants, the popularity of *chai*, and world music, Lavie and Swedenburg rightly remain skeptical.

More frequently, the presence of diasporic groups appears to fuel racism and cultural nationalism; this, despite the fact that these groups are present in relatively small numbers. As migrants confront two or more national states, their identities and practices are interpreted through categories of race and ethnicity that are embedded in the framework of each of these states. Paul Gilroy, an especially insightful observer of racial and nationalist politics in Britain, notes how tensions around immigration are leading to new expressions of racism.[30] He suggests that the novelty of this "new racism" lies in the capacity to link matters of patriotism, nationalism, xenophobia, Englishness, Britishness, gender, and militarism.

Gilroy argues that the politics of race are charged with the rhetoric of national belonging and racial homogeneity so as to blur the distinctions between nation and race. The problem of race is seen as the result of immigration, and the question of how long is long enough to be a true Brit is unanswerable for racially marked black groups, regardless how long they or their families have been in the nation. At other moments, racism is endorsed more as a matter of culture and identity rather than skin color, and directed toward those accused of not being sufficiently assimilated in the "British community." For Gilroy, what is notable is how this racism is preoccupied by the dynamics of inclusion and exclusion in the national imaginary.

The problem with this racialized cultural nationalism is its attempt to reimagine the national community in ways that narrow definitions of citizenship. Taking questions of citizenship out of the political context, they seek to reverse the logic of civic nationalisms: citizenship is the outcome of cultural, racial, and historical affinity rather than political community. The fracture between the promise and reality of political citizenship is further exacerbated. The circumstances in which these cultural nationalisms occur have local, regional, and historical implications. They are related to state actors, state policies, and the distribution of social resources. The problem is that these cultural nationalisms define notions of belonging and citizenship in unrealizable ways: national belonging and citizenship can only come with assimilation but meaningful assimilation is withheld through the denial of equal rights and privileges of citizenship.

Clearly, my position in relation to the question of nationalisms, nations, and states is that the discourse of globalization obscures their continuing salience. My aim is to question the shift from the national and internal to the global, not to question the importance of cross-border flows of finance, trade, people, and cultural ideas. Hierarchies of national states, the strengthening of some states and the weakening of others as a result of the increasing economic and political interdependence are equally important concerns. We ought to be concerned about cultural nationalisms, but, as the foregoing discussion and the previous chapter suggest, in ways that allow us to question internal battles over national belonging and citizenship. If there is one point to be derived from the arguments laid out in this book, then it is that we need to develop analytical tools that can address the internal inconsistencies of nationalism and its external challenges, that can identify its inherent limitations but also can turn our attention to the possibilities of alternative models of community and belonging lurking at the margins. I believe that such possibilities do not exist in the discourse of globalization and its prophecy of waning states, nations, and nationalisms. To imagine their alternatives is the next challenge of encountering nationalism.

NOTES

1   Harry Magdoff, *Imperialism: From the Colonial Age to the Present* (New York: Monthly Review Press, 1978), esp. pp. 69–72.
2   Eric J. Hobsbawm, *Nations and Nationalism since 1780: Programme, Myth, and Reality* (Cambridge: Cambridge University Press, 1990), p. 183.
3   The term is David Harvey's. See his *The Condition of Postmodernity: An Enquiry into the Origins of Cultural Change* (Oxford, and Cambridge, Mass.: Blackwell, 1989).
4   Saskia Sassen, *Globalization and Its Discontents: Essays on the New Mobility of People and Money*, with a foreword by K. Anthony Appiah (New York: The New Press, 1998), esp. "Introduction," pp. xix–xxxvi.
5   Amnesty International, "AI on human rights and labor rights," in Frank J. Lechner and John Boli (eds.) *The Globalization Reader* (Oxford: Blackwell, 2000), pp. 187–90, esp. p. 187.

6   Philip McMichael, *Development and Social Change: A Global Perspective*, 2nd edn. (Thousand Oaks, Calif.: Pine Forge Press, 2000), esp. p. 96.

7   Joseph Kahn, "Losing the faith: globalization proves disappointing," *New York Times*, March 21, 2002, p. A6.

8   Tim Weiner, "Monterrey's poor sinking in rising economic tide," *New York Times*, March 21, 2002, p. A8.

9   Martin Shaw, *Theory of the Global State: Globality as an Unfinished Revolution* (Cambridge: Cambridge University Press, 2000), esp. pp. 12–14.

10 David Held, "The decline of the nation state," in Geoff Eley and Ronald Grigor Suny (eds.) *Becoming National: A Reader* (New York and Oxford: Oxford University Press, 1996), pp. 407–17, esp. p. 407.

11 Linda Weiss, *The Myth of the Powerless State* (Ithaca, NY: Cornell University Press, 1998), esp. p. 11.

12 Ibid., esp. ch. 6.

13 George Steinmetz, "Introduction: culture and the state," in George Steinmetz (ed.) *State/Culture: State-formation after the Cultural Turn* (Ithaca, NY and London: Cornell University Press, 1999), p. 11.

14 Held, "The decline of the nation state," p. 412.

15 Bob Jessop, "Narrating the future of the national economy and the national state: remarks on remapping regulation and reinventing governance," in Steinmetz, *State/Culture*, pp. 378–405, esp. p. 394.

16 Leslie Sklair, "Sociology of the global system," in Lechner and Boli, *The Globalization Reader*, pp. 64–9, esp. p. 64.

17 Dennis Altman, *Global Sex* (Chicago and London: University of Chicago Press, 2001), p. 18.

18 Linda Basch, Nina Glick Schiller, and Cristina Szanton Blanc, *Nations Unbound: Transnational Projects, Postcolonial Predicaments, and Deterritorialized Nation-States* (Langhorne, Pa.: Gordon and Breach Publishers, 1994), esp. pp. 3–7.

19 Liisa Malkki, "National geographic: the rooting of peoples and the territorialization of national identity among scholars and refugees," in Geoff Eley and Ronald Grigor Suny (eds.) *Becoming National: A Reader* (New York and Oxford: Oxford University Press), pp. 434–53.

20 Sassen, *Globalization and Its Discontents*, esp. ch. 3.

21 Mike Featherstone, "Global culture: an introduction," in Mike Featherstone (ed.) *Global Culture: Nationalism, Globalization and Modernity* (London, Thousand Oaks, Calif., and New Delhi: Sage Publications, 1990), pp. 1–14, esp. p. 1.

22 Benjamin Barber, *Jihad vs. McWorld: How Globalism and Tribalism are Reshaping the World* (New York: Ballantine Books, 1995), esp. ch. 5.

23 Ibid., pp. 80–1.

24 Stuart Hall, "The local and the global: globalization and ethnicity," in Anthony D. King (ed.) *Culture, Globalization and the World System: Contemporary Conditions for the Representation of Identity* (Minneapolis: University of Minnesota Press, 1997), esp. pp. 27–39.

25 Janet Abu-Lughod, "Going beyond global babble," in King, *Culture, Globalization and the World-System*, pp. 131–7, esp. p. 136.
26 Hall, "The local and the global," p. 25.
27 Ibid., p. 26.
28 Barber, *Jihad vs. McWorld*, esp. pp. 8–12.
29 This point was first made by Kristin Koptiuch and reiterated by Smadar Lavie and Ted Swedenburg, "Introduction: displacement, diaspora, and geographies of identity," in Smadar Lavie and Ted Swedenburg (eds.) *Displacements, Diaspora, and Geographies of Identity* (Durham, NC and London: Duke University Press, 1996), pp. 1–25, esp. p. 2.
30 Paul Gilroy, *There Ain't No Black in the Union Jack: The Cultural Politics of Race and Nation*, with a new foreword by Houston A. Baker, Jr. (Chicago: University of Chicago Press, 1987), esp. chs. 1 and 2.

Index